ALSO BY JAMAICA KINCAID

At the Bottom of the River
Annie John
A Small Place
Annie, Gwen, Lilly, Pam and Tulip (with Eric Fischl)
Lucy
The Autobiography of My Mother
My Brother
My Favorite Plant: Writers and Gardeners on the Plants They Love (editor)
My Garden (Book):
Talk Stories
Mr. Potter
Among Flowers: A Walk in the Himalaya
See Now Then
An Encyclopedia of Gardening for Colored Children (with Kara Walker)

Putting Myself Together

Putting Myself Together

Writing 1974–

JAMAICA KINCAID

Introduction by Henry Louis Gates, Jr.

 Farrar, Straus and Giroux   New York

Farrar, Straus and Giroux
120 Broadway, New York 10271

EU Representative: Macmillan Publishers Ireland Ltd, 1st Floor, The Liffey Trust Centre, 117–126 Sheriff Street Upper, Dublin 1, D01 YC43

Copyright © 2025 by Jamaica Kincaid
Introduction copyright © 2025 by Henry Louis Gates, Jr.
All rights reserved
Printed in the United States of America
First edition, 2025

Photograph on page 49 by Benno Friedman.
Illustration on page 88, *The Skating Party*, used with permission of the Edward Gorey Charitable Trust.

Library of Congress Control Number: 2025004090
ISBN: 978-0-374-61323-5

Designed by Abby Kagan

The publisher of this book does not authorize the use or reproduction of any part of this book in any manner for the purpose of training artificial intelligence technologies or systems. The publisher of this book expressly reserves this book from the Text and Data Mining exception in accordance with Article 4(3) of the European Union Digital Single Market Directive 2019/790.

Our books may be purchased in bulk for specialty retail/wholesale, literacy, corporate/premium, educational, and subscription box use. Please contact MacmillanSpecialMarkets@macmillan.com.

www.fsgbooks.com
Follow us on social media at @fsgbooks

10 9 8 7 6 5 4 3 2 1

To Aabid Allibhai,

Without whom this collection of articles would not exist in almost diary-like form of my very earliest efforts of trying to assert myself, a self I did not then know I had, or that a self was even possible. In my whole life then there is only one thing that I was ashamed of and it is that I exist! For now that I exist I have allowed others to know what I really have been thinking. To see my earliest expressions of my thoughts makes me shudder a little, but not too much. I am surprised now, not proud (Pride is not a beautiful garment), that I ploughed through all sorts of difficulties that stood in my way, one of them being I was a Black Girl! But I did not know I was a Black Girl, I had always been Black and for the first sixteen years of my life I was a Girl.

This conversation does not really belong in my gratitude to Aabid, who was so devoted to me and full of admiration and love, but because of him many things came back to me in the form of Memory. I owe him not a thing money can buy. I owe him my admiration and support and dedication to his future as a scholar.

And so to Aabid Allibhai, with gratitude in all the ways we Human Beings have to express it and to say it: Love!

Contents

Introduction by Henry Louis Gates, Jr.	ix
The Triumph of Bad and Cool (1974)	3
Erotica! (1975)	8
If Mammies Ruled the World (1975)	12
Pam Grier (1975)	15
The Labelle Hustle (1975)	23
Last of the Black White Girls (1976)	27
Jamaica Kincaid's New York (1977)	32
Antigua Crossings (Fiction) (1978)	50
Ovando (Fiction) (1989)	62
Athol Fugard (Interview by Jamaica Kincaid) (1990)	72
The Finishing Line (Fiction) (1990)	88
Foreword to *Babouk: Voices of Resistance* (1991)	91
On Seeing England for the First Time (1991)	96
Biography of a Dress (1992)	109
An Antiguan Election Journal (1994)	118
Christmas Pictures from a Warm Climate (1994)	131
Introduction to *The Best American Essays, 1995*	135
The Little Revenge from the Periphery (1997)	140
Introduction to *Generations of Women* (1998)	147
Introduction to *My Favorite Plant* (1998)	154
Introduction to *Poetics of Place* (1998)	159
Looking at Giverny (1998)	164
Those Words That Echo . . . Echo . . . Echo Through Life (1999)	169
Islander Once, Now a Voyager (2000)	175
Sowers and Reapers (2001)	181
Her Best Friend Provokes Her to Write About Her Garden (2002)	190

Splendor in the Glass (2002)	194
The Garden the Year Just Passed (2002)	198
The Lure of the Poppy (2002)	207
Gardening (2003)	211
Living History in Vermont (2003)	217
Desert Blooms (2004)	220
Jumby Bay (2004)	223
Introduction to *The Best American Travel Writing, 2005*	226
Formal Meets Folly (2005)	234
Foreword to Ian Frazier's *Gone to New York* (2006)	236
Captain's Farm (2006)	243
Foreword to Alexandre Dumas's *Georges* (2007)	246
Dances with Daffodils (2007)	249
Her Infinite Variety (2008)	252
The Estrangement (2009)	256
Lack, Part Two (2009)	260
Tide (2011)	263
Introduction to Simone Schwarz-Bart's *The Bridge of Beyond* (2013)	268
The Kind of Gardener I Am Not (2018)	273
The Walk to Robert Frost's House (2019)	277
A Letter to Robinson Crusoe (2019)	283
I See the World (2020)	288
Inside the American Snow Dome (2020)	292
I was never really making a garden so much as having a conversation (2020)	296
The Disturbances of the Garden (2020)	302
Acknowledgments	313

Introduction
by *Henry Louis Gates, Jr.*

JAMAICA KINCAID was born Elaine Potter Richardson in St. John's, Antigua, on May 25, 1949. Her mother, Annie Victoria Richardson, was born in Dominica; her father, Roderick Potter, was an Antiguan taxi driver and chauffeur. Annie Richardson—and the fictionalized version of her—would be key characters in her daughter's work. Kincaid barely knew her birth father. She lived with her mother and the man who would eventually become her stepfather, David Drew, a cabinetmaker. (Annie Richardson and David Drew did not marry until 1967.)

Kincaid recalled her mother doting on her when she was a child. Annie taught her to read, made her clothes, and ensured that she received an education. Her relationship with her mother changed after the birth of her three brothers in 1958, 1960, and 1962. Kincaid believed that her mother lost interest in her and instead spent her time caring for her sons and her ill husband. Her resentment grew when she was removed from school, first to help out at home, and then, in 1965, to move to the United States to work as an au pair in Scarsdale, New York. Her mother ordered her to send money home. Kincaid refused.

Kincaid furthered her education in New York. She took classes at Westchester Community College in Valhalla, New York; Franconia College in Franconia, New Hampshire; and the New School for Social Research in New York City. In New York City she worked several short-term jobs while publishing her writing in *Ingenue*, *Ms.*, and *The Village Voice*. During these years she adopted the name Jamaica Kincaid, which she believed gave her the freedom to write whatever she wanted, especially about her family. She spoke about fiction versus nonfiction in 1992, saying, "I write about myself for the most part, and about things that have happened to me. Everything I say is true, and everything I say is not true. You couldn't admit any of it to a court of law. It would not be good evidence."

Kincaid began contributing to *The New Yorker*'s Talk of the Town column in 1974. She was a staff writer at the magazine from 1976 until 1996. Her first published story, "Girl," appeared in *The New Yorker* in June 1978. It would become the first story in her first book, *At the Bottom of the River*. In 1979 she married Allen Shawn, the son of her *New Yorker* editor, William Shawn. They had two children (Annie, born 1985, and Harold, born 1988) and would divorce in 2002.

I first read "Girl" when it appeared in the magazine, which I could read only casually during summer vacation, at my own pace, sometimes skipping around from article to article, at other times reading it straight through—at least, trying to. "Girl" I seem to have stumbled on, without actually glancing at its author's name. I should explain that by June of 1978, I had just submitted my PhD thesis to the Faculty of English Language and Literature at the University of Cambridge and was anxiously awaiting word of its approval, which would allow me to become an assistant professor of English and Afro-American studies at Yale. Exhausted by that ordeal, leisurely leafing through the splendid pages of *The New Yorker* was welcome relief.

By this time, I was beginning to see that African American literature was in the midst of what we might think of as a renascence, a burst of irresistibly vigorous belletristic creativity from a younger generation of writers, in the wake of the ideologically driven Black Arts Movement of the late 1960s, a small but growing body of creative literature that seemed to be as much, if not more, about other great literature, about aesthetics, as about content. Black Arts literature unapologetically privileged *content*, for sure, and the critical theory and practice that arose around it was excessively, perhaps overweeningly, scornful of any text that seemed to be privileging form, or in dialogue with the canon of Western (read: *white*) literature. In its wake burst a few writers who would, in retrospect, inaugurate a new period in African American literary history, including, to name just two of the most important, Toni Morrison (with *The Bluest Eye*, *Sula*, and *Song of Solomon*), and Ishmael Reed, whose forays into satire (especially *Mumbo Jumbo* and *Flight to Canada*) were works of stunning originality, indeed, like Morrison's, works of literary genius. These works, all published between 1970 and 1977, were clear signs that something dramatically *new* was manifesting itself in black literature, something unexpected and quite exciting—and that "something" would be propelled by the writing of black women.

By the time I submitted my dissertation, a younger generation of literary critics, trained in English departments and American studies programs, had begun the search for a critical language worthy of this emerging literature, worthy, as it were, of this emerging moment, which was impossible not to notice, not to be swept up in. Criticism, in other words, was being invigorated, too, especially by the theories of structuralism, post-structuralism, and deconstruction that were making their way across the English Channel from the continent and across the Atlantic from Europe. Like other scholars of literature, we were caught up in what, in retrospect, was most certainly an age of critical theory. And it was exciting!

At the first conference at which new theories of African American literature were presented, at Yale in the summer of 1977, the venerable scholar Eleanor Traylor, close friend of Toni Morrison, Maya Angelou, and James Baldwin, and most recently the chair of the Department of English at Howard University, said something, almost as an aside, that struck me with enormous force: she said it was time for black writers to "assume their propositions, and stop feeling the need to *claim them*." That they should, in other words, make the fact of their "blackness" the default, and write about what it means to be black and human, what it means to be a human being who also happens to be black . . . or not! That black writers should stop feeling the need to plead our people's *case*, or to refute centuries of racist dogma about our supposed "natures." Black creative writers, she argued, needed to get on with *making literature*, first and foremost, and leave the revolution-making to those better suited to it, people such as politicians, ideologues, and propagandists. Aspire to the mastery of craft as sublime as that of our greatest jazz musicians, she said.

It is difficult for me to think of a bit of wisdom that has affected me more profoundly than this comment by Eleanor Traylor. In fact, decades later, it would be these words, ringing in my ear, that first convinced me that the author of a holograph manuscript called *The Bondwoman's Narrative* was, in fact, as she claimed to be, an African American female former slave. Why? Because she introduced her black characters without any reference to their race, whereas the whiteness of her white characters was somehow signaled or marked. Blackness was this author's default! As unlikely as it was, I was convinced by this fact alone that this handwritten manuscript had been written by a black woman who most probably was who she said she was.

And it was with Eleanor's curious charge in my subconscious, I think, that I stumbled upon "Girl":

This is how to make a good medicine for a cold; this is how to make a good medicine to throw away a child before it even becomes a child; this how to catch a fish; this is how to throw back a fish you don't like, and that way something bad won't fall on you; this is how to bully a man; this is how a man bullies you; this is how to love a man, and if this doesn't work there are other ways, and if they don't work don't feel too bad about giving up; this is how to spit up in the air if you feel like it, and this is how to move quick so that it doesn't fall on you; this is how to make ends meet; always squeeze bread to make sure it's fresh; *but what if the baker won't let me feel the bread?*; you mean to say that after all you are really going to be the kind of woman who the baker won't let near the bread?

It is difficult for me to express how astonished I was reading this story. Was the author *black*? Could this author *be black*? She had with great determination refused to say what she was. There were clues, certainly, but very subtle ones, such as dishes like "pumpkin fritters" and food like "salt fish," and something that one sings called "benna," but her reader would only learn the meaning of that by looking it up. Her world, the world she had created and was describing in this short story, was self-contained. Only the author's first name, "Jamaica," surely a nom de plume, convinced me that this author could be a black woman. (For a brief moment, I have to confess, I wondered if the author were actually a white woman, after all, and since nobody could actually have been named by their parents "Jamaica," was using the first name "Jamaica" to disguise her real identity, to put us off the trail . . .

So *this* is what Eleanor had been talking about the summer

before, I remember thinking! And that same effect, this same practice of "assuming her propositions," in the curious phrasing that Eleanor Traylor had used at that seminal conference about new ways of reading black literature, can so beautifully be gleaned in the following passage from "The Circling Hand," certainly my favorite short story of Jamaica's, published five years after "Girl" and to my mind one of the most beautifully written stories in the whole of English literature:

> When I got to our house, I rushed into the yard and called out for her, but no answer came. I then walked into the house. At first, I didn't hear anything. Then I heard sounds coming from the direction of my parents' room. My mother must be in there, I thought. When I got to the door, I could see that my mother and father were lying in their bed. It didn't interest me what they were doing—only that my mother's hand was on the small of my father's back and that it was making a circular motion. But her hand! It was white and bony, as if it had long been dead and had been left out in the elements. It seemed not to be her hand, and yet it could only be her hand, so well did I know it. It went around and around in the same circular motion, and I looked at it as if I would never see anything else again. If I were to forget everything else in the world, I could not forget her hand as it looked then. I could also make out that the sounds I had heard were her kissing my father's ears and his mouth and his face. I looked at them for I don't know how long.

It may sound like an exaggeration, but I don't think that any black writer before Jamaica Kincaid had successfully foregrounded a very small instance of an episode in a character's life or a character's emotion intended to reveal an aspect of the complexity of discovering one's humanity—in this case, a certain inevitable alienation between mother and daughter—without, in some way, tying it to the larger world of black-white race relations. Never. And revealing that emotion, let's say, is what the story was *about*. It was not about a black mother and her black daughter on some island, difficult to pronounce correctly, floating somewhere in the Caribbean. No, it was about itself, as it were; an act of language, first and foremost. And if I am correct, that is both an astonishing fact and an astonishing achievement. "We must write less of issues that are particular and more of feelings that are general," the freeborn black poet Frances Ellen Watkins Harper pleaded, in a letter that she sent to Thomas Hamilton, the august editor of *The Anglo-African*, in 1861. "We are blessed with hearts and brains that compass more than ourselves in our present plight." But, to my mind, no black author had successfully managed to do this, to write, as it were, not exactly beyond race, but with one's "blackness" assumed, an uncommented-on default, in the same way that we talk to each other "behind the Veil," in Du Bois's marvelous phrase. And here, finally, it was, the fulfillment of Harper's plea, I remember thinking, barely able to contain my excitement, as I read "Girl." And that sense of stunned amazement would recur over the next few years as I read her next seven stories published in *The New Yorker*, before reading and re-reading "The Circling Hand," in my opinion, her masterpiece.

What binds these short essays and writings, beginning in 1973 and running up to the present, is a striking voice, mordant, irreverent, and generous. Ranging through topics in black life and culture, African America, American America, the African West Indies, despised England, the history of colonialism especially in the Caribbean, writing itself, friendship, gardens, her mother, her children, and herself, Kincaid approaches these personal and political subjects with a driving, unremitting eye—though never without humor. These pieces, written for venues such as *The Village Voice*, *Ms.*, *The New York Times*, *The New Yorker*, and most recently *Architectural Digest*, measure that simultaneously serious and sarcastic posture by meting out irreverence to all the objects under her contemplation: Muhammad Ali, Monet's garden, or the marred history of colonialism. She blends reportage and personal experience with a deep understanding of history, showing how events "out there" can be felt in "here." "Dear Mr. Crusoe, Please don't come," she wrote in a piece in 2019. She laughs at the things that are meant to frighten her: "Once, as I was walking down a street and just about to pass by a man, he said to me, 'Hey sugar, you coming at me like a fresh baked cake.' When I didn't say anything but kept on walking he crept up behind me and whispered in my ear, 'Speak Devil, speak.' I looked at him and I laughed out loud. Every time I think of this, I smile to myself."

This body of work conveys a powerful zest for living. "How thrilling it can be to find yourself in a place among things that remind you of some of the difficulties involved in being a human being and, at the same time, some of its pleasures," she writes in "Living History in Vermont." Elsewhere, after the death of her father: "I despise death and consider it a humiliation and in any case much overdone and so plan never to do it myself and plan never to have anything at all to do with it, for it is so contagious," she wrote in *The New York Times* in 1999. Desiring death is a luxury, she warns; living is urgent, not to be taken for granted.

Jamaica's collected nonfiction falls generally into four broad but intertwined categories: racism and colonialism; motherhood; the relation between literature and life and death; and, most certainly, gardening. These themes often blend into each other, upsetting the imagined purity of categorization. Gardens, language, and her relationship with her mother all seem to her coterminous—part of the constant work of life. But her nonfiction, nevertheless, is not at all vague: it is, at all points, pinned in place by a deep sense of history and the stubborn irreducibility of the past.

Without doubt, however, her great subject is her mother, and the powerful ambivalence that that relationship generates. "Then again," she wrote in *Harper's Magazine* in 2009, having just announced that she was not thinking of her mother, "I am always thinking of my mother; I believe every action of a certain kind that I make is completely influenced by her, completely infused with her realness, her existence in my life."

And her estrangement from her mother remains throughout these essays the source of a deep and abiding grief. It is also the major condition for their possibility; it is into that breach that she writes. She also lost a brother to AIDS, and notes that he was unable to look after himself properly when going out into the world; their mother doted on him when sick in a way she never had in health, giving detail to the powerful but complicated love she gave. Kincaid speaks of her own, different relationship with her children with great warmth and power.

Gardens become a central preoccupation later; she regards the work of cultivation as a kind of weaving and unweaving of life itself. She invests horticulture with a sense of the matter that binds all life: "a great divide has fallen on our life, on my life certainly and on the way I see the world: in life itself there are lots of dead in it, the kingdoms of mammals, vegetable, mineral, and all the others, are all in the living sometimes but in the dead all times" ("I See the World," *The Paris Review*, April 2020).

She has a sense of what it takes to become a person, to put yourself together. Becoming is an act of invention, tested by the real. She calls on what I think of as a seductively lyrical accessibility in her writing, with its continual pull between drawing distinctions and toppling them: her rhetorical strategies show an interest in drumming up contrasts and pulling the rug, as when she writes: "The color black and the color white are not ultimately the colors of the imagination; the colors black and white are so useful, they are the colors of work, the colors black and white are the best way for the harshness of reality (and the real is always so harsh if only because it is its true self); in the beginning, the one to which we are, for good and bad attached, the words are black written on paper which is white" (introduction to *Poetics of Place*).

She feels she has won, fought for, stolen her place in the canon: "I do not come from a family of writers. I never knew a writer. We are oral people." She relishes her plot. Books were, she confesses, the only things she ever truly loved, and literature—writing—has saved her life.

Talking to an interviewer, Alyssa Loh, for *American Reader* in 2015, Kincaid reflected on the persistent effort to characterize her writing as angry. How wrong that assessment seems after spending time with this rich body of work, which bristles with rage, wonder, and so much else. "You make me realize that I am pissed. Not at you, but at this perception that I am pissed—I'm really pissed at it," she said to Loh. "That's the way I write. It's never going to stop. And the more it makes people annoyed the more I will do it. And it's actually really good writing. I'm a good writer. They should just say that: 'She's a great writer.' I am."

Putting Myself Together

The Triumph of Bad and Cool

'Cos black is so bad
And white is so sad.
Ah said it
Ah meant it
Ah really re-pra-sent it.
—Street jive heard in Cambridge, Massachusetts

BLACK BOYS ARE BAD. They are bad and they are cool. They are so bad that sometimes they do indescribable things. White boys are not bad and they are not cool. But sometimes they like to think they are. When white boys want to play bad they walk through Central Park at midnight and then write about it. That is not bad and anyone who makes a living that way should be paid in Puerto Rican furniture.

Last week Muhammad Ali did a few things to show that he was the baddest and coolest. He beat that chump of a champ George Foreman in eight rounds: he became the only authentic, living hero on the face of this planet, and then he proved himself to be the only

1974, Nov. 7. "The Triumph of Bad and Cool." *The Village Voice*: 22.

viable personality left over from the sixties. It was just glorious. Allah now has oil and a world boxing champion. Could any god ask for more?

I saw Muhammad Ali do those things at the Victoria Theater in Harlem on Wednesday night. So did a number of other people, most of them men who bore the marks of former bad boys. In any case, they spoke that way. They used the word nigger very loosely and they made it sound worthwhile and respectable. They also used the word faggot a lot which they did not make sound worthwhile and respectable. In these circles, I discovered, faggot has replaced the word mo'fucker.

It was a very un-slick audience. No one looked as if they had gotten dressed up for the event. The closest thing to being glamorous anyone came was one man who walked around with an orange-colored Panasonic cassette player. Lots of people carried brown paper bags which held bottles of stuff. Yes, it was a low-tone crowd, but a very bad low-tone crowd.

Most people were for Ali. You could tell because no one bought the Foreman posters. That wasn't a good sign for Foreman. A bad man ought to have the bad people behind him. Well, Foreman might be bad, but he wasn't the baddest. People were going crazy in the aisles telling each other how Ali would do it, in what time, in what style. It wasn't entertainment, it wasn't politics, it was going to be vindication. Ali became a redeemer of sorts.

There were lots of guards in the theater and they all wore dark glasses. It made them look very ominous but they were really quite nice. They saved choice seats for themselves. I sat next to one named Michael Finch. There were some things he wanted me to know.

"Muhammad represents all black manhood. He's got the pride of his people. He fought against America for himself and for his people. Aside from all that, I just dig his poetics. But I tell you he gonna give that Foreman what's his. He gonna open his eyes, then he gonna close them, then he gonna put a tin cup in his hand and put him on a street corner where he belong."

Then, "What would happen if the picture won't come on? I tell you if that picture don't come on you'll see hell up in Harlem. Hell. I'd throw off this stuff and pretend I'm one of you all."

Michael Finch had an opinion on everything. When the image of David Frost, who acted as one of the hosts, first appeared on the screen, he said, "What's that faggot doing up there? He don't belong in no fight. He should be home with his wife drinking coffee and dipping doughnuts."

He called Joe Frazier a faggot and a turkey. He called George Foreman a faggot and a monster. He called everyone he didn't like a faggot. When he saw Muhammad Ali in a pre-fight interview, he said, "He's a terrible nigger, man, I tell you that nigger is bad."

I learned a number of things that evening.

1. Muhammad is the cool way of referring to Muhammad Ali.

2. When a black person uses the word nigger it can be a positive or a negative thing. It all depends on a number of complicated variables. White people in general, however, are not allowed to let the word even cross their minds. Michael Finch said that nigger is a bad word and white people just don't measure up as far as badness is concerned.

3. The announcer said that other people had said it (and I think he meant the fight) couldn't happen in the deepest part of Africa, but here it is. This was followed by random film clips of downtown Zaire. Well, it is happening in the deepest part of Africa. Downtown Zaire has wonderful, big skyscrapers. It looked just tremendous. The World Trade Center may be hideous in Manhattan but it would look just fabulous in Zaire. Skyscrapers, like polyester, may be the birthright of Third World consumers.

4. Zaire has an authenticity program that promotes and encourages native customs that Europeans used to consider vulgar and primitive. Before the fight the closed-circuit as well as the audience

were entertained by Zairians performing their own various tribal folk dances. It was very elaborate and suggestive and you saw that the Soul Train Dancers didn't invent the Funky anything. Perhaps it goes to prove that this particular racial group is just all round rhythmic. Michael Finch said he liked the way those people get down. In any case the fact that authenticity programs and skyscrapers can exist side by side and find appreciation under the same national umbrella is somehow remarkable.

5. The Zaire River used to be called the Congo River. I don't know why they changed it. Congo seems like such a nice name for a river.

6. President Mobutu, the president of Zaire, is very stylish and very handsome. He wears a leopard skin pillbox very well.

Around ten o'clock, Muhammad Ali entered the ring. The audience in the theater rose to its feet and cheered. Actually, they said, "Ali bomaye." The tribal spirit is very contagious. He looked like a movie star, the way he strode into the ring. His face looked smooth as a peach, his hair was nicely done—no split ends. Then he took off his robe and flexed the muscles in his arms. Gosh! He has the best pair of collarbones you have ever seen on any screen. Muhammad Ali before the fight looked so precious. Muhammad Ali after the fight was a little rough in spots. He clowned a little and led the audience in the Ali bomaye chant. It was quite heroic. I thought he was just wonderful, he said he was just wonderful, the audience in the theater told his video image he was just wonderful.

Five minutes or so later George Foreman entered the ring. The audience booed at him. He didn't have the grace of Ali at all. And besides he had lots of split ends. He just doesn't have the face of a hero. In a pre-fight interview, Ali said that the way he psyched himself up for this fight with Foreman was to watch lots of old horror movies like *Horror of Dracula* and *The Return of the Werewolf.* Well, it is true that Foreman looks like a big black mound of brute force which is not the sort of thing you want to meet alone in a deserted alley. Foreman fell into the unappealing low-tone category. Ali was high-tone all the way and you can't get any badder than that.

At the end of it all Foreman the chump was beaten by Ali the Champ. That was bad enough. But really the baddest thing in that whole fight was Ali leading the crowd in the Ali bomaye chant somewhere between the fourth and fifth round of the fight. Now that is so bad and so cool. It took the concept of bad and cool further than you ever dreamed it could go.

Foreman is now so ashamed of himself that he goes around telling people that Ali is a credit to his family, race, and boxing. Maybe. But Ali says he is a credit to Allah. I believe him. It is the year of Allah and all you foolish people who think someone else is coming, good luck. But just remember, I told you first: when he comes he'll be riding a camel, not carrying a cross.

Erotica!

Recent research casts doubt on the common belief that women are vastly less aroused by erotic stimuli than are men. The supposed lack of female response may well be due to social and cultural inhibitions against reporting such arousal and to the fact that erotic material is generally oriented to a male audience.
—Report of the President's Commission on Obscenity and Pornography, 1970

HISTORICALLY, EROTIC EXPRESSION IN ART has been a no-woman's-land. Male painters and sculptors have prevailed, and they have metamorphosed, allegorized, and idealized women as sacred virgins, passionate romantics, or seductive sorceresses.

Realizing that women's image has been distorted and rendered alien to the way *we* see and know ourselves and our sexuality, a growing number of women artists have been turning to erotic imagery to express and celebrate femaleness.

1975, Jan. 1. "Erotica!" *Ms.* Vol. 3, iss. 7: 30–33.

Often the artist trying to make an erotic statement finds herself combining politics with aesthetics and hassling with some difficult questions. How can one explore the vulnerability of sexual relations, concealing nothing, without being voyeuristic or titillating? How can one make the distinction, if there is one, between eroticism and pornography?

"Pornography titillates, eroticism stimulates. The erotic theme to me," explains painter Joan Semmel, "is one of communication—two people expressing their humanity to each other. A man's point of view is more concerned with aberrations, the objectification of women. Women are almost always passive and in a nonparticipatory position. I think women will be more comfortable with erotic imagery now that women artists are doing it. We have not responded before because it's been done by men for men, mainly to exploit women."

Betty Dodson, on the other hand, calls herself a pornographer. She has exhibited her explicit classical-style drawings, showing human bodies copulating and masturbating, under the "pornographic" label. "I call myself a pornographer," she says, "because I think the word ought to be legitimized. 'Pornography' has been a dirty word, and I think that anything that has to do with sex should be good. Sex is something people do, and there should be nothing bad about showing it. If women shy away from this kind of art, it's only because of their conditioning."

Indeed, pop artist Marjorie Strider was making erotic drawings ten years ago, but, she says, "I was ashamed of them." In her current erotic work, she takes off on the motifs of ancient Greek vases. By combining eroticism and humor, Strider produces works that are inventive and irreverent.

Symbolic and political elements occur frequently in the erotic art of contemporary women. Using commercial images for inspiration, Rosalind Hodgkins explores and documents myths that exploit women. "The more I explored the role of women in society, the more I had to deal with eroticism. I wanted to show how our sensuality has been perverted, and I wanted to redefine our sex in art."

If women are staking new claims on the erotic landscape, they are also widening the erotic vocabulary. Hannah Wilke sculpts layers of latex rubber into an abstraction of female sexuality, as a rejection of what she calls "the rigid impotence" of male erotic art. And Maureen Connor makes gigantic "breathing flowers" of satin and velvet to expose the biological vulnerability of a woman. The flowers, which quiver in response to electronic stimulation, invite the viewer to touch.

Women artists are giving us new views not only of women but of men as well. Sylvia Sleigh and Eunice Golden are two artists who are each dealing with the subject of the male nude. "After all," Sleigh says, "men have been showing us their ideal woman; it's about time we showed them our ideal man. Women should see more of men; we should see more of what we're getting." A realistic painter, she handles the subject straightforwardly, often by using classical themes and poses. She notes that men's reactions to her work are almost always angry. "They've always thought of the male nude as something very private."

Eunice Golden provokes an even angrier reaction. She paints the male nude, accentuating that most vulnerable appendage of male anatomy—the erect penis. "We live in a guilt-ridden society, and in doing the male nude I wanted to get to the core of that guilt. My nudes are active, frontal, energized forms. The work is erotic because it involves all the senses and it's advocating a new vocabulary, a new way of seeing and dealing with eroticism."

The biggest obstacle facing the woman erotic artist is the reluctance of many museums and galleries to show her work. The idea of showing the male nude—as perceived by the female artist—is in particular disfavor. The pattern of exclusion from muscums was clear enough for artist-activist Anita Steckel to mobilize her sisters to publicize and speak out against this "sexism and puritanism."

Museum directors—almost all of them men—defend their rejection of the male nude (and other sexually explicit work done by women) by saying the art "lacks quality." Perhaps the male ruling class just isn't ready for vulnerability—to let the world see it with its pants down. It may be a situation analogous to the *National Geographic* magazine's rule of skin: the only acceptable naked woman is a "native" naked woman. For the museums it seems to be: the only good nude is a female nude.

While established museums were nervously evading the issue, the art historians Phyllis and Eberhard Kronhausen opened the International Museum of Erotic Art in San Francisco in 1973, and began actively acquiring the works of women artists for their permanent collection. The public response, from women in particular, has been overwhelmingly positive, and the Kronhausens report that more and more women are participating in the museum's educational programs.

Many of the women making erotic art today are changing the scenario, giving us a defiant, double-edged, yet often kinder view of the sexual experience. In the process, they are liberating erotica from its voyeuristic, underground ghetto.

If Mammies Ruled the World

I SAW *GONE WITH THE WIND* last week for the fourth time, which means that I like the film very much. I am sure at one time, when the film was made, it was meant to be a melodrama. Now it seems a very colorful comedy. But I don't like this film because of Scarlett (petulant little bitch), or Rhett (dashing chump—what do you really think of a man who says to a woman he knows is clearly no good, "I love you Scarlett, in spite of you and me and the whole world going to pieces around us") or Melanie (a dull martyr) or Ashley (silly wimp). What I really like about this film is Hattie McDaniel, the Mammy.

A Mammy, I think, is different from your mother because while your mother is expected to love you, Mammies love you for no reason at all. A Mammy is fair, loving, loyal, nurturing, supportive, protective, generous, and devoted. Ideally, she is a big black woman, who wears big, full skirts that are good for burying your face in. Aunt Jemima was one of the best Mammies and even if she was not

1975, May 5. "If Mammies Ruled the World." *The Village Voice*: 86.

really responsible for giving us the pancake, the credit does not look very good on anyone else.

A Mammy is the sort of person who will pretend to be listening to you as you jabber away about all the insane things happening in your life, but what she's really doing is just looking at you, thinking, isn't she wonderful, isn't she great?

A Mammy is the sort of person to whom you can say, I just raped fourteen children and I killed eight of them, and she'll say, isn't that terrible, I love you anyway.

A Mammy always seems to have her own rhyme and reason about the way things are supposed to work. "Mammy says that if you put a knife under the bed, it will cut the pain in two!" Really. Mammy says, "You eat!" or "You better take your nap right now," or "You better come in out de cold or you gonna catch your death."

Black people do not like the image of a Mammy anymore, but they haven't liked anything wonderful about themselves in a long time. At least not publicly. They don't seem to like acknowledging the fact that they sing and dance better than anybody else; that they really can shuffle their feet; that no one else has quite mastered the beauty of rolling the eyes, hands on the hips, shaking the head from side to side, and muttering, hmmm, hmmm, all in one stroke. They have sat back pathetically while Fred Astaire pawned himself off as the greatest lap dancer of the century. For true!

The fact is that black people, in all their various stages, are just fabulous. The other fact is that white people are not so fabulous, but I don't think there is anything wrong with that. At least I hope not. White people are a little bit normal and a little bit ordinary. I'll give you an example. Did you know that the Charleston started in Charleston, South Carolina, where black people were parodying the way white debutantes danced. I say, can you beat that?

What I imagine black people are really objecting to when they disapprove of Mammies, tap dancers, and moochers is the system that produced these things. Richard Goldstein told me that he thought *Gone With the Wind* was the first disaster movie. I hadn't really thought of it that way but God, did the Old South ever need destroying. The Old South remains one of the most vivid examples of why white people in America won't be able to look themselves clearly in the eyes for a long time. White Southerners have always appeared to me to be savages of the North American continent. I first heard about George Wallace standing in the school door when I was about ten years old. My teacher read it to us from *Time* magazine. She asked us what we thought of such a person and I told her that since Alabama was on the other side of the Mississippi, it must be a part of the jungle, therefore George Wallace was a savage and we should send him little Gideon Bibles. I didn't know civilized people behaved in that way. Scarlett and Rhett and Melanie and Ashley were not civilized people and that's why they didn't deserve a Mammy. But the worst part of it is, they have successfully ruined for us any ideas about having Mammies. We may not be civilized people either, but I promise you that if Gerald Ford were a Mammy we would all be a lot happier.

I personally would like to have a Mammy for a lot of reasons, but my favorite reason for wanting one is so she could tell my editors, "Now you-all look here, don't go messing with my little Jamaica's copy or I'll make you all take to your bed like white on rice."

Pam Grier

THE MOCHA MOGUL OF HOLLYWOOD

PAM GRIER IS ONE OF three "bankable" movie actresses in Hollywood. The people who invest money in movies believe her name on the marquee insures box-office profits. The other two actresses whose names inspire that kind of confidence are Barbra Streisand and Liza Minnelli. But while they came to the screen with substantial reputations and wide appeal, Pam Grier's success has been more traditional. She had minor parts in a number of films before making *Black Mama White Mama*—the 1972 film that brought her public attention.

Pam Grier's success remains very marginal, however; you would most likely have to be black or regularly read such publications as *Black Stars* or *Right-On* to know of her. Her films—*Black Mama White Mama, Coffy, Foxy Brown, Sheba, Baby*—have been enormously successful financially. But "black" movies almost always

1975, Aug. 1. "Pam Grier: The Mocha Mogul of Hollywood." *Ms.* Vol. 4, iss. 2: 49–53.

make money. So, is it *her* or the *pictures*? The people in Hollywood say it's Pam Grier.

Although she has not demonstrated that she possesses the talent of a Cicely Tyson or a Ruby Dee, she has an extremely valuable asset—"star quality." She can so effortlessly dominate a scene that everything and everyone else in it becomes incidental. You are struck by how extraordinarily beautiful Pam Grier is and though her films tend to be shabbily put together, she comes across in them with intelligence and charm.

Pam Grier is the most winning example of a miscegenated person I have ever seen. She says she is part Caucasian, part Negro (on her father's side), part American Indian, part Asian (on her mother's side). Her skin is the exact color of the pancakes in the Little Black Sambo book. Her nose is the kind that was meant to flare when someone disgusts her. She has the kind of lips that look comfortable smiling, pouting, or pursing. She has big, dark, almost almond eyes, dark hair, long legs, and long arms. She has the sort of body that press agents like to promote as a sex symbol. "Me, sexy?" she says. "I'm just plain ol' red beans and rice." She has a very noncommittal accent but every once in a while, usually when she wants to make fun of something, she slips into a black syntax.

Pam Grier lives in a very large house in Los Angeles with a panoramic view of Mandeville Canyon. To enter the house, you must pass through an electronically controlled gate with a sign on it saying ATTACK DOGS ON DUTY. The house has such a sensitive burglar-alarm system that it is activated by any moving object over a few pounds. The house itself conveys a kind of modernness the newly rich are fond of. It's done up in a rather fresh and expensive department-store style. Large healthy plants are in appropriate corners; skins of wild animals are scattered in set places; and there are plenty of big chunky chairs, sofas, and cushions. On the walls are paintings and reproductions of modern graphics—and a copy of Norman Rockwell's *Family Tree*. The fare on the bookshelf ranges from art to dentistry to copies of *Gun Digest* and *The Book of Knives*.

Someone comes to clean the house regularly, and a man delivers drinking water, the way a man used to deliver milk. Three gardeners arrive twice a week to look after the grounds, which are nicely set off by a swimming pool in the shape of half a star.

Pam Grier shares this house with a man. Though I visited the house several times, I never saw him and was never aware of his presence. When I asked her about him, her reply was abrupt. "My boyfriend is a dentist. He is my Number One man and I want to tell you that he's very understanding and very smart. He's no one important or special. He's only special to me. But I date a lot of people in the business." And that was it. She didn't give me his name, and she didn't say who the other people she dated were. Once, though, as we were driving down Sunset Boulevard, talking about cool men, I told her I thought Teddy Pendergrass (lead singer of Harold Melvin and the Blue Notes) was the coolest person I could think of. And she said, "Teddy? Hey, I got his number." And she not only had his number, but she had two numbers for him. I was quite impressed.

Pamala Grier was born on May 26, 1949, the second of three children, the older of two girls, in Winston-Salem, North Carolina. When Pam was five, her father, a maintenance mechanic for the United States Air Force, was transferred to a base in Swindon, England. She lived on American military bases in Europe until she was fourteen years old.

Europeans, she says, loved her because she was dark-skinned and American, and she loved them because they had Coca-Cola. But after nine years, when the Griers came back to the States and settled in Denver, Colorado, she seemed decidedly "foreign." She spoke English with an accent; she liked having afternoon tea; she wore and thought fashionable a style of clothes seen only in illustrations of old adventure stories for girls; she had a certain "dicty" way of carrying herself that made her seem haughty and standoffish; she had been given a solid primary education and she loved reading books. Charming, yes, but popular? No, not in that neighborhood in Denver.

"Denver," she says, "wasn't bad—it was rough. I wasn't very big then and I found that you had to fight all the time. I mean you had to fight for your lunch money or act like you didn't have any. You couldn't even put money in your penny loafers. You had to put it in your socks or tape it under your shoes or something. It was pretty rough, especially for a young kid who had been sheltered on air force bases."

And then there were more normal teenage complications. "I thought I was too tall, too thin, too awkward. I had bow legs, and I thought they looked like stringbeans. My knees were the biggest thing on me. I used to dye my stockings with coffee because I had read somewhere that dark stockings give your legs a fuller look. I used to wear a color of lipstick my mother called 'asshole' pink. I wasn't popular with boys, and I almost didn't have a date for the senior prom. I felt strange, and I just couldn't find a balance."

At eighteen, she entered Metropolitan State College in Denver, spending a year there. She hoped to become a doctor. It was then that she entered a beauty contest, not because she felt any more attractive, but because the prize money would support another year in college. Though she wasn't judged the most beautiful contestant—she was the only black girl competing—she did win a prize for her singing and dancing. She was also seen by a Hollywood agent, who told her, "You ought to be in pictures." But David Baumgarten, head of the Agency for the Performing Arts, was serious. He offered to take her to Hollywood. She said no, but her mother said yes. Pam Grier went to Hollywood, where Baumgarten became her agent (which he still is), sent her to acting classes, and gave her a job as a switchboard operator with his agency.

Every day on her lunch hour, she would go for readings, but producers told her that she did not possess that elusive quality known as "Negro enough," that the space between her two front teeth might, on film, prove too distracting, that she was too fat or too thin.

One day, while going through the classifieds in a trade paper, she saw that a studio needed a switchboard operator. The studio was American International Pictures, and the job paid $25 more per week than she was making—an overwhelmingly appealing combination. She told the AIP personnel director that she could work a large, complicated switchboard. Then she came in forty-five minutes before anyone else on her first day, and successfully taught herself how to operate it.

"When I started working at AIP," she says, "I knew I wanted to learn about the business because I wanted to be in the business. I started listening in on calls, and I got to know a lot about what was going on. I wasn't doing anything new. People do it all the time, but if they have no use for the information it doesn't do them any good. I had use for the information. I wanted to see how things work, what makes a success and what makes a failure.

"When I relieved the production secretary, I would study the storyboards in the production room. I got to know who was doing what, where they were doing it, and how long it would take. Everything went click, click, click in my head. I was a little monster for the information."

But Pam Grier then wanted to be a movie star, not a producer or director. So she went to see Roger Corman, a notoriously successful producer of first-rate grade "B" pictures, who was casting a new film. She had no idea what it was about or what she could do in it. But she landed a minor role in *The Big Bird Cage*, and she has never answered anybody's telephone for a living since.

That was in 1969. It would be three years and bit parts in films like *The Big Doll House*, *The Twilight People*, and *Beyond the Valley of the Dolls* before she got to star in Corman's *Black Mama White Mama*—a women-in-prison film broadly based on *The Defiant Ones*. American International Pictures, who had forgotten they once had a switchboard operator named Pam Grier, released it. While "White Mama" seemed to drift into a haze, people took notice of "Black Mama," Pam Grier. AIP went on to package the films that have Grier confronting villainy unlike any other screen heroine.

In *Coffy* she blows off the head of the pusher who has made her sister hopelessly addicted to heroin. In *Foxy Brown* she avenges the cold-blooded slaying of her brother and boyfriend by castrating the villain, putting his penis in a jar filled with pickling juice, and making a present of it to his girlfriend. In *Sheba, Baby*—the newest and most middle class of the three—she saves her father's loan company from a gangster takeover. They kill her father. She cleverly manipulates them into killing each other, saving Mr. Big for herself. She gets him with a spear gun.

These films have never received critical notice, but they were not meant to. They are mostly simplistic, sensational, violent, and technically faulty. But *Coffy*, *Foxy Brown*, and *Sheba, Baby* have one outstanding redeeming value—they are the only films to come out of Hollywood in a long time to show us a woman who is independent, resourceful, self-confident, strong, and courageous. Above all, they are the only films to show us a woman who triumphs!

But does that kind of triumph provide a model worth following? In a narrow and specific way, yes. When I was a little girl in Antigua, I saw an Eve Arden film. She played a woman with plenty of brains, authority, and style. She had a number of younger men working for her, who would behave in a very silly manner whenever she left them on their own. It was only her sharp orders that shaped them up.

I liked that woman. It's not that I cared for the way in which she ordered people around, but I cared very much that she had ability, presence, brains, and what seemed to me the courage to control and impose order on a world outside the house. I have wished many times that I could propel myself through life with the same spirit as that celluloid image.

It is, I believe, that same kind of triumphant spirit and character that holds *Coffy*, *Foxy Brown*, and *Sheba, Baby* together.

"When I was a little girl," Pam Grier says, as she skillfully maneuvers a Mercedes convertible onto the crowded San Diego Freeway, "my mother used to give me lots of advice but she told me one thing I'll never forget. She said, 'Work hard and learn to be independent because you have to make your own way in this world. Use your own strength and no one will ever be able to take advantage of you. When you allow someone to take advantage of you it's another form of slavery.'

"I have done nothing but work hard. I don't have a press agent to put things out for me that mean nothing. What I have are four phones that start ringing at seven o'clock in the morning. I take my business seriously, not just as an actress but as a filmmaker. And that's why I am where I am today." Grier has recently formed her own production company, called Brown Sun Productions after the pet name her grandmother gave her. Her immediate motive isn't to change the image of women in films so much as it is to change the image of Pam Grier in films. That image—of the "black sex goddess"—has been fostered by AIP's handling of her films.

"When they first saw *Coffy*," she recalls, "no one thought it would make any money. They said it was too depressing, that the character was too strong and too serious. So they cut it up—taking out the most important parts, like tender scenes between me and my sister. So all you see is *bang, bang, bang*, shoot 'em up tits and ass, *bang, bang, bang*, shoot 'em up tits and ass. But they kept saying, people will love it now. It's entertainment.

"AIP's policy is to give the niggers shit. They don't like me but they want to work with me because I make them money. They don't like that I talk about the cheesy way they work or that I say the movies that I did for them were jerk jobs. They think I am being ungrateful because they discovered me and made me a star.

"The people in Hollywood don't understand where I am coming

from. They don't understand where I have been. They have lived in Beverly Hills for too long, and they don't know from nothing because they are not exposed to anything. My movies were the first they had done with a strong woman character, not to mention black. Once they saw the grosses, they wanted to do every one of them like that. I was angry. You can't give people the same thing all the time. You made money on one thing so the next time you go for something a little better than you had before.

"I set up my own corporation. Should I sit around and wait for these cigar-smoking-conservative-high-water-Bostonian-wing-tipped-shoes-businessmen-lolling-in-their-studios to give me a job? I don't wait for anything."

Grier's energy and drive are enormous. When I arrived at her house at half-past nine one morning, she had already been up three hours—which included an hour's worth of jogging. Then she got dressed, went to see her agent, stopped off at the publicity offices of AIP to autograph promotional photos of herself, posed obligingly at the switchboard for the photographer, drove to Inglewood to have her skis repaired and ski boots refitted. Later that evening, she and her cousin Rosey Grier, who is a liaison between the city's black youth and the office of the mayor of Los Angeles, were to attend a charity benefit. I left her at half-past five and in all that time she had only a cup of coffee. She says that she eats only one meal a day.

But it is enough fuel to keep Pam Grier going—reading scripts for herself and others, and getting her drum-playing in shape for a forthcoming nightclub act. "I'm experimenting," she says. "I haven't had the chance to expose myself before because I am black and I am female. But I am ready now. I made a lot of money that I could have spent on stuff for me, but I have invested it in my future."

She slows up for a moment, then blurts out, "God, I hope I haven't told you anything you don't want to hear. People are always telling me to be mysterious. I say, 'Me, mysterious? That's like trying to hide Mount Everest.'"

The Labelle Hustle

LABELLE—Patti LaBelle, Sarah Dash, and Nona Hendryx—is a group of black singers widely credited with being firsts: *first* black group to give a concert at New York's Metropolitan Opera House; *first* black group to give a concert at the Harkness Ballet Theater; *first* "black-girl group" to be successful without the traditional "black-girl group" props—the extravagant hairdos, the sequined gowns, patterned dance steps, charm-school manners. Labelle has succeeded in areas and on levels where others haven't even tried, and for a group of black women whose talents are so very medium, that is an impressive achievement.

Labelle has a past that they now seem desperate to repudiate. It is not a particularly illustrious or memorable one in the manner of, for instance, the Shirelles or the Ronettes—groups who were popular around the same time as Patti LaBelle and the Bluebelles. That's what Labelle used to be called, and as such, are best remembered for their hit song, "I Sold My Heart to the Junkman." It's a past that included too much hard work for too little money. Black audiences had a lot less money then—that may be the reason why they were so much more discriminating than they are now. In any case, Patti LaBelle and the Bluebelles got thoroughly disenchanted with that phase of their career so they consolidated their name and persevered until they found the next thing.

"The next thing" was to realize this: white audiences have much more money to squander on whatever sounds vaguely entertaining; white audiences recognize the superiority of most black entertainment and will readily buy it, provided it fulfills certain white expectations. (For example: take James Brown and his sweat and greasy hair and his big black girls with their tight shorts and their leather boots and their Woolworth's basement wigs. Not only does this act not meet white expectations, but it often seems vicious and threatening.)

Here's what Labelle did. With the help of Vicki Wickham, their white English manager, they billed themselves as a new kind of hip blackness—and this was long before Minnie Riperton and her birds. This was different from the old kind of hip blackness in that it appealed primarily to whites. They recorded songs by Cat Stevens and songs about "the revolution." They toured with the Who. They sang backup for Laura Nyro on *Gonna Take a Miracle*. (On that album, Laura Nyro tried to fulfill what I imagine is a lifelong ambition of hers: being a black girl in a black group, singing songs like Smokey Robinson's "You've Really Got a Hold on Me," "Dancing in the Street," and "Jimmy Mack.") What "Moonshadow," "the revolution," the Who, and Laura Nyro had to offer Labelle was a devoted, affluent, hip white following. What it didn't quite offer them was anything remotely near the "black experience," but they must have felt they had had enough of that particular hustle.

In 1974, *Nightbirds*, their third album as Labelle, was released. It was notable for Allen Toussaint's production and for the hit single "Lady Marmalade." By that time they had their own devoted, affluent, hip white following, and they had developed their own special kind of props. These involved costumes that had an "outer-space" syntax, which were just as fussy and extravagant as the gowns they had so pointedly abandoned. They referred to themselves as space queens and to their music as future music. It was pretentious, but then there is nothing—absolutely nothing—more charming than pretension in black people. Of course, in some circles, this sort of thing is simply called jive.

Labelle at the Harkness Ballet Theater. The Harkness combines two aesthetics: a large, overdone, old-fashioned "ladies' room," and the interior of an expensive box of chocolates. Everything is done in baby-blue velvet. The walls are white with gold trim. A large, vulgar mural of mostly naked men graces an arch over the stage. Into all this sashays Labelle, wearing those space-age silver costumes—looking like a Puerto Rican's idea of Negroes from Mars. They are very attractive. They sing "Somebody Somewhere," "Can I Speak to You Before You Go to Hollywood," "Nightbirds," "You Turn Me On," "Lady Marmalade," "What Can I Do for You." They sing all these songs to a beat more suited to Kiki Dee (the white singer who recently had a hit called "I Got Music in Me," proving that she did have some music in her but it wasn't *the* music) than to three black American girls. In any case, they do prove this: if you put three black girls into one room you will find that they can sing, that they have a lot of energy, that they can shake around to a recognizable beat, and that they can wear anything stylishly.

As performers, Labelle is a common bunch. Each number is given an equal dose of "energy," something they have, and continue to confuse with real talent. Every song they sing ends up in a sweat. They sweat so much they have to take off piece after piece of clothing, tossing each, one by one, on the floor. But that isn't the only vulgarity they indulge in. They beg their audience to love them. They beg and they beg and they can't stop begging, not even after the love comes. Not for one moment did they convince me that they knew what they were doing, or that they were in control.

What *does* the spacey costuming mean? What *do* they mean when they call their music "R&B, but with a rock energy . . . none of that slick, polished jive"? R&B with rock energy is a musical category that no self-respecting black performer aspires to be in. If Mick Jagger were black, he would sing R&B. Because he is white, he chooses second best—he adds rock 'n' roll to R&B. No group before Labelle has pursued the Number One spot in the Number Two category with so much vigor. I suppose one ought to admire them for that.

Jamaica Kincaid is a Negro who learned to do the Watusi from Tan *magazine.*

Last of the Black White Girls

LAST WEEK DIANA ROSS OPENED a two-week engagement at the Palace Theatre. The opening show went like this: Diana Ross, wearing a white dress, her real hair pulled tightly away from her face and caught in the back by a false chignon, first appeared onstage accompanied by three mimes. She sang "Here I Am." Then she sang "I Wouldn't Change a Thing," and while she sang this the mimes unraveled a large rectangular piece of fabric from the back of her gown. This was also the same fabric as the gown, and it became a movie screen upon which images of Diana Ross in her past-Supremes period were projected. Then the mimes helped her out of her white outfit and under it was a gold body-fitted pantsuit. In that costume, she sang, without interruption, "The Lady Is a Tramp," "Touch Me in the Morning," "One Love in My Lifetime," and "Smile." Then she sang "Love Hangover," her current hit single, and midway through that she left the stage to change into a purple gown that was quite spectacular, and finished singing the song. After that she introduced her three half-white daughters, Rhonda Suzanne, Tracee Joy, and Chudney Lane Silberstein, who were seated in the balcony, and she sang, for them, "Girls." She didn't say that a few days earlier she had filed for divorce from their father. Next, using appropriate costumes and props, she impersonated Billie Holiday, Josephine Baker, Ethel Waters, and Bessie Smith. She said that these women and Langston Hughes and Lorraine Hansberry and Duke Ellington and Count Basie had prepared the way for her. After an intermission she came back and did a history of Motown in song starting with "Money" by Barrett Strong and ending with the Jackson 5's first hit, "I Want You Back." Then she sang some of her biggest and best hits from the Supremes—by far the best thing she did all evening. She talked about the Supremes and not once did she mention the dead Florence Ballard or Mary Wilson, who is credited with actually founding the group. "The good old days," she said. "Me a little skinny kid from Detroit wanting to take a giant step." She sang some more songs and ended with a hysterical "Ain't No Mountain High Enough." Then, in a pathetic, shameless, and cute way, she said to the audiences, "You know, you know before I came out here tonight I was scared. I was scared because I wanted to be what you wanted and more." And in unison the audience said "Ooooooooooh" and applauded wildly.

What Diana Ross sounds like was second only to *Tan* magazine in my adolescent fantasies. It was from *Tan* magazine that I learned to do the Watusi and it was from *Tan* magazine that I learned about cool black girls. I was about fourteen and had just started wearing brassieres and I had my first boyfriend. He was the pianist for our junior choir and every Tuesday and Thursday before and after choir practice we used to meet in the small dark space behind the church organ and do silly things. I felt funny all the time. Around that time "Where Did Our Love Go?" came out. It was great. Shortly after, I heard "Baby Love" and that was the greatest. Because just the way Diana Ross sounds on that particular record was just the way I wanted to be. It was so cool, so sexy, so sweet, so pretty, all of these things for two and a half minutes. I was so full of lust, it was sad. I think you had to be a teenage girl or a teenage boy wanting teenage girls to understand what she meant. She was awfully subtle and decent, yet she seemed to promise everything. No girl anywhere has ever sounded like that. It was the voice of a young girl wanting everything yet not knowing what it was that she wanted or what it was that she would get.

Diana Ross was the special one. There had never been anyone quite like her because there were *two* things that made her special: not only was she a young woman who conveyed the innocence of a girl, but she was a black person who had mastered, without the slightest bit of self-consciousness or embarrassment, being white. They both worked for her in ways no one could have imagined. At the time, in the early sixties, there were dozens of black girl singers. They were all more or less good and successful but their popularity depended not on their unique talents, but simply on their ability to sing a good song. There is no reason to think that the Ronettes couldn't have made a hit out of "Soldier Boy." But I don't think that anyone else could quite make of "Baby Love" all that Diana Ross made out of it. To make the girlishness work in an interesting and lasting way, to prevent it from becoming obviously erotic and possibly cheap, it had to be more. There are two things a black girl can do and be really cool. She can be Bad. Or she can be White. Diana Ross turned into a great black white girl with an incredible single-mindedness. On early Supremes records like "Run, Run, Run" and "Buttered Popcorn" her singing had a slight bit of grit. But by the time she made "Where Did Our Love Go?" and "Baby Love" there was not a trace of anything relatively black in her voice. There was none of the church experience that almost all black performers have in their past. No street experience.

Certainly one would never know that she grew up in a housing project. It's true that every Motown artist had to attend the Motown charm school where they were taught good manners, how to conduct themselves in public, and everything else that would prevent people from saying, "Oh, those Negroes again." But for her, charm school was just polishing up. Black people always say that they have one face for white people and when they are by themselves they are real. I have never for a moment thought that there was a Diana Ross more real than the one I could see.

It's possible that she knew there is something awfully neat about a black person being white. This has nothing to do with political correctness or incorrectness. And it has nothing to do with black faces in idiotic detergent commercials or equal opportunity to be boring. It has to do with being high-tone and dicty and knowing the rules of the game that they made. It's much easier for a white person to play at being black than it is for a black person to play at being white. It's much easier for Mick Jagger to play at being James Brown than it is for James Brown to play at being Mick Jagger. For a white person it becomes an exercise of the intellect resulting in maybe a parody, maybe a tribute. But for the black person who has the most to lose in terms of cultural identity it's deadly serious business. The approach is never one of serious study but a devotion to imitation.

Diana Ross, of course, did this when it was completely unfashionable, and even dangerous, to do. In the sixties an awful lot of people didn't want to be white. Certainly no black girl of note wanted to be white. Black girls wanted to be bad, bad professionals or bad revolutionaries. Still she pressed on. She sang one song after another about teenage love and heartbreak and making up. Sometimes she would sing "The Impossible Dream." Sometimes she would wear a tightly curled wig that was supposed to be an Afro. The closest she came to making a social awareness record was "Love Child," a song about not making love before you're married because you might get pregnant and the baby would be born out of wedlock. This in 1968 when lots of young girls were living together and lots of single women had decided to give birth to children they were carrying.

I haven't much liked anything she has done since she left the Supremes. All the things about her then that seemed fresh and innocent became hard and calculating. It's almost as if she figured out what it was that had made her great and decided to exploit it. When she was young she sounded beautiful and sexy; now she is known as a "beautiful" and "sexy" woman. But in fact she is a small woman with huge lips on a bony face; she has a flat chest, a mere rise for an ass, and stringy arms and legs. But somehow she does manage to look great onstage. Her show was brash and disturbing and she changed costumes so much that it disrupted her singing. The most warmly received songs were the ones she had done with the Supremes, and although they weren't as good as they were years ago, they were good enough to make things as common as "Theme From Mahogany" forgivable.

I suppose now she can do anything. After all, everybody gets a chance to be cool for two minutes and some people never bring it off at all. But Diana Ross was cool for at least five.

Jamaica Kincaid's New York

THERE ARE EIGHT MILLION STORIES IN THE NAKED CITY, AND THIS IS ONE OF THE BETTER ONES

The Antigua Girls School, St. John's, Antigua. 1958.

WE ARE A CLASS OF TWENTY GIRLS or so in Form 2A. Our teacher, Miss Hill, is asking us what is the capital of America. We all know that the capital of America is Washington, D.C., but we have decided to tell her that the capital of America is New York. We have decided to tell her this because we do not like her and try to give her as many wrong answers as possible to the questions she asks us. We call her "the Snout" behind her back, because in a profile her mouth sticks out like a pig's snout, and she in turn calls us, to our face, "the Little Baboons." She goes down the line of girls all seated behind old oak desks modeled after, I am sure, the desks of stupid schoolchildren in England: Cynthia, Gweneth, Christophene, Fernella, Joycelyn (Bow), Evangeline

(Vangie), Vanda, Janice, Clydie, Annie, Hilary, Vanessa, Elaine, Annette.

Then she points at me and says, "And what makes you think that the capital of America is New York?"

I say in my best British West Indian voice, "Well, Miss, the capital of the United States of America has to be New York because New York is where all the interesting people in America live. It says so in all the magazines and films too, as far as I can see. It's the way the capital of England isn't Manchester. It's London because all the interesting people in England live in London. France too. The capital of France is Paris because all the interesting people in France live in Paris. Even here. Look at us. The capital of Antigua is St. John's and not All Saints or Liberta or even English Harbor. That's because everything is here. So that's why the capital of America has to be New York City because all the interesting people in America live there."

It isn't clear at all to me now what exactly I meant by "the interesting people," but I do know that it wasn't like anything I am seeing in front of me . . .

I came to America in 1965. I was sixteen and a half years old. I came here to be a student. At the time there was nothing in the world I hated more than the idea of being a student. But I didn't let that matter much to me. After all, I was in America, the place I had always wanted to be more than any other place in the world, so what did I care what I was masquerading as? I lived with a family, the Masons, in a town in Westchester. They were very nice and protective toward me, and my mother would remind me how lucky I was that I had such nice people to look after me while I was in America. From the very first moment I got here, though, I would say to them, "How far is New York City from here?" and they would say, "Just forty-five minutes or so away by train." I would then say, "Really, just forty-five minutes away by train?" And they would say, "Really, just forty-five minutes away by train." Then they would laugh at me because they said it was so amusing the way I would always ask about New York.

That was the first thing I wanted to do, take the train to New York. The first thing I did, though, I bought a girdle with a large red rose decorating the front paneling. I had never seen a girdle or known anyone who wore a girdle before. But from magazines and films I had gathered that all up-to-date American women wore girdles. I, at the time, was 5'11" tall and I weighed 107 pounds. Along with the girdle I bought a padded brassiere that made the nipples of my breasts look like newly sharpened pencils. Then I had my hair straightened with a cream for the first time (before I had it pressed with a heated comb), and I had it styled in a way that made me look like the pictures of Negro American girls I had seen in *Tan* magazine. Of all the things I had wanted to be when I was little, being a Negro American girl like the girls in *Tan* magazine was one of three that I was most serious about. The girls in *Tan* magazine looked to me to be tough and bad and worldly, and in my mind girls like that didn't live in Chicago or Detroit or Cincinnati. Girls like that lived in New York.

My first letter home to my family:

December 1965

My Dearest Mamie,
    I am here at last and everything is so wonderful. The weather is very cold, though, colder than we could have imagined. The trees have no leaves on them at all and the grass is brown and it is such a strange sight to see. How are you all? I miss everybody already. I am very excited because it is almost Christmas, and everybody is preparing for it, and it all looks

just like greeting cards. The Masons say that as soon as they get their Christmas preparations underway we are all to go to New York City and visit Rockefeller Center, which they say gets very dressed up for Christmas, and also that we will visit some other places. This morning a funny thing happened to me. I got up and the sun was shining so brightly that you could see shadows of everything. I put on a cotton dress and some tennis shoes and stepped outside for a walk because it was such a nice sunny day. Well, the step outside was like stepping into a deep freeze. It was so cold. You see, the sun shining here doesn't mean a thing in winter. The sun is shining and you can still freeze to death. When I told the Masons they laughed so much. Oh, also it is for certain that I will start school after Christmas. I send my love to everyone, especially to you, my dearest mother.

    Your loving daughter

It wasn't true that I missed them. My family was the last thing on my mind. I felt a little ashamed by this and every once in a while I would make a big fuss about my home. I would say, "It's nice here, but really I miss my home. It's so warm there, you know."

They would say, "Well, do you want to go back?" I would say, "Oh no, at least, not right away."

I was in fact making up my mind not to go back at all and wondering how I would ever get to New York.

This is my second letter to my mother, written in January 1966:

My Dearest Mamie,

    How are all of you? I am well, thank you. I can't stop saying it, the weather is so cold here. I know what you are going to say but I am enjoying myself, really I am. I had a wonderful Christmas. I received all sorts of things, including a warm coat, boots and gloves. But the thing I got that I like the most is a red dress that has smocking and little pearl buttons on the blouse. I have finally been to New York City itself. Where we live is only 45 minutes away from New York, and it is called a suburb of New York City. Doesn't suburb sound like a laxative and liver salts? But I really was in New York City. The heart of it. All the buildings are very tall and thin. Just like me. I know if you were here you would want to give them tonics and try to fatten them up. All the people move very fast, just the way you see them do in the cinema. I have now been to the Empire State Building, the Pan Am Building and Rockefeller Center. I bought some shoes in New York City, exactly like the ones you thought were too extravagant for me to have last carnival. Don't be angry. In America it's acceptable to dress this way. Please don't worry too much about me. Remember how you used to be so proud that I was really capable and could look out for myself? Well, I remember all the things you ever taught me. I send all my love to everybody and most especially to you.

    Your loving daughter

That is what I wrote home. But my reaction to my first visit to New York was much different from that. To begin with I was really excited in an almost childish way to find myself walking down Fifth Avenue, walking across 42nd Street, walking up Broadway, standing at the corner of 42nd Street and Madison Avenue, and peering up Madison Avenue. Madison Avenue sounded even better now that I could see it written on a painted yellow street sign. I bought bags of chestnuts (until then I had only seen chestnuts in pictures) and ate them greedily even though I hated the way they tasted. I thought all the people looked alike, that the white people and the black people looked more like each other than they looked like white people and black people I had seen outside New York. They all had the same gait, the way they would walk toward each other with such ferociousness, looking as if they were hell-bent on colliding, but seconds before the actual collision they would veer away from each other. It looked like a game. People didn't seem interested in each other; they didn't stop and stare at what the other was doing, or listen to what the other was saying. They didn't butt into each other's conversation. It was the complete opposite of everything at home, and just what I wanted: the complete opposite of everything at home. And the buildings. People actually lived and worked in them really, not just for The Pictures. And the way it smelled, so wonderful, even though all the cars (so many of them, I had never seen so many cars in one place before) made my eyes water. For years and years, at night when I said my schoolgirl prayers I would add that God would let me see all this and now I actually was seeing it. At that moment I was the only person I had ever known who had wished and prayed for something bigger than a new yellow organdy dress for Harvest Sunday and have the wish and the prayer come through.

It was the first time in my life that I was genuinely excited about something and not told my mother. I had lied to her and done all the things that convince parents you want to send them to an early grave. But I had never before not blurted out to her immediately about anything that really affected me in some way.

Back at my new home I started school and it was decided that if I did well I might try to attend a nursing school. A long time ago it was decided that a good profession for me would be nursing. I couldn't stand the sight of blood, and when I would see someone ill I would sympathetically develop their symptoms. My mother said that I was just weak but that as I grew older I would grow out of it. I didn't grow out of it and I didn't want to be a nurse, but I had never heard of anyone passing up an opportunity to what my mother called "bettering yourself" just because they didn't like whatever was offered to them. I had never in my life heard someone say that they were dissatisfied with their job. I kept going to school so that one day I might be a nurse.

At the school the strangest thing happened. All the white people liked me and thought me charming, particularly the way I spoke English. All the black people hated me and thought me ridiculous, particularly the way I spoke English. I didn't think twice about it. I became very good friends with the people who liked me.

I met Sally at a YWCA social in Yonkers. The socials were held every so often so that young girls could meet each other and meet some young men from a nearby military academy. Sally didn't come to meet other young women or the young men. She had come to keep her friend Margaret, a girl from Scotland, company. All the girls, including me, looked very conventional and pleasant. Except Sally. She wore navy blue, tight, bell-bottom pants; navy blue turtleneck sweater; ankle length, brown vinyl boots; and colored beads around her neck. She had long, brown, straight hair which she wore parted in the middle. The hair always seemed to be in her face and then she would use both hands to tuck it behind her ears. The ends of her long, brown hair were bleached to a blond color. She wore frosted pink lipstick and frosted pink nail polish. She smoked Marlboro cigarettes continuously, and often she would keep a lighted cigarette in the corner of her mouth for long periods of time. She didn't like any of the men at the social, and she told me that it was because they all had short hair. I was so impressed. Fancy not liking a man because of the length of his hair. When one of them approached her, she would greet whatever he said with, "Oh yeah! Oh huh! You gotta be kidding!" We started to talk to each other because we were the only two girls who were not asked to dance, she because she didn't want to, me because it was clear to everybody that I couldn't. I can remember some of the first things she said to me. "These guys are a bunch of jerks," and "Do you go to the city a lot?" and "You like Dino Valenti?" I could see immediately what she was. A bad American girl. A tough American girl. I fell in love with her and her ideas about everything.

She told me that she lived in Purchase with her parents and her brother; that they lived not far from the railroad station; that her father worked for the railroads; that her brother was a mechanic; that her mother was a housewife; that they were Irish and Catholic; that she worked as a secretary for the state government in Yonkers; that she read quite a bit; that *Valley of the Dolls* was her favorite book; that she knew that she could write a book like that if she wanted to; that she went to New York City every weekend; that she liked the Jimi Hendrix Experience, Cream, the Doors, and Quicksilver; that she didn't like girl singers.

I had never heard of the Jimi Hendrix Experience or any of the other groups that she mentioned, and I had always preferred girl singers, particularly black Americans and the Beach Boys, but I didn't say any of this to her.

She said, "I bet Jim Morrison is a real piece of ass."

An ass to me before had been another name for a donkey but just the way she said it I knew exactly what she meant.

We became very good friends and would speak to each other on the telephone for hours every day. I began to dress more or less like her: bell-bottoms, turtleneck shirt, though I wouldn't go so far as the vinyl boots. We would come into the city every Saturday night and go straight to Greenwich Village. When we got there we would walk up and down 8th Street. Up and down, up and down. Sometimes, Sally would stop and speak to someone she recognized. Sometimes we would stop in at a store so that she could buy something or speak to someone, usually a man she was interested in. Sometimes we would go to a party she had somehow heard of. When we went to these parties it was certain that we would leave with boys. She was very good at this, picking up boys. I still didn't know the first thing about men, so when she found a boy for her she would make sure to find one for me, too. When we would leave the party with these strange boys, we would go back to their apartments, which always seemed to be just around the corner, and smoke marijuana. Nothing would happen. We would all fall asleep.

After this we would never see them again unless we ran into them on the street.

It was such a strange New York for me. It wasn't the stores on Fifth Avenue, or 42nd Street, or Broadway, or Madison Avenue. I had never seen this in the cinema or read about it in magazines. These weren't people I had even had so much as a hint of. People talked about anti-this and anti-that. I didn't understand anything. Less than two years earlier I had been a schoolgirl in Antigua worrying about how much starch to put in my gray linen uniforms. There was one thing I liked about this new way of living that I was seeing: it was the way the people I met seemed free. I didn't know what they were free from, but I liked the way they moved about, and I liked the way that they seemed happy and the way they seemed to come and go with no questions asked. I thought that I might like my life to be like that. But then there were things about them that I didn't like. They were little things but they annoyed me just the same. I didn't like the way they burned candles and incense all the time. It reminded me of obeah women. I didn't like the way people expected to share a cup or the same bottle you were drinking from. I didn't like the way strange people would embrace me and after only knowing me for five seconds, tell me that they loved me. When I was little my father, who liked Americans very much, used to tell me that if an American should ask me if I could do something and I couldn't do it, I wasn't to say no. I was to say instead that I would try. I could tell that these people would never understand that. I trusted and admired my father's views on things like that.

I don't remember if there was any one moment when I decided that I would and could move to New York and be on my own. I know that I did begin to set it up. I started to act strange and disagreeable. I said out loud that I thought school was "a drag," and that I didn't want to go anymore. My letters home to my mother and my family were no more than, "Dear Mamie, how are you all? I hope you are all fine. I am well thank you." My mother would write back and ask about progress I was making in school and how was my life going on other fronts. I started to hate her letters and would curse to myself as I read them. Then I wrote a letter to them saying that I didn't want the life they had hoped for me. My mother wrote back and asked if it was a man, and reminded me that she had warned me about men and the things they could do to women. But a man was the last thing on my mind and I didn't write her after that for two years. I decided to move to New York, really. When I told Sally this, she said that she was thinking of moving too, but to California. She said things were more interesting there. I didn't want to go to California. We parted.

I didn't know what I would do in New York, because there wasn't anything that I actually knew how to do. I had never learned to do anything except what my mother called "fend" for myself. She would say to me, "You must learn to fend for yourself." I couldn't do anything. I didn't even know how to type. When I was thirteen my mother made me take typing and Gregg shorthand lessons. She had said, "You never know when it might come in handy." I took these lessons for two years and at the end of that time I didn't know how to type and I couldn't take shorthand. I hated to remember anything that I had to remember; I hated numbers, I hated knowing dates, and I hated analyzing things. There was only one thing that I actually loved. I loved books. I had learned to read before I turned seven. I would read the Bible at home and the *London Times* at the library. My mother spent every Thursday evening at the St. John's Library from six to eight o'clock reading books, mostly about religion and nutrition, her favorite topics then. She would take me with her (then she took me everywhere she went and we were such a little couple, people used to comment on it) and I would sit there with the *London Times* and one day I could just read it. When my mother found this out she was so pleased that she went out and bought me a copy of the *Concise Oxford Dictionary*. She wrote in it: "To My Darling Daughter, who will one day make me proud of her." I took my dictionary with me everywhere. None of my friends had one, so naturally I had to be a big show-off. I read everything I could get my hands on. When I found a book that I liked but couldn't keep I would steal it, and hide it under our house. Then I used to think that my love of books was such a good way for me to pass off my laziness. Sometimes now I think it saved my life.

So I moved to New York. My ignorance was on my side. I wasn't afraid. I didn't know what to be afraid of. I did one thing, I did another. I did what I now call crashing about. One day I started to write.

But about Sally. She went to California, lived in Newport Beach, and worked as a secretary at a toy company. When she left I missed her very much and would make her call me on the toy company's telephone. I felt so alone and so much was happening to me and I had nobody to tell anything. Then in the summer of 1969 I went to visit her for two weeks. She was just the same. She still liked Jimi Hendrix, Cream, and Jim Morrison. I didn't like hearing about that in the same way anymore. I had changed a lot but she didn't want to hear about it at all. All the time I was there we took Seconals. We haven't seen each other since, but every year we send each other season's-greetings cards. She still has the same address.

Marjorie turned nineteen today. Ma Christian is so glad that God has spared her life so she could live to see her only daughter become a "big woman."

"Nineteen. You mean she is nineteen and still living in her mother's house?"

"Oh? And what do you think you will be doing when you are nineteen? Where do you think you will be living?"

"When I am nineteen I am going to be living in New York. Just wait and see. I am going to be living in New York."

To myself, I say, I'm going to live in New York and wear high heels and nylon stockings and hats, lots of hats. I'm going to be a smart woman who lives in New York. Mamie has already told me that it is better to be a smart woman than a pretty woman. She says, "Lots of pretty women around and they come so cheap and they act so foolish. But a smart woman. Not many of those. Just take a look. Go ahead. Take a look."

It turned out to be true. At nineteen I was living in New York. Sometimes people say things in anger, or in jest, or even in innocence, and they will turn out to be true. When I said that, I wasn't more than nine years old, and I said it just to give backchat to my mother. How did I exist? How did I support myself? Mostly what I did was to live as if I was all alone in the world. When I was little (again, when I was little. I hope I don't spend my whole life saying "when I was little" even if it turns out to be the most interesting thing to happen to me) and would protest to my mother that a task she had set for me to do was really beyond me, she would say "But what if we were dead? What would you do if you didn't have us to take care of you? Would you know how to do for yourself? You mustn't depend on us so. Life takes many strange turns and you never can tell."

As usual she has been so right. Life did take a funny turn. I live in New York all by myself and I earn a living writing. My family doesn't understand this. When I tell my mother that I am probably able to do this because of her "what if we were dead" act, she says, "Little did I know you would turn it against me." My mother sees my life in New York as turning against her. In some way she is right. She must know that if only I had gone to London or even, say, Cincinnati, it would have been impossible for me not to write to them for two whole years and that when I started to write again I presented them with a completely new and different child from the one who had left them off two years earlier. She must know that I couldn't have lost one self and found another and still pass for a nonlunatic in any other place but New York. It must be this that people know about New York; that what is lunacy every place else doesn't matter much here at all.

I do not come from a family of writers. I never knew a writer. We are oral people. We talk to each other a lot, and when we talk we touch the person we are talking to. All the things I know about my family and about everybody else, people told me. The people in my family are banana and citrus-fruit farmers, fishermen, carpenters, and obeah women. My schoolmates are so much more well thought of than I. My mother would like to say to her friends, "My daughter, who now lives in America and holds a responsible position with a shipping firm, sent me this dress and it came just in time for Easter Sunday, too. You remember her, how troublesome she used to be? Well, she grew out of it." But she can't say this.

When I say to her that I write because it satisfies me in some way, that it makes sense to me, she ignores this completely. She writes to me to tell me she thinks the prime minister of Antigua is an evil old man and an ass.

In New York, I live in an apartment that has two rooms plus a kitchen and a bathroom. It faces the south. The apartment has three windows and the three windows have window seats and the window seats would look very pretty if they had nice-looking cushions in them, but they do not have nice-looking cushions in them so they do not look very pretty. In my apartment there is a fireplace with a marble mantelpiece. There are plants, some hanging in the window, some just standing around. The ones standing around do not look as if they are standing in the perfect spot. There are a lot of records and books piled up on the floor because I cannot afford to buy bookshelves in which to store them. There is a television set standing on two telephone books, which in turn is standing on a chair so that I can watch it comfortably while lying in bed. There are two boudoir chairs that I bought in a sale. They used to be furniture on a cruise ship during the forties. Then there is a night table, a chest of drawers that matches it, and a coffee table, also from the sale from the cruise ship. There is a typewriter that sits on an old office typewriter table. There is a kitchen table with a blue and white enamel tabletop and four matching chairs. There are photographs of people I used to know hanging on the walls. I took these photographs myself. In the kitchen there is a white refrigerator. It has two doors. In the freezer there is nothing but ice trays filled with ice and a bag full of chicken necks and giblets. When I buy a whole chicken I save these because I think that I will one day use them for something. I never use them for anything. In the other part of the refrigerator is yogurt, brewer's yeast, fruits and vegetables, thirty-two bottles of different vitamins and other things that women eat because they don't want to get fat. There is a stove that lights up immediately when you turn on the gas. The kitchen is so small that you can't turn around in it with outstretched arms. The bathroom is bigger and it has a tub that when filled with water will cover to just below the breastbone. In my apartment, I smoke Lucky Strike cigarettes.

This is where I go when I say to my friends, "And now I am going home." Sometimes when I take a good look at my home it makes me feel very big and very strong. Sometimes when I take a good look at my home I feel very small and very vulnerable. Not long ago I had mice in my house and for two weeks I couldn't live there. When I started to live there again, I would stand on a chair to get dressed, I would stand on a chair to get undressed, I would stand on a chair to put on my makeup, I would stand on a chair to make myself some dinner. And this was after they had been caught.

A man and a woman I know, friends of mine too, are always telling me that I am to be admired because I have lived for so long by my wits. I know what they mean, I know they mean it as a compliment but just the same I don't like it when they tell me this. "Lived by her wits." I think it makes me sound like someone who has been up to now a successful embezzler. Lived by my wits, indeed. First of all, let me be the judge of whatever it is I have lived by. But the other thing, you mean people are going to think that the years I spent not knowing my head from my ass amount to my living by my wits. It wasn't that way at all. I have lived the way I have lived and done the things I have done because I didn't know anything else. I would go from one thing to the other, one thing to the other, and when things didn't work out I would just pick up and go. But I didn't think of it as wits. If anything, it was that I wasn't afraid.

About these interesting people. Where did I get such an idea. But it is true that they all live here. I see them all the time on the street passing me by, I have dinner with them, they have dinner with me, we chat on the telephone, I go to parties with them. I even have disagreements with them. I think I am now one of them; that is I am a New Yorker. If I think about it, this is what passes through my mind:

The women. I know so many women. We sit and chat for hours. We sit and chat about men, mostly. We say that there aren't any good ones around. We say how much they don't live up to our expectations. We say how much ahead of things we are, compared to them. We say how we must be independent of them. We say how much we can't live without them. What we say amounts to this: "Anytime you look there are going to be only two or three good men around. You can count them on one hand and still have fingers left over." These are my mother's words exactly. Sometimes I think that all women are going to be just like my mother. Even as I write this, a woman I know has just told me that her new boyfriend makes love the way James Taylor sings "Handy Man." So this is what will be the end of us? *"Sigh! He makes love the way James Taylor sings 'Handy Man.'"* But the worse thing about it is how it can't be helped. It just can't be helped.

Once, as I was walking down a street and just about to pass by a man, he said to me, "Hey sugar, you coming at me like a fresh baked cake." When I didn't say anything but kept on walking he crept up behind me and whispered in my ear, "Speak Devil, speak." I looked at him and I laughed out loud. Every time I think of this, I smile to myself.

I try not to go to parties. I am afraid I will like them and become a New York partygoer. When I go, I try to behave as badly as possible so that I won't be asked back. The other day at a party I was introduced to a man, a writer. On being introduced to him I said, "Oh, so you are that man who writes those articles. I thought from your writing you wore Hawaiian shirts." It's true too. I really did think that. He writes about what rich Parisians are doing in New York. What rich writers are doing in the Hamptons. What the rich and the social are doing here, there, and everywhere. I couldn't believe that that's how a grown man thinks is a way to make a living. And he was a grown man. He wore a well-tailored three-piece suit and a tie, and from a distance he looked like a gentleman. But from his writing I thought he was a boy who wore Hawaiian shirts. I don't like rich people and I am always glad when it looks as if the future won't be so bright for them.

At another party I met an Englishwoman. First of all, I am not a big fan of the English. They made me sing too many "Rule Britannias" in the hot sun, and the thing about that song is that it has a line in it that goes, "Britons never, never shall be slaves." But we were not Britons and most of our ancestors were slaves. When this woman found out that I was from the West Indies she said, "West Indians are the best cricketers in the world today. They even beat us."

So I say, "Yes, that's the trouble with Negroes. White people teach them something and soon as you turn around the Negroes can do it better. Just wait until we learn physics."

I do not see a psychiatrist. I have never been to one. I think about it, though, because a lot of the people I know see one. I don't think I could stand it. I don't want to know why I hate my mother so, and why I love her so. I don't want to know why I think my mother's love is like a poison. If I know why I feel my mother's love is like a poison

I might not be able to say it anymore. I like the way it sounds. "My mother's love is like a poison." I could say it all day. And actually it is true but that's only part of it. She really loves me too. Besides I have a sort of tradition to keep up. My pediatrician in Antigua was once a psychiatrist. He came to Antigua in the thirties, a refugee from Czechoslovakia. He came as a psychiatrist but people there had never heard of a psychiatrist before and besides it's fun to be crazy in Antigua. Bands of schoolchildren congregate outside your house and follow you around wherever you go, taunting you. He became a children's doctor. He and his wife (an Englishwoman who also served as his nurse) were a sight to see, the way they hated children. I know they did because he would always prescribe purgatives.

I have seen three girls standing on the corner of 123rd Street and Eighth Avenue singing a song. They sang the song over and over. As they sang, they would clap their hands and slap each other's palms, all in perfect rhythm. The words to the song they sang go like this:

> Judy, you make my heart shine
> You make my Dick on the bone
> You make it greasy baby.
> Roaches, your mother's titties fly
> Her ass is bigger than mine
> That bitch is funky, baby
> 5, 10, 15 more
> The Dick got slime in the bathroom door
> The mother scream
> The Dick turned green
> And that's the end of my ding-a-ling.

Sometimes I sit by myself in the dark and for hours I think of all this in exactly the sequence that I have written it down here.

This is not a photograph of me. It is a photograph of the clothes I would be wearing if this were a photograph of me. They asked for a photograph of me, but I said no. When I was a little girl in Antigua, my friend Josephine Defoe's mother killed her husband's mistress (who lived all the way in Montserrat) by using a photograph.

Also, someone has told me that this is the way South American authorities display the clothing of South American guerrillas they have killed.

A long time ago there was a photograph of me in a magazine. At the time I had forgotten about Josephine Defoe, her mother, her father, and her father's mistress.

—JAMAICA KINCAID

Antigua Crossings

A DEEP AND BLUE PASSAGE ON THE CARIBBEAN SEA

(Fiction)

THE CARIBBEAN SEA IS SO BIG, and so blue, and so deep, and so warm, and so unpredictable, and so inviting, and so dangerous, and so beautiful. This is exactly the way I feel about all the women in my own family. I am twelve years of age now and I have never been swimming in the Caribbean Sea. I have never been swimming in it because I do not know how to swim, I am the only person in my family who doesn't know how to swim. My mother has tried to teach me, starting when I was two years old and stopping when I was ten. She told my father behind my back that I was too lazy. But it wasn't that I was lazy at all. I was too frightened of the sea.

We live on an island, Antigua, and on one side runs the Atlantic Ocean and on the other side is the Caribbean Sea. The Atlantic Ocean does not matter much to us. It comes from too far away and it shares itself with too many other people who are too different

1978, June 29. "Antigua Crossings: A Deep and Blue Passage on the Caribbean Sea." *Rolling Stone*. Iss. 268: 48–50.

from us. The Caribbean Sea is ours and we share it with people who live on islands like us, islands that are sometimes made out of coral, sometimes made out of dead volcanoes. All these islands surround the Caribbean Sea like a ring-around-the-rosy-pocket-full-of-posey game, preventing it from spilling out into the larger world of seawater. I know that there are other seas which must seem more important and more special, but they exist for me only in books.

What is an Isthmus? What is a Peninsula? What is an Ocean? What is a Sea? What is a Channel? What is an Island? What is a Continent? And you, Little Miss, with the sly mongoose smile on your face, make sure you get it right.

In school I have been told things about the Caribbean Sea. I have been told how it got to be the Caribbean Sea; the many different kinds of fish and fowl and turtles and plants and other things that live in it; how deep it is in some places and how shallow it is in other places; how old it is, how it comes and how it goes. I do not remember well any of these things. I only remember how the Caribbean Sea came to be called the Caribbean Sea. It's like this: When Columbus discovered the West Indies he met two tribes of Indians, the peace-loving Arawaks and the warlike Caribs. At the time the Caribs were migrating up from South America, moving to islands that were already inhabited by the Arawaks. The Caribs easily conquered the Arawaks, taking the women and children as wives and slaves. Sometimes they would eat a particularly brave Arawak because they believed that if you ate a brave man you would receive his braveness and because the Caribs were cannibals.

The Caribbean Sea was named after the Carib Indians who conquered the Arawaks; the Caribs who were later almost completely killed off by the Spanish, the English, and the French; the Caribs who ate the explorer Verrazano.

I know this because my grandmother is a Carib Indian. She is very tall and very dark and very fierce looking. She comes from Dominica and it is there she lives with her husband (my grandfather) and it is there my mother grew up. At the end of every day, just before the sun sets completely, my grandmother sits on a little bench in front of her house and stares out at the sea. She sits there and she stares and stares and says nothing at all to anyone. Every so often she spits a big spit and I am always surprised at the force of it. It's the same sort of spit that she spits when she has just passed someone who is an enemy. Then just as it starts to get dark, she gets up and shakes out her big skirt (all her skirts are big skirts) as if it has gathered something unpleasant while she has been sitting there. My grandmother is a Christian now and she goes to church regularly but all of this is just to please her husband who is a lay minister in the Methodist church. I have seen the way she hunts agouti and I know that she has not forgotten the history of her ancestors and it makes me glad.

I would like to say that I have sailed the Caribbean Sea. It's such a nice way they have of putting things in books. *"I have sailed the Caribbean Sea."*

But I haven't sailed the Caribbean Sea. I have been put on a steamer and sent to stay with my mother's parents in Dominica. I have been five times. Always, I leave Antigua at six o'clock in the evening, and by six o'clock the next morning Dominica is in sight, and two hours later we land there. I do not like going to Dominica and I am never sent because it is the holidays and it would be nice for me to see my grandparents. I am sent to Dominica because my parents think I am an overly troublesome child and that my overly troublesomeness comes about because enemies of my family are working obeah on me. I have seen one of these enemies. It's a woman who says that my father is the father of her only child. My father says that it isn't true at all. I have seen that woman's only child, now a grown man and a waterworks meter reader in the Public Service. His name is Strickland, which is also my father's name, and he has a petal-shaped nose, which is also the shape of my father's and the shape of my nose. My father has four different children named Strickland by four different women and only two of these Stricklands he says are his children, but from the shape of their noses and other things you can see that he is the father of all these boys named Strickland.

But this is what happened: I had just turned nine when it seemed to my mother that I talked so fast she couldn't understand me anymore and that maybe the reason I did that was because I had something to hide. She said to me, "I better keep an eye on you because all fast chatters are liars." Then just like that I started to lie and so brazenly too, even when there wasn't a chance that I could get away with it. So when she found out what a notorious liar I had become she said, "I better keep an eye on you because where there's a liar there's a thief." So I started to steal and I especially liked to steal money from her, and why, I don't know since she has such a hawk's eye for her own money. My mother said that none of this happened to me like that and she wrote Ma Chess and asked her what she thought of me. Ma Chess said, "The Little Ma must cross the water. There is nothing else for it. She must cross some sea water and then stay on the other side for a year. It's best that you send her to us, though, and that way you can be sure she'll be all right." This is exactly what she wrote in a letter to my mother and this is exactly what I heard my mother read aloud to my father one night when they were sitting on the front steps and I was pretending to be completely preoccupied with a silly little *crapo* (frog) who was jumping around in the patch of white head bush but really hearing every word that passed between them.

Dickenson Bay Street, St. John's, Antigua

25th March, 19—

My Dear Elizabeth
    How are you? How is all that rain treating you? I see from Ma Chess' letter that the banana crop was good. The mangoes

too. I am glad. It means that you can come and see us and take a holiday a bit from that louse Latigue. I hear from Ma Gertrude that he was in Portsmouth the other day sporting about with a new woman. What to do with him? Just what to do with him? I know only too well, but it's true, as everyone says, that you are by far the nicer sister. We are all fine here in spite of this everlasting drought. It's still been so long since it rained and the water situation is so bad that we have to line up at the pipes for water. But we have managed to get some drinking water from the cistern up at the Moravian church. We had a couple of earthquakes in the middle of the night on top of everything, and soon after that a big fire started in some cane fields over in Ottas. We could see the sky all orange-y. The children are all fine and growing so much, though the baby almost died from being eaten up by red ants. They came in through the windows from the okra trees where they have been living. Thank God Mignonette heard him crying so much and went to take a look. His whole face was covered with them. They were even in his eyes. I don't know how he survived it, the poor little thing, but he's doing all right, eating so much and carrying on with all sorts of baby antics. Strickland is finally recaning the dining room chairs and repairing the Morris chairs. After all this time of me getting behind him to try and make the house look respectable he is shaping up. He and Oatie have jobs building up the new hotels out in Parham. I don't know if Mignonette wrote to thank you for the bracelets and the earrings and the little basket you sent her yet. She is very proud of them and tells all her friends that the earrings and bracelets are made of gold from British Guiana. The basket she has reserved for Sunday afternoon walks exclusively. We are very worried about her. She still has the bed-wetting problem you know. It's that weak back of hers acting up again. We have tried everything: soursop heart, turtle berry bark baths, tonics and even some rigamarole exercises which Strickland suggested. But nothing works. Ma Francis says soaking the back in seawater at 'fore day morning is a good remedy for weak backs, so starting next week we are going down to Rat Island and we'll see what happens. The water down there is very clear. Give my best regards to Ma and Pa Chess and tell Ma Chess I will send her a letter as soon as I get a chance. Also, tell her that I could use some dasheen if she has any extra ones since the ones around here don't taste as good and they always make your throat scratchy. Please take care of yourself and don't worry about that shadow of a man Latigue.

    Your loving sister,
    Victoria

    This is a letter my mother has written to her sister. They write regularly to each other. It takes a full week from the time my mother posts it to get to my aunt Elizabeth, who lives in Mahaut, Dominica, with her husband and my grandparents, all of them in the same house. The letter will most likely get to Dominica on a steamer called the *M. V. Rippon*, and it is this steamer that carries me to Dominica on all my trips. My mother and her sister are named after queens of England. Ma and Pa Chess are my grandparents, though why they are called that I don't know since that is not their real names. My grandmother is named Josephine Claudette and my grandfather is named Albert Alfred. Mr. Latigue is the name of my aunt's husband. He is a magistrate in Dominica and because of that he has to travel all over the island. It is not a good marriage and it makes my aunt Elizabeth very unhappy. When I ask my mother about it she says that it is another story altogether and too much for a young girl like me to understand. I know it would make her mouth drop wide open if she knew how much about everything I know. My name is Mignonette and my aunt Elizabeth did receive a thank-you note from me for the bracelets and the earrings and the basket but the thank-you note is in my mother's handwriting. It is my mother who tells people that the bracelets and the earrings are made of gold from British Guiana and it is my mother who makes me take the basket with me on my Sunday afternoon walks. My mother thinks the basket is so attractive and will set off my Sunday clothes. I think the basket looks as if it was made by hand in Dominica. Quite often my grandmother makes up a package of fruits and vegetables and nuts and sends them to my mother. Sometimes by the time they get to us most of the things in the package are half rotten but this never stops my grandmother from sending things and my mother from asking for them. My mother says that nothing in Antigua is as good as things in Dominica. Once as a joke my father asked her why if she felt that way she came here then and why did she stay. But I don't believe he meant it as a joke since many times I have felt like saying the same thing to her and a laugh is always the furthest thing from my mind.

My mother came to Antigua when she was either eighteen years of age, or nineteen years of age, or twenty years of age, or twenty-one years of age. Every time she tells the story of leaving Dominica she is one of these years of age or another. It's not that she means to lie about it. It's just that it has been so long ago—twenty years or so—and so many things have happened to her since she left and came here. Anyway that's the explanation she gave me a long time ago when I pointed out to her that she changed her age every time she tells this story. I didn't point it out in a rude or scornful way since it goes without saying that I love my mother very much even if we hardly ever see eye to eye about anything, and also this is my favorite of all her stories. It is quite like a story I might have read in a book, and every time she tells it she uses the same words exactly.

"The first time I crossed the water wasn't like it is for you. I didn't have any nice people waiting to greet me at the other end of the road. All I had was a room at Dr. and Mrs. Bailey's. They were very good friends of Ma and Pa Chess when they lived in Mahaut years before that but even so they were not the nicest people in the whole world. I remember the day so well as if it was just yesterday but it was way before you could even dream to be born. The night before I was to leave in the boat, a Saturday night, Pa Chess took me to Roseau so that I wouldn't miss the boat which was leaving early the next Sunday morning. It was raining of course, just the way it always is, and Pa Chess said that it was a bad sign, but how could it be a bad sign when there was nothing unusual about it raining. It always rains in Dominica just as the sun always shines here. But Pa Chess didn't want me to leave because it wasn't so long ago that Johnny had died, of what, to this day, no one knows. We spent the night at Aunt Gertrude's who at the time lived in Roseau not far from the river and in quite a nice house too. I didn't sleep very well, no, I didn't sleep at all, I was so excited. You see, I had never been anywhere before and I was looking forward to never having to carry a hand of plantains on my head for miles again. Of course I didn't know then that I would have to carry you or maybe I would have thought twice about it. (Here she will stroke my cheeks and laugh or do something to show me she doesn't really mean it at all.) I have never seen time fly by so fast and as soon as it was 'fore day morning me and Pa Chess were off to the wharf. I was wearing a red dress with a big flounce skirt and I had my hair done up in corkscrews. I looked like I was going to mass ball, which is just what Pa Chess said and it didn't please him at all. Pa Chess took me on board the steamer. At the time it was a boat called the *Caribee* and it traveled up and down the sea just the way the *Rippon* does now. He took me over to the captain, who was a white man from Scotland but not such a good white man or he wouldn't be running a steamer in the West Indies, and he asked the captain to keep an eye on me since this was my first time on a big boat and I was so young. Shortly before we were to leave the church bells started ringing because it was Sunday morning after all, but Pa Chess said that the way they were ringing wasn't such a good sign. He said, 'For whom the bells toll, yes Little Ma, just tell me for whom those bells toll.' He said this over and over again and so I had to tell him that it had nothing to do with me and my trip. The last thing he said to me before he left was that I was to be careful that my joy didn't turn to sorrow, and it's true that by the time we reached Guadeloupe I had thrown up so much and all over my beautiful dress and my hair was standing up on my head making me look like a wild bull. Then I couldn't remember the day that the thought of crossing the sea had made me happy. When days later we reached here—because things were so much slower then—it was weeks before ground felt steady under my feet. And that's why I have never gone back home, not as Pa Chess thinks, because I don't get along with him."

I know this story so well. I know it back to front, front to back, inside out, and so on. Pa Chess is right that the reason she never goes to see them is because she doesn't get along well with him. I wish I knew what their falling-out was about but I don't. And though I don't think that my mother wishes Pa Chess anything bad, just the other day when she got a letter from Ma Chess telling her that Pa Chess wasn't feeling up to mark that day and was suffering from constipation, she burst out laughing and said out loud to herself, "So the great man can't shit." She doesn't know I heard her say this. I don't know what to make of a woman who laughs at her own father.

It was on a Saturday that I went to Dominica for the first time. Also it was in June and I had just turned nine years old. Since the boat I would sail on left at six o'clock, we had an early dinner, and since it was a Saturday, we had for dinner pepper pot with fungi and sliced breadfruit, all things I hate so much. My mother said that instead of eating dinner I could eat a bowl full of yellow plums.

All through dinner my father kept whistling a song about harbor lights and the whistling made my mother furious and she said to him that it was bad enough the way he kept his hat on at the dinner table but to whistle too, and what a bad example he set for me. But he didn't say anything to that because she was always bothering him about where he should and shouldn't wear his hat and he continues to wear his hat wherever he likes and whenever he likes too. In any case being furious at my father is like being furious at my mother's stone heap. There is never a reply. And when my mother wasn't correcting my father's manners, she told me things to do and things not to do when I was with her family. She said that I was to try hard not to bring shame on her and my father. I said the appropriate "Yes Mamie, No Mamie, Yes Mamie," but if you were to ask me now exactly what it was she said to me then I couldn't say, since it all went in one ear and came out the next, just the way she always says I take her advice.

In a corner I could see my grip packed to the brim with all my little things. It had my name and my address in Antigua and my address in Dominica written all over it. It was then I felt very sorry for all the things I had done and almost said, "Oh please, don't send me away. I won't do it again and I love all of you so much." But I didn't. And what would have been the use of that when the way I was behaving wasn't even my own fault. It had been decided weeks ago that my father would see me off to the boat. This was because it was a Saturday and my mother would be too busy. That's what she told me but I heard her tell my father that it would be better if he took me to the boat because if she did she might not be able to send me off.

But there we were, my father and me, off to the boat, my little hand in his. As I said goodbye to my mother, she plastered my unruly braids to my head again, removed a spot of dirt from my chin with a finger wet with her own spit, told me how to behave (again), asked God to bless me, and gave me a big kiss. Then she stood in the middle of the street and watched us go and the last thing I saw, just before I turned the corner, was her standing there wearing a dress that had a big flared skirt with red butterflies and red hibiscus and shouting to me, "Be a good girl. Write, write . . . And remember not to bring shame on your family." Did my father and I say anything to each other on the way to the boat? No, except he told me that Dominica wasn't such a good place to play cricket and also that they didn't have good Guy Fawkes Day celebrations there.

When we got to the boat this is what my father did: he went over to the captain and said, "Please take good care of her. She is our daughter and sometimes she is a little mischievous." This much of it I heard and if I didn't feel so sad I could have laughed. Isn't that nearly what Pa Chess said to the old Scottish captain so long ago, long before I could even dream to be born. Sometimes things are better than in a book. But this captain wasn't a bad white man because later that night I could hear him whistling a song from *Pinafore*, the same song from *Pinafore* that my father whistles when he is in his shop planing mahogany wood that he will soon turn into a beautiful piece of furniture. So what did my father and I have to say to each other just before he left me?

"Goodbye, Mr. Strickland. God bless you."

"Goodbye, Little Miss. God bless you and be good."

On the boat, and such a big boat at that, they had hands of bananas wrapped in plastic bags everywhere. There was a man minding a big basket of the hated breadfruits. There was a woman and three children, three bad children because she had to use the life belts to tie them to their seats. There was also a cooly haired man who kept walking up and down and singing a song about a twopence ha'penny woman. Later I could see that he was a part of a group of steel band players because they brought out their steel drums and they played the song about the twopence ha'penny woman that the cooly haired man had been singing all by himself. It went like this:

Twopence ha'penny woman
Lie down on the bristol
De bristol le' go boom boom
And it knock out she big fat poom poom

They were going to Martinique and later that night as I thought I would die from seasickness and I threw up in the little bowl the captain had given me they played that song over and over.

As for the sea, I couldn't hear or see it but I could feel it in my stomach. I felt as if the whole sea had decided to settle in my belly and when it got tired of that it would rush up in my ears and my eyes. I was sure that my eardrums would break and that my eyes would be forced out of me. But on and on it went all night. The steel drum players, drunk from drinking too much white rum by this time, kept playing and playing. Let me just say that not in my whole life do I ever want to hear that song again.

The harbor in Dominica is deep so the boat came all the way up to the jetty. I could see my aunt Elizabeth and my grandmother waiting there for me. Even if I had never seen pictures of them I would have recognized them as my mother's family. They don't look alike at all. My aunt Elizabeth has flame red hair, my grandmother is taller than her two daughters, and she is much blacker skinned than any black skinned person I have ever seen. But just the same I can see that all these women belong in the same family. I waved to them. By that time I was looking quite presentable. When I met them they kissed me and my grandmother asked how was my trip.

I said, "Well it was quite pleasant. The moon was bright, the stars were shining, and the water was quite lovely to look at."

But she didn't listen to what I was saying. Instead, she marched me over to the far side of the jetty, the part where the water was deepest, and she made me spit in the sea three times.

Ovando

(Fiction)

A KNOCK AT THE DOOR.
It is Frey Nicolas de Ovando. I was surprised. I was not expecting him. But then on reflecting, I could see that though I was not expecting him, he was bound to come. Somebody was bound to come. On reflecting, I could see that while I sat I thought, Someone will come to me; if no one comes to me, then I will go to someone. There was that knock at the door. It was Ovando then. Immediately I was struck by his suffering. Not a shred of flesh was left on his bones; he was a complete skeleton except for his brain, which remained, and was growing smaller by the millennium. He stank. Immediately I was struck by his innocence: for he had made himself a body from plates of steel, and it was stained with shades of red, blood in various stages of decay, and he thought I would not know the difference. He carried with him the following things: bibles, cathedrals, museums (for he was already an established collector), libraries (banks, really, in which he stored the contents of his diminishing brain), the contents of a drawing room.

"Ovando," I said, "Ovando," and I smiled at him and threw my arms open to embrace this stinky relic of a person. Many people have said that this was my first big mistake, and I always say, How could it be a mistake to show sympathy, to show trust, to show affection to another human being, on first meeting? How can my action, then, with its foundation fixed in love, be judged a mistake? For I loved him then, not the way I would love my mother, or my child, but with that more general and spontaneous kind of love that I feel when I see any human being. As I shall show you, my first actions should not have been rewarded as they were. But wait here a minute and I shall show you what happened next.

With a wave of my hand I threw the door open and said, "Come in." I did this with great exaggeration, for it was unnecessary. You see, he was already inside. And so too when I said, "Sit down, make yourself at home, in fact think of this as your new home," not only was he already sitting down but he said, "Yes, this is the new home I have been looking for, and I already like it so much that I have sent for my relatives in Spain, Portugal, France, England, Germany, Italy, Belgium, and the Netherlands. I know that they will like it here as much as I do, for they are just like me, we have met the same fate in the world." So many things at once seemed wrong to me that it was hard to know where to begin. I could not see his eyes; they were shut. Any number of things could explain this, I thought: perhaps he was blind, perhaps all his deeds so far had left him in a permanent state of inner bliss. And as for the relatives! Imagine whole countries populated by people with not a shred of flesh left on their bones, complete skeletons inside bodies made from plates of steel, people who had lost the ability to actually speak and could only make pronouncements, their brains growing smaller by the millennium, their bodies covered with blood in various shades of decay; whole countries of people coming to visit me even though I had not invited them, whole countries of people sitting down in my house without asking my permission!

The most confusing thing was that he had used the word *fate*. I gathered then that merely reasoning him out of his plans would not work. ("Ovando, look, let us be reasonable. All of your words and deeds toward me so far have been incredibly unjust. Already, just in the first few moments of our meeting, you have done me irreparable harm. Stop now, let me show to you the grave errors you have made." "Really, there is nothing I can do about this. A power outside and beyond me has predetermined these unalterable events. All of my actions have been made for me in eternity. All of my actions are divine.")

I could have brought a stop to what was an invasion to me, a discovery to him; after all, I too knew of divinities and eternities and unalterable events. But I looked closely at him. He was horrible on a scale I did not even know existed before. I sat at his feet and helped him take off his shoes.

For a very long time Ovando believed the world to be round. It suited him to believe that, for from his point of view he could see only horror and misery and disease and famine and poverty and nothingness. If the earth were round, thought Ovando, he could go away, far away from his immediate surroundings, far away beyond the horizon, which would prove not to be a ledge over which he would fall into a sea of blackness. For a while, then, a round earth spun on its axis in Ovando's mind's eye. At first this world was small and bare and chalk-white, like a full moon in an early evening sky; it spun around and around, growing into perfection and permanence until finally, awake or asleep, alone or in a procession, in silence or in battle, Ovando carried this round, bare, chalk-white world. Then, after a few hundred years of this, Ovando filled his earth with seas, across the seas he placed lands, the lands were covered with mountains and rivers, and the mountains and rivers hid enormous treasures. When Ovando's imagination brought forth the round earth and then the seas and then the land and then the mountains and then the rivers, he acted with great calm. But in imagining the treasures he grew agitated, and then he fainted. He took this to be a sign from his various divinities, for all visionaries take as a sign of affirmation a momentary loss of contact with the ordinariness of daily life.

"Ah, then," said Ovando, as he entered a small room. He sat at a desk and proceeded to fill countless volumes with his meditations on the spheres, divine assertions, liberation from bonds spiritual and physical, and phlebotomy. To say that his meditations were nothing more than explanations and justifications for his future actions might seem unfair, for after all is it not so that all human beings are, from moment to moment, vulnerable to overwhelming self-love? When Ovando emerged from this small room, his eyes were half shut. The lights had burned out many, many years earlier, but he had continued his work of filling up the volumes in the half dark, and not once did he get to sleep. In his hands now he carried a large piece of paper, a piece of paper that was as large as a front lawn, and on this piece of paper Ovando had rendered flat the imagined contents of his world. Oh what an ugly thing to see, for the lands and the seas were painted in the vile colors of precious stones just ripped from their muddy home! It looked like the effort of schoolchildren. It looked like a fragile object that had been dropped on a hard surface and its pieces first swept up in a dustpan and then gently but haphazardly placed on a tabletop. It looked like sadness itself, for it was a map. Ovando spread his map out before him. Using the forefinger of his left hand, he traced on his map a line. Months later his finger came to a stop. It was at a point not too far from where he had started. Removing his finger from his map, he let out a long, satisfying breath, and then he looked up. At that moment the world broke.

From where I sit the world looks flat. I look out to the horizon. The world ends in a sharp, flat, clear line where the seas and the sky are joined. I look out on my world. I accept it in its flatness. I am not tempted to transgress its boundaries. My world bears me no ill; on the contrary, my world bears me only goodness. I accept the goodness that my world bears me. My world with its goodness is not a burden; on the contrary, I find grace and light and comfort in my world. I find the things I need in my world. And yet—; for all hearts contain within them an eternal yearning, a yearning for a peace that is not death, a yearning for an answer to a question that cannot quite be asked. My heart is no exception and so my world is not infinite. To the stranger's eye (Ovando's) my world is a paradise. To the stranger's eye (Ovando's) everything in my world appears as if it were made anew each night as I sleep, by gods in their heavenly chambers. The climate in which I live is unchanging and kind; it does not exhaust me with extremes of hot and cold. I have by now lost interest in knowing the exact number of trees that bear me food; so, too, in the number that bear me only flowers, and in the ones that bloom only at nights and only when the moon is in its full phase.

I sit in the morning sun. I idly rub my toe against the earth beneath me, and a large vein of gold is revealed to me. I walk in the warm evening air. I stumble over the glittering stones that are scattered in my path. What can I do with all that I am surrounded by? I can fashion for myself bracelets, necklaces, crowns. I can make kingdoms, I can make civilizations, I can lay waste. But I can see the destruction of my body, and I can see the destruction of my soul. Then in my flat world I am blessed with a certain vision. I see the end in everything around me. I see its beginnings, I see its ends. I see the way things will always be. For me then, all discovery results in contemplation. I see a thing I have never seen before, I place it in the palm of my hand; eventually I see the many purposes to which it can be put, eventually I see all its many purposes brought to an end, eventually I see it die. I replace the thing I have never seen before in the exact place in which I found it. Again let me say: I see an object, I see its myriad uses good and bad, I see it rise up to great heights. I see it hold sway, the foundations of vast enterprises are laid in it,

I see it reduced again to its humble origins, a thing I can hold in my hand. In the many things I have held in my hand, from time to time I see my own humanity: I can hold religious beliefs, I can extol a moral value, I can prevent myself from entering the dungheap that is history. My world is flat. I accept this. Its borders are finite. I accept this. The flatness of my world is kind to me.

"My Sheer Might!" said Ovando loudly and then fell silent. Those three words rushed out of his mouth and vanished into the silence of things so completely that Ovando did not believe that he had said them. He had spent many years in preparation for this moment, the moment in which these words could be said. The moment in which the words could be said was the moment in which the words would be true. And so for a long time Ovando stood in front of a mirror, more in the stance of a child at play than an actor in preparation for a great part, and he tried to say the words "My Sheer Might!" At first he could only see the words glowing in the darkness inside his head. Then the words burned in a cool, soft way, an indication that they were at the beginning of their life span. In the meantime—that is, during the time Ovando stood in front of the mirror, a mirror, by the way, that reflected nothing but his own image—my own world in its flatness heaved up and down in the way of something alternately freezing and thawing out. I looked at my world: its usually serene and pleasing contours began to change before my eyes. The roots of trees were forced out of the ground. The grasses were ablaze with a fire that I did not know how to put out. The streams dried up, and the riverbeds became barren tracks. The birds all hovered overhead and blotted out the light of the sun. The unwinged creatures stood up and cried into the charged air, but their own sounds disturbed them so that they then lay down and buried their heads in their stomachs. I said, "What is it? Who is it?" and then without speech I observed this frightening wonder, waiting for the moment when my world would return to the way it had always been, waiting for the moment when I would doubt that what I saw before me had really taken place. Ovando said again, "My Sheer Might!" and this time the words did not vanish into the silence of things. This time the words became like a poisonous cloud of vapor, and they spread out, swallowing up everything in their path. In that moment the mirror into which Ovando looked, the mirror which reflected only Ovando, broke into thirteen pieces in some places, into six hundred and sixty-six pieces in other places, and in still other places into different numbers of pieces, and in all of these places the breaking of the mirror signified woe. In that moment, I, my world, and everything in it became Ovando's thralls.

One morning, Ovando arose from his bed. Assisted by people he had forcibly placed in various stages of social and spiritual degradation, he prepared a document, which, when read to me, would reveal to me my real predicament. He had by this time grown an enormous tail, which he would cause to flail about in the air whenever he was amused. What amused him was predictable: the endless suffering he could cause whenever he wished. He had also grown horns on either side of his head, and from these he hung various instruments of torture; his tongue he made forked. The document that he had prepared for me was only six inches long and six inches wide, but it was made from the pulp of one hundred and ten trees and these trees had taken ten millennia to reach the exquisite state of beauty in which Ovando found them: their trunks were smooth, and so thick that two arms wrapped around them would just meet, and they glowed ruby red in the sunlight. At the very top the leaves and branches formed globes of yellow and green that also glowed in the sun; they perfumed the air but not pervasively, not enough that one could become accustomed to it. These trees Ovando had ordered cut down so that only stumps remained, and boiled and pounded and dried, and the process repeated again and again until they were reduced to something that measured six inches by six inches. Holding it up to the light, he said, "Do you see?" and I understood him to mean not only that he could reduce these precious trees to something held between the tips of two of his fingers but that he also held in his hands the millennia in which the trees grew to maturity, their origins, their ancestry, and everything that they had ever, ever been, and so too he held me. Then on this paper Ovando wrote that he dishonored me, that he had a right to do so for I came from nothing, that since I came from nothing I could not now exist in something, and so my existence was now rooted in nothing, and though I seemed to live and needed the things necessary to the living such as food and water and air, I was dead; and so though I might seem present, in reality I was absent. This document consisted of hundreds of articles and each of them confirmed my dishonor, each of them confirmed my death, each of them confirmed my nothingness. I listened to him carefully, his voice the sound of metal rapidly corroding. At the end of this I stood up and made an extremely long and incoherent speech, so shocked I was at the brutality of tone and language of Ovando's document, so unused to such cruelty, such barbarism, such harshness. In my long and incoherent speech, which I delivered in a heartfelt and sorrowful and earnest way (for should I not be touched by my own pain, should I not be moved on seeing a picture of myself humbled by a power over which I had no desire to triumph, a power I wished would stay out of my way?), I tried to point out to Ovando that since the ideas of Honor, Death, and Nothingness were not within my view and so held no meaning for me, he could not really rob me of anything; since these ideas constituted some of his deepest beliefs it was himself then that he dishonored, it was himself then that he made dead, it was himself then that he consigned to nothingness. But Ovando could not hear me, for by that time his head had taken the shape of a groundworm, which has no ears.

Ovando has conquered the ages and placed them in medallions he wears around his neck, his waist, his wrists, and his ankles. After consulting for a long time the one he wears around his left wrist, Ovando said, "I shall raise the curtain, and my relatives shall now make their appearance." Of course, such a thing as Ovando's curtain was invisible to me. Ovando made an enormous flourish with his hands and, as if a curtain really had been parted, there suddenly, in what used to be an empty space, now stood a covered floating vessel. Ovando smiled at me, his face splitting with pleasure and conceit. Ovando's relatives arranged themselves into pairs of male and female and then began to leave their covered floating vessel. As they did so they announced in loud voices, as if it were a curse, the names of the places from which they had come: Spain, France, England, Belgium, the Netherlands, Germany, Portugal, Italy. As they entered the earth they kissed the ground, not as a sign of affection but rather as a sign of possession. They looked around and at last they saw me. In unison, like a clap of thunder, they all said, "Mine!" Ovando, seeing the danger in this, said, "Draw lots," but the people who drew my head really wanted my legs, and the people who drew my arms wanted my insides, and so on and so on until they fell on each other with a ferociousness that I could not have imagined possible. This battle now lasted for hundreds and hundreds of years, at the end of which time they should have exterminated themselves, but wherever their blood was spilled new versions of themselves grew up. It was in this way that they multiplied, by spilling blood over the earth itself.

Ovando speaks his own name. He says, "Ovando!" His name then gently leaves his lips in a long sigh, a delicious parting. Saying his name, Ovando runs his hands through his hair; saying his name, Ovando caresses his face; saying his name, Ovando gently passes his hands down his own back, through the crevices of his private parts, gently unmatting the tightly curled hair that grows in thick sworls and covers completely his child-size penis; saying his name, Ovando gently runs his hands down one leg and up the other, across his chest, stopping to pinch sharply first one flattened breast and then the other; then raising his hands to his nostrils, he inhales deeply, and then bringing his hands to his mouth he kisses and sucks them until he feels content. His desire for his own mortal self fulfilled, he falls into a state of bliss, into a deep, deep sleep.

Ovando then lived constantly in night; but it was not a quiet night, a night that bore a soft sleep in which dreams of a long-ago-lived enchanted childhood occurred; it was not the sort of night that the day angrily interrupts, jealous of the union between the sleeper and the borderless, soft tapestry of blackness; and it was not a night of nature, which is to say the progression from the day to the opposite of day; it was not the night of just after sunset or the night of just before the sun rises. Ovando lived in the thickest part of the night, the deepest part of the night, the part of the night where all suffering dwells, including death; the part of the night in which the weight of the world is made visible and eternal terror is confirmed. In this night, Ovando's body was covered with sores (sores, not wounds, for the hand that inflicts wounds may be an unjust hand and injustice calls forth pity); he lay on a bed of broken glass bottles (not nails).

Who will judge Ovando? Who can judge Ovando? A true and just sentence would be imbued with love for Ovando. The sentence must bear within it sympathy and identification, for only if the judge resides in Ovando and Ovando resides in the judge can an everlasting judgment be passed. Ovando cannot pass judgment on himself, for, as is to be expected, he loves himself beyond measure. Such a love is a worm asleep in every heart, and must never be awakened; such a love lies like kindling in every heart, and must never be lit. A charge against Ovando, then, is that he loved himself so that all other selves and all other things became nothing to him. I became nothing to Ovando. My relatives became nothing to Ovando. Everything that could trace its lineage through me became nothing to Ovando. And so it came to be that Ovando loved nothing, lived in nothing, and died in just that way. I cannot judge Ovando. I have exhausted myself laying out before him his transgressions. I am exhausted from shielding myself so that his sins do not obsess and so possess me.

Athol Fugard

(INTERVIEW BY JAMAICA KINCAID)

WHAT DO YOU SAY TO PEOPLE you admire? I met Athol Fugard, the South African playwright, on a Sunday afternoon in New York. He is someone I admire. He is not someone with a zillion dollars, but he comes from a tribe of people that has zillions of dollars. The reason I admire him is that he does not let them forget the crimes they have committed in acquiring their fortune.

It was easy to speak to him. He gave the impression that doing the right thing was easy, that doing the right thing made you feel alive, that it was as easy as breathing to know the right way from the wrong way. Of course, it's the way people who have survived real adversity behave—Big World kind of adversity, that is.

At the end of the conversation I could see that you can say thank you to people like this. They don't need it, but you can say it all the same.

1990, Aug. "Athol Fugard." *Interview*. Vol. 20, iss. 8: 62–69. (Interview by Jamaica Kincaid.)

ATHOL FUGARD: *Are we going to sit and relax over here?*
JAMAICA KINCAID: Yes, why not?
AF: *O.K., and we put this tape recorder in between the two of us?*
JK: Yes . . . The thing I always like to know about someone is what they were like as a child.
AF: *Um [clears throat], a certain amount of that was written into the character of my little white boy in "Master Harold" and the Boys. And I don't know how good your memory is, but that self-portrait of the artist as a young, obnoxious [laughs] child indicated somebody who was lonely. Who already, at a very early age in his life, delighted in words, played with words, knew that somehow his life was going to be about words—the spoken word, the written word, words on paper, words on the stage. And who was also confused. Growing up in South Africa was a complicated experience for me, for one very simple reason. I think—I don't quite know how it came about—but I think at a fairly early age I became suspicious of what the system was trying to do to me. I knew the way it was trying to pull me. I became conscious of what attitudes it was trying to implant in me and what prejudices it was trying to pass on to me. You know, in South Africa at that point—and it was certainly that way right up until recently—all the institutions in your life made you feel that you were a white, and they bore down on you and tried to get you to think and feel in a certain way. And there was something in me which sort of questioned that, which made life quite difficult and complicated.*
JK: When you say you were lonely, you seem to be describing the life of a brilliant child. I think that children who are very smart are lonely because they know things don't add up. They don't really enjoy the things that children are supposed to enjoy. What were your parents like?
AF: *Both, in their own way, very beautiful people. My father was an invalid, a cripple. And drinking was a great problem in his*

life. He was a gentle man. A very, very beautiful man. But a very weak man. He had one extraordinary thing, and I think that had a decisive influence on my life: he was a marvelous storyteller. And we had a very close relationship. There were three children, incidentally, an older brother and a younger sister, but I was the closest to my father. My earliest memories are of the very delicate, very painful relationship I had with him, because it's hard for a young boy, who needs a role model, to discover that his father is weak and not strong and is enormously flawed. So it was a very delicate, very pain-filled relationship, but also a very beautiful one. Because I never hated him or anything like that. My earliest memories of that relationship are of sitting at his bedside, and he used to get a terrible pain in the stump of his amputated leg—terrible pains in the hip and in the muscles that were left on the section of the thigh. And late at night he'd wake me up and ask me to massage it and try to just ease the pain a little bit that way. And in return for that, while I was massaging his leg, he would tell me stories. He would condense the books he had read down into simple little child's versions. I think he passed on a certain gift for storytelling. So that was my father.

My mother was a monumental woman. She was obviously the stronger of the two parents. She was the breadwinner in the family. And she was extraordinary in that coming from typical Afrikaner stock—she was an Afrikaner peasant, she had almost no education, could barely read and write—she was also very questioning of that whole system. And one of the most extraordinary experiences in my life was how, from about the age of eight or nine, when the questions about that society began to become very urgent and real for me as a young white boy, my mother then shared those questions with me. She too began to look at and examine that society. And how then, until she died ten years ago, she kept pace with me as I tried to emancipate myself from the prejudices of that society. She ended up a monument of decency and principle and just anger. Oh, she was an extraordinary woman! She had total faith in me as a writer. At a certain point—I think I was eighteen years old—I said to her, "I'm going to be a writer." She said, "I believe you, and I will do anything I can to help you." And she was as good as her word. She gave me the most extraordinary support, then and through the rest of my life, until she died.

JK: Amazing.

AF: *So, those were my parents.*

JK: But how did they get to be that way?

AF: *Beg your pardon?*

JK: How did your parents get to be that way?

AF: *Well, what I've said about my mother doesn't really apply to my dad. My dad stayed very much in the old mode of the typical white South African.*

JK: Really!

AF: *Yes. He wasn't a cruel man in any sense, but—*

JK: Was he an Afrikaner, too?

AF: *No, he was English-speaking South African. But he never tried to emancipate himself from the prejudices that one associates with white South Africa. That was just my mother.*

JK: I see.

AF: *And it became a sort of conspiracy between myself and my mother. We never really spoke openly about it, say, between the years of eight and twenty, until I really broke out. It wasn't something that we flaunted publicly, if you know what I mean.*

JK: Yes.

AF: *It was like a conspiracy between the two of us, the way we would talk about the society, the way we would question it, the way we would report to each other on the injustices we had seen.*

JK: Just the two of you?

AF: *Just the two of us.*

JK: Was it just sort of natural, just in passing? The two of you would have a conversation and you'd find yourselves talking about these things?

AF: *Just find ourselves talking. I was very close to both. I think that I was unquestionably the closest of the three children to my father, and I was the closest to my mother. But there is one other thing about my mother which I should mention, which is that she was an enormously ambitious woman. Powerfully ambitious. She wanted to do something with her life, but she never got the chance. The responsibilities and the obligations in terms of raising three children, supporting a family—she was never free to do any of the things that she wanted to do. Now I don't think she deliberately looked at her three children and said, "Which one is going to make it?" I don't think it was as deliberate as that. But I think something instinctively said to her, "Athol is the one"—or actually "Harold," because my first name is really Harold. "Harold is the one who's going to make it." And that forged a special bond between the two of us, which wasn't there between my mom and my sister, or my mom and my older brother.*

JK: What were they like?

AF: *Oh. They are thoroughly decent human beings. And they have passed through periods of confusion and uncertainty and anxiety—like the rest of South Africa—and now, like the majority of white South Africans, they realize that the time has come for enormous changes. And that the old system was monstrously unjust and cruel and evil, and that a new South Africa is very painfully laboring its way into life.*

JK: What made people change? What happened? I mean, I know what happened, but I am outside.

AF: *Well, you see, there is a question still. A special degree of vigi-*

lance is still very necessary, and is even more necessary now than in the past. There's a difference now, but I still need to be persuaded that what we are being confronted with is not a change in policy but a change in heart. Because until there is a change in heart, *I will remain very suspicious of that government and what it's doing. When I am convinced that there has been a change in* heart, *yes! Because a change in policy is obviously easy. I mean, if you find your power and your life threatened because you are pursuing a policy which involves the economic stagnation of the society, then it's very easy to change policy in order to preserve all of those things, to preserve the good life. And that's not a very significant change, as far as I'm concerned. What South Africa has needed is a change of heart. And I do believe that that is taking place. How does it happen? I think it happens when people stop getting frightened. I think fear is the single most potent factor in prejudice. And I think, for example, that when Nelson Mandela—that* dreaded *man, that leader of the evil empire— when that man was released and he stood up there, all of white South Africa sat on the edge of their seats and* looked *at him for the first time. And they saw a gentle man, a beautiful man, a man prepared to forgive. They began to say, "Now, hang on." If I had lost twenty-seven years of my life in a jail I doubt very much if I would have come out with forgiveness in my heart.*

And so I think that white South Africa has had its fear eroded by encountering situations like that, by seeing Nelson Mandela and discovering that he's a man that actually talks about peace and brotherhood and people coming together. And they see, as has happened progressively under the awesome pressures of urbanization in South Africa, that black people have moved into areas of what was exclusively white South Africa and have taken up residence—illegally, but they have nevertheless taken up residence—and that the world doesn't fall apart. Then they go on to discover that their children, in the case of private schools, are sitting next to a black child from some privileged black family and come home and talk with love about their black schoolmate. So a process of disarming has taken place.

And you ask, and it's the first time I've been asked that question: "How has it happened that white South Africans—these arch, archetypal representatives of racial prejudice—now seem, in fairly significant numbers, to be prepared to abandon those prejudices?" My answer would be that I think circumstances, history, and events have made them less frightened. Knowledge.

JK: Yes. It's very interesting. That man, how do you pronounce his name? Turn—?

AF: *Treurnicht. Terrifying man, that! Terrifying!*

JK: Yes, he really is. But it's very interesting that he now seems to say to his constituents that what the black people will do to the white people—the things he describes—are the things the white people did to the black people.

AF: *Yes, exactly! Can you believe it?*

JK: Really! It's astonishing! It makes you want to say to him, "Well, it was good enough for you to do. So why not me now?

AF: *Well, it's our turn now! It's our turn! But he reflects accurately, I think, how delicately balanced the situation in South Africa still is. I mean we cannot, at this point, talk about a situation which is going to move quickly and without bloodshed toward a just and decent society. I think there are still powerful forces that could wreck the process.*

JK: How have you lived in South Africa all that time?

AF: *You end up with a survival mechanism.*

JK: Were you ever banned?

AF: *My plays were banned.*

JK: But you yourself?

AF: *No. The harassment that I've had to put up with is having my* *passport taken away, having my mail opened, telephone tapped, being under surveillance, having my house searched.*

JK: You *have* had that.

AF: *Yeah. You know, in the middle of the night.*

JK: So you must know something about terror. There were moments when you experienced terror?

AF: *Yeah, sure. You can't sort of be in active opposition to the government and not—no, they make you know about it.*

JK: It makes you wonder how it is that some people can identify, the way you do, with suffering, and some people cannot. What is it that makes someone that way, your way?

AF: *I don't know. And one of the ironies is that South Africa has gone through all the dramatic phases of its history in the past thirty to forty years, and now, with the emergence of powerful, militant, black political organizations and the growth in black consciousness—if you want to put it that way—there is, of course, an enormous amount of resentment, leading, in fact, to rejection of me by black people—*

JK: Oh! That is ironic.

AF: *A rejection of my writing.*

JK: That is incredibly ironic.

AF: *Oh, absolutely.*

JK: So you have to bear that too.

AF: *Oh, yeah, sure. Absolutely. I am nobody's hero. It's as simple as that. I mean, white South Africa sees me as—somebody told me they overheard somebody else saying, "Oh, don't pay any attention to him. He's a communist!" [JK laughs] And in the same token a young black writer whom I have done my best to defend in the past had an opportunity to speak publicly in Washington recently, and he said, "Fugard's writing had no validity. He's a white man." I mean, I can understand where he comes from. I understand what's being said.*

JK: Yes.

AF: Yeah. I'm caught in the cross fire. But you know, that's life. And life's too short, Jamaica, to worry about those things.

JK: Do you think of leaving South Africa?

AF: *I could leave. The government took away my passport at one stage to try to force me to leave permanently. I didn't. You end up with a survival mechanism. I can remember coming to New York for the first time and moving around the city as an innocent and getting into some pretty hairy situations once or twice, and then realizing that I didn't have a survival mechanism for this city. And I had grown up with a survival mechanism for South Africa. And what does a South African survival mechanism amount to? Here's a good question. All right, let's try and deal with it. Laughter is one of them. Interestingly enough, the preparedness to stand up and be counted, when the situation arises, is another one of them. Because if you feel the need to protest but don't protest, I think you're distilling a poison in yourself.*

JK: Yes. And then you die of it.

AF: *And then you die; you will destroy yourself. Regretfully, a certain callousness becomes a survival mechanism.*

JK: How do you mean, "callousness"?

AF: *All right. I was going to use an illustration, and I talk about it with a degree of innocence because it is a process inherent in life itself. I mean, if you're going to bring your hand up [slaps hands on table] consistently against some hard surface, you're going to end up with calluses. If you're a man who handles bricks every day, you are going to end up with calloused hands, because that is the way life is going to protect itself from permanent damage. Maybe it is different for other people. But something like that has been* my experience in terms of my—*I don't know what word we are going to use . . . "soul"? To a certain extent, watching injustice—the humiliation, the mutilation, whatever vocabulary you want to use—of people* daily, *simply because they happen to have the wrong skin* *color, a certain desensitization takes place. Let me put it to you this way: I didn't go into a state of trauma every time I saw an unjust arrest. But that never removed the anger. I mean, I hope that my writing is evidence of the fact that I am as angry today as I was when I first arrived at a clear understanding of what my society was about and how wrong it was. I just developed a certain* callousness *about it.*

JK: Yes.

AF: *I was able to look at things without crying every time.*

JK: Did you cry at first?

AF: *Oh, oh! And to this day I still cry when it is too much.*

JK: What would be something too much?

AF: *What sort of things have made me cry recently, in terms of anger? I'm a runner. I was in Port Elizabeth, which is my home, a little seaside town on the Indian Ocean side of South Africa. Very small town. That's where I go and write. But I'm a runner, and I was running along one of the country roads, and I happened to pass a little black child who was sitting on the side of the road, playing with a few little stones. A little child in rags. A little child that looked up and smiled at me with such radiance and joy as I passed, and we greeted each other. And I realized how the system was stacked against that child. How I most probably passed an individual with some extraordinary potential inside of himself—it was a little boy—potential to do extraordinary things with his life, and that he might never get a chance, because of the system. And that was almost too much for me. That was a hard one. And that sort of thing keeps on recurring. By and large, as I say, you get a sort of callousness which allows you to look at what is happening without cracking up.*

JK: Um-hm.

AF: *But just occasionally [laughs quietly] something gets past those calluses, and you do crack up.*

JK: Did your mother or father have any conflicts about their different views, or did it never come up?

AF: *Never came up. My father died in his sixties, but my mother was still only in the middle of her journey. She hadn't reached the point, which she did in her later life, where she would argue with anybody about the injustice of that society. I mean, I can remember sitting [laughs] in front of a television set, looking at the white Afrikaner prime minister of South Africa making a speech, and her swearing at him as he was making it. So she was really prepared to argue in the later years of her life, but it never surfaced as an issue between my mother and my father.*

JK: Did your father see your plays?

AF: *He died after I had written the first of the plays to start giving me a reputation, a play called* The Blood Knot, *which was about twenty-seven, twenty-eight years ago. I was in the process of staging it in Johannesburg with the South African actor you might know, Zakes Mokae. Well, you saw Zakes in* "Master Harold."

JK: Yes, that's right.

AF: *Zakes and I were in the process of doing that in Johannesburg when my father died. And he already knew that I was trying to start a literary career.*

JK: And he knew your views.

AF: *And he knew my views.*

JK: But you never discussed them?

AF: *No. No.*

JK: Isn't that odd?

AF: *It was. You see, I would argue with my mother. With my mum I had furious arguments! It was indicative of a strange sort of relationship I had with my dad, which was a relationship based on the recognition of a kind of pain.*

JK: There's something I want to ask you about—arguing with one parent and not the other. And I'm wondering if it isn't because you must have instinctively known that that bond with your father, if it was violated in any small way, might have given way to a permanent break?

AF: *That could well have been. I've also wondered whether it wasn't possibly because I, without saying as much to myself, knew that my dad was incapable of that journey. I knew my mother was! No question about it. I knew that I could challenge my mother, as she, in turn, challenged me. That we could challenge each other to the limit! Perhaps unconsciously I realized that my father wasn't capable of that journey, and therefore to leave it alone.*

Do you know where I encountered the relationship between my father and myself? Or a resonance of it? In a memoir by V. S. Naipaul about his childhood.

JK: Oh, yes! Yes.

AF: *He was writing about his father, and I recognized the same territory.*

JK: But unlike him, you don't scorn your history. I mean you're not ashamed of it.

AF: *I know!*

JK: He's very—

AF: *I can't understand that!*

JK: I can't understand it.

AF: *I can't understand that, and he saddens me enormously.*

JK: Oh, it's very sad. I'm awfully glad he got a knighthood out of it, though [laughs]. Work well done.

AF: *Yeah, yeah. But what I was going to say is I've sometimes wondered—because I'm so aware of the nuances of that relationship with my father—I've wondered, what writers in America would deal with a relationship like that? And what's very interesting is that it is always in writers from the South that I find the sort of artists who go into that territory: Carson McCullers. Eudora Welty.*

JK: Truman Capote.

AF: *Truman Capote! Absolutely, Truman Capote!*

JK: So what is it, then?

AF: *I think it's—I think it's—oh, I don't know. My guess is, are we talking about the possibility that that vein, that very rich vein in American literature, deals more certainly with ambiguity than any of the others? I don't know!*

JK: I don't know either.

AF: *I don't know what it is. I've always felt a greater affinity with some of those writers than I do with others.*

JK: Oh, absolutely. Yes. Well, the other writers are very much of the First World. And—

AF: *I think you've got it! That's a damned good observation! First World! You see, I haven't got a First World identity.*

JK: I've always thought the South is very odd. It's very much—

AF: *And the South is Third World.*

JK: Yes, yes. [both laugh] They've never freed themselves from that tradition of slavery.

AF: *No, no, no, no!*

JK: Well, I often think that what makes up the Third World isn't so much economics but that relationship of domination and conquest.

AF: *But I think one of the decisive factors in South African political life, and certainly in terms of the future, is that black South Africa has no experience of slavery. I mean in their experience of oppression. They have experience of the most cruel, mutilating oppression, but not slavery. Is there a difference? Maybe there's no difference.*

JK: Maybe there is no difference, and maybe there is.

AF: *You see, what I know, what was my experience from that moment, as a seven-, eight-, nine-year-old child, when I first began to look at the society in South Africa and began to think to myself, "Now look here, something's wrong"—I was looking at* men and women who had their dignity intact! The most unbelievable weight of oppression and injustice was bearing down on them, but they never lost their spirit! Now, at no point could I have said to myself, no matter how terrible—and I've seen some unbelievably awful situations in South Africa—could I point and use the word "slave." And I think the very power and strength of the liberation movement—the presence of Nelson Mandela, Walter Sisulu, and all the others—makes me inclined to say, "Look here. There is some distinction. Some important distinction."

JK: Yes.

AF: *I'm not trying to minimize anything. Or in turn to magnify anything. I just think there is a difference. And of course another factor about slavery is that you have been taken away from your home. The land of your birth, of your father's and mother's births.*

JK: Yes, yes. Your history. It's a living death.

AF: *That's it! You see, the history and tradition of black South Africa [claps] was never taken away from them.*

JK: Yes. And I wonder why it could *not* be taken away.

AF: *Because they stayed on their land. They might have been herded into small enclaves—*

JK: Yes, but they were there.

AF: *—but they were there.*

JK: Earlier you mentioned writers from the American South. Did you have a great interest in America, as a child?

AF: *Oh yes! I wish I could remember the specifics of it, but my home away from a very troubled home was the Port Elizabeth public library. It's a beautiful old Victorian building. There's a main floor area, and then there are a series of galleries with a wrought-iron balcony running around them. Do you understand?*

JK: Yes.

AF: *Like a second floor, and then a third floor, and a fourth floor. And the books are spread out on these galleries and on the ground floor. And as a little boy of eight or nine, I think, I first discovered the Port Elizabeth public library, and for the next ten years it was my home. I just prowled endlessly. And there was a period when I was addicted to all the westerns, you know, the cowboy stories. But more significantly, there came a point when I found my first William Faulkner.*

JK: Ah!

AF: *And I just read everything.*

JK: Yes.

AF: *And I have, I think, read everything about three times— started at the beginning again and just gone right through.*

JK: Isn't that amazing? That moment when you realize what's possible? You yearn for it, and there it is!

AF: *Exactly. When you realize what—what a voice can do!*

JK: Yeah.

AF: *Now Faulkner showed me territory.*

JK: Yes.

AF: *He's a regional writer, Faulkner. He hasn't written about the whole world. He hasn't taken on everything. He has got a focus on this one little county down there in the South—*

JK: And yet you recognize that county.

AF: *Oh, it transcends. And that gave me the courage to just focus on my little corner of South Africa. And tell my stories about that corner, without compromising them. Without saying, Oh, now I must remember that I'm hoping Americans will read this, so therefore let me simplify. No! Just tell it. Tell it in the very first instance, as if you were telling it to yourself. Tell it to your own people. If you're a good storyteller, you end up telling it to everybody. But in the very first instance, tell it to your own people.*

JK: Yes. I have to say I know that feeling very well.

AF: *What was your moment of discovery?*

JK: It was reading, I think, strangely enough, *Jane Eyre*, when I was about eleven years old or so. And I've never gotten over reading it.

AF: *I know what that feels like.*

JK: It's a beautiful book. I remember always one word from it: "gloaming."

AF: *"Gloaming." What a* great *word!*

JK: It is such a great word, and the thing about it is that it's not possible to have a situation of gloaming in the West Indies because—

AF: *[laughs] You don't have a long twilight.*

JK: Yes, we don't have a long twilight. [laughs] But for my whole life, you see, that's a word that just stuck with me.

AF: *You know, it's lovely to hear that, because I've just written a play which is in the process of being performed in the black ghetto areas of South Africa. My daughter is acting in it. And it contains my literary testament—my literary testament is summed up in one moment in the play. When this aging schoolteacher, who obviously is Fugard in disguise, confronts one of his pupils, a young, radical black who is going to start boycotting classes. And early in the play, the schoolteacher has tried to say to the boy, "Use words. They are* powerful! *They are the most powerful things." And he quotes a Confucian scholar who said that, using only words, a man can right a wrong, judge and execute the wrongdoer.*

And then at a later moment in the play, and actually the climactic moment in the play, he confronts the young boy with a choice. In his one hand he has a dictionary, in the other hand he has a stone. And he says, "Choose. Which one do you want? Choose!" He says, "In this hand"—holding up the stone—"I'm holding a stone! In this hand I'm holding the whole English language." [strikes the table] It's my literary testament.

The Finishing Line

(Fiction)

THE MAN ON THE FAR LEFT, STANDING. The seated woman. The standing woman on the left. The standing woman on the right. The fiery contraption with two legs, silent. The small boy. The man on the far right, standing.

1990, Dec. 2. "The Finishing Line." *The New York Times Book Review*: BR18. (1990, Dec. 2. "Have Yourself a Gorey Little Christmas: Nine Writers Create Stories for Edward Gorey's Christmas Illustrations." *The New York Times Book Review*.)

"The women are grouped together tightly, too tightly, more than I like women to be," said the man on the far right, standing.

"People say I have a glow about me," said the man on the far left, standing.

"I feel that I am alone in the world, I feel that even though I am in the company of people who, for reasons not clear to me, are fond of me, I am alone in the world," said the small boy.

"The skirts of the women who are grouped tightly together intermingle, creating a powerful flow, a strong current feeding into a mysterious source that is just beneath this very surface," said the man on the far right, standing.

"After I have taken a walk in the rain, small beads of water cling to me almost as if with affection, and I glisten, but only briefly, for soon they disappear," said the man on the far left, standing.

"I can see all the people who came before me, but no one seems to come after me," said the small boy.

"I want the women to be nice, not vinegary; I want the women to be kind, not cruel; they are already beautiful in a way I can understand," said the man on the far right, standing.

"I like things that come from far away," said the standing woman on the right.

"I like you and you are so close to me right now," said the standing woman on the left.

"I used to be able to stand up," said the seated woman.

"I like oranges, I like limes, I like coffee, I like tea, I like cane sugar, I like things that come from far away for they are always subject to the powers of cartels," said the standing woman on the right.

"I like you and you are standing so close to me right now and I can smell on your breath all the things that you like and all the places they come from," said the standing woman on the left.

"When I was able to stand up I used to forge alliances; I was benign sometimes, I was malevolent sometimes, but always in an underhanded way of course, always in a way that did not draw suspicion," said the seated woman.

"What would Mr. Wilson say?" said the man on the far left, standing.

"Mary's father or the retired lunatic in the cartoon," said the man on the far right, standing.

"In August I will stage a pantomime based on the slow but definite decline of my ancestors, ending with me in my small boy-ness for I know I shall never grow any more," said the small boy.

"What would Mr. Wilson say, What would Mr. Wilson say," said the man on the far left, standing.

"Mr. Wilson would say, that the teacup you are carrying in your hand is a teacup and it can only hold tea or something that is like tea, but it can never be used to hold another kind of beverage, like a fruit juice for instance, and it can never take the place of a water goblet at the dinner table, it can only be a teacup, only a teacup, always," said the man on the far right, standing.

"Where is the finishing line, I shall race you to the finishing line," said the man on the far left, standing.

"The finishing line is with me, I am standing on the finishing line," said the small boy.

"The finishing line is long and thin and white," said the seated woman.

"And . . . . ," said the man on the far right, standing.

"Indeed. . . . !" said the seated woman.

Foreword to *Babouk: Voices of Resistance*

THIS BOOK IS ABOUT A SLAVE (a man named Babouk), slavery itself, and the world of a people (Europe and its inhabitants) who profited from it. The slavery business, the institution of slavery, has been around for so long that it is clear that no piece of literature, no matter how great, has been able to put a stop to it. It would seem that the thing we call civilization can't be achieved without uprooting whole groups of people from everything they have ever known—who and what they know their individual and collective selves to be; the place they have always lived; their mothers, their fathers, their children—and forcibly made subject to the will of others.

Why this is so is not a mystery to me. I look at it this way: Suppose I am living in a nice village situated in a nice forest, or, say, my nice village is surrounded by some beautiful mountains, their tops

---

1991. Foreword to *Babouk: Voices of Resistance*, by Guy Endore. New York: Monthly Review Press. v–viii. (Afterword by David Barry Gaspar and Michel-Rolph Trouillot.)

changing color with the changing position of the sun. I go fishing every day, and every day I catch some fish—just the right number to satisfy me. I cultivate a small plot of land and I always have as much food from this land as I need, so that I never have to have a larder. To keep myself company, I make up some tales about how I got here and where I will go when I am not here anymore. This is a nice little setup I have here, my definition of contentment; and the thought of going off somewhere to pile brick upon brick in the hot desert sun to make monuments commemorating vicious people and their vicious deeds, or working in someone else's fields, or doing any of the horrible things that a civilization requires in order to be a civilization—none of this appeals to me at all.

Now, then, I try to imagine this: I am living somewhere that's not in the least nice—the weather is terrible (England); the people in other countries like your country better than they like their own because something more than the weather is terrible about where they live; I am surrounded by plenty but still I feel very greedy; I want more than I have; I have heard about all sorts of things somewhere else on the other side of the world and I would like to have them and I would like to have them for nothing. I have ideas about a lot of things. I feel I know how the world ought to look, the language most people ought to speak (my own), the sort of god they should believe in (my own again), and so on and on. Unfortunately, none of the things I want for myself or the things I want to do, none of my desires, can be realized where I am, so how terrific, how nearly perfect to find a defenseless people somewhere to be mere instruments of my will, some people over whom I have complete dominion. Who can resist this? No one has ever done so.

Different people require different things from life. Let me explain what I mean: here is the opening paragraph of a book called *Africa Explored: Europeans in the Dark Continent, 1769–1889*, a collection of biographies of some of the restless parasites who came to Africa from all over Europe, hoping that the experience would rescue them from the meaninglessness common to every human life:

> Near the end of Pall Mall there once stood a fashionable tavern known as the St. Alban's. Early one summer evening in 1788 nine rich and distinguished members of a small dining club met here to enjoy one of the excellent meals provided by the establishment. During the course of the evening the conversation turned to Africa, that mysterious continent of which so little was then known; and before the club members parted they had decided to form "an Association for promoting the Discovery of the Interior parts of Africa," in the belief that "so long as men continued ignorant of so large a portion of the globe, that ignorance must be considered as a degree of reproach on the present age."

I would think that some people sitting in a nice warm club, eating some good food (even if it is English food), drinking a good claret, would be reasonably contented—I mean, taking all the things I know about life into consideration. But obviously I am wrong. For there was poor Africa, sitting contentedly in all its innocence and beauty, attracting the gaze of the powerful and miserable.

Here is another paragraph, this from the autobiography of a slave named Gustavus Vassa. He is describing the place he comes from and the people who lived there:

> Our land is uncommonly rich and fruitful, and produces all kinds of vegetables in great abundance. We have plenty of Indian corn, and vast quantities of cotton and tobacco. Pineapples grow without culture; they are about the size of the largest sugar loaf, and finely flavored. We have also spices of different kinds, particularly pepper; and a variety of delicious fruits which I have never seen in Europe; together with gums of various kinds, and honey

in abundance. All our industry is exerted to improve these blessings of nature. Agriculture is our chief employment; and everyone, even to children and women, is employed in it. Thus we are habituated to labor from our earliest years. Everyone contributes something to the common stock: and as we are unacquainted with idleness, we have no beggars. The benefits of such a mode of living are obvious... Those benefits are felt by us in the general healthiness of the people, and in their vigor and activity... Our women, too, were, in my eyes at least, uncommonly graceful, alert, and modest to a degree of bashfulness; nor do I remember to have ever heard of an instance of promiscuity amongst them before marriage. They are also remarkably cheerful. Indeed, cheerfulness and affability are two of the leading characteristics of our nation.

And so to *Babouk*, this work of fiction, the life of a free man living in reasonable contentment in Africa, of his capture by other Africans (a point not dwelt on long enough, in my opinion), who sold him to European slave-traders, his journey to a world of hells, his life as a slave, the rebellion he led to free himself and his fellow slaves, and his death in its defeat. From the point of view of "great literature," this is not a great book, but to people caught up in a catastrophe that was not of their own making, a catastrophe that five hundred years after it commenced shows no sign of abatement, great literature is nice but essentially useless. At a certain point in life it is better to read this book than *Remembrance of Things Past*, just to name one example of great literature. In fact, after you read *Babouk*, you may wish that the author of *Remembrance of Things Past* were still alive so that you could point out to him a number of things he seems to have missed, such as the source of the money that allowed his characters to live such lives of moral worthlessness.

Here are some other reasons to read this book instead of one of the titans of our times: you will be reminded that twelve years after Christopher Columbus landed in this part of the world, over a million of the people he found living here were dead. In addition, so many Africans were thrown overboard on voyages from Africa to this part of the world that it would not be an overstatement to say that the Atlantic Ocean is the Auschwitz of Africa. It is hard to turn a page of *Babouk* without finding reports—drawn from actual history—of beatings, murders, people nailed to posts by their ears, all because they tried to escape the brutality that had fallen on them; or of women with child stretched out on the ground so that they can be severely beaten for some task not properly carried out, the ground hollowed out to accommodate their protruding stomachs. Who is the savage here, and who is the uncivilized? This superior Western civilization, did it pass over the heads of some of these Western civilization people?

On Christopher Columbus's tomb, someone wrote: "For him the known world was not enough, he added a new one to the old, and gave to heaven countless souls." Indeed! I found this quote in *Babouk*. The author, Guy Endore, placed it at the head of a chapter, and it made me feel that if I had met him I would have liked him. He was a white man and he wrote a work of fiction, a passionate human account of the life of an African slave. He also wrote screenplays in Hollywood, and at some point in his life he was publicly censured and humiliated for the views he held about American society. I am glad the author of this book was a white person. I think that every white writer should write a book about black slavery, as I think every writer who is not a Jew should write a book about the Holocaust. Perhaps someday someone will produce a work of such overwhelming literary merit that it brings the machinery of slavery and holocaust to a complete halt.

On Seeing England for the First Time

WHEN I SAW ENGLAND for the first time, I was a child in school sitting at a desk. The England I was looking at was laid out on a map gently, beautifully, delicately, a very special jewel; it lay on a bed of sky blue—the background of the map—its yellow form mysterious, because though it looked like a leg of mutton, it could not really look like anything so familiar as a leg of mutton because it was England—with shadings of pink and green, unlike any shadings of pink and green I had seen before, squiggly veins of red running in every direction. England was a special jewel all right, and only special people got to wear it. The people who got to wear England were English people. They wore it well and they wore it everywhere: in jungles, in deserts, on plains, on top of the highest mountains, on all the oceans, on all the seas, in places where they were not welcome, in places they should not have been. When my teacher had pinned this map up on the blackboard, she said, "This is England"—and she said it with authority, seriousness, and adoration, and we all sat up. It was as if she had said, "This is

Jerusalem, the place you will go to when you die but only if you have been good." We understood then—we were meant to understand then—that England was to be our source of myth and the source from which we got our sense of reality, our sense of what was meaningful, our sense of what was meaningless—and much about our own lives and much about the very idea of us headed that last list.

At the time I was a child sitting at my desk seeing England for the first time, I was already very familiar with the greatness of it. Each morning before I left for school, I ate a breakfast of half a grapefruit, an egg, bread and butter and a slice of cheese, and a cup of cocoa; or half a grapefruit, a bowl of oat porridge, bread and butter and a slice of cheese, and a cup of cocoa. The can of cocoa was often left on the table in front of me. It had written on it the name of the company, the year the company was established, and the words "Made in England." Those words, "Made in England," were written on the box the oats came in too. They would also have been written on the box the shoes I was wearing came in; a bolt of gray linen cloth lying on the shelf of a store from which my mother had bought three yards to make the uniform that I was wearing had written along its edge those three words. The shoes I wore were made in England; so were my socks and cotton undergarments and the satin ribbons I wore tied at the end of two plaits of my hair. My father, who might have sat next to me at breakfast, was a carpenter and cabinetmaker. The shoes he wore to work would have been made in England, as were his khaki shirt and trousers, his underpants and undershirt, his socks and brown felt hat. Felt was not the proper material from which a hat that was expected to provide shade from the hot sun should be made, but my father must have seen and admired a picture of an Englishman wearing such a hat in England, and this picture that he saw must have been so compelling that it caused him to wear the wrong hat for a hot climate most of his long life. And this hat—a brown felt hat— became so central to his character that it was the first thing he put on in the morning as he stepped out of bed and the last thing he took off before he stepped back into bed at night. As we sat at breakfast a car might go by. The car, a Hillman or a Zephyr, was made in England. The very idea of the meal itself, breakfast, and its substantial quality and quantity was an idea from England; we somehow knew that in England they began the day with this meal called breakfast and a proper breakfast was a big breakfast. No one I knew liked eating so much food so early in the day; it made us feel sleepy, tired. But this breakfast business was Made in England like almost everything else that surrounded us, the exceptions being the sea, the sky, and the air we breathed.

At the time I saw this map—seeing England for the first time—I did not say to myself, "Ah, so that's what it looks like," because there was no longing in me to put a shape to those three words that ran through every part of my life no matter how small; for me to have had such a longing would have meant that I lived in a certain atmosphere, an atmosphere in which those three words were felt as a burden. But I did not live in such an atmosphere. My father's brown felt hat would develop a hole in its crown, the lining would separate from the hat itself, and six weeks before he thought that he could not be seen wearing it—he was a very vain man—he would order another hat from England. And my mother taught me to eat my food in the English way: the knife in the right hand, the fork in the left, my elbows held still close to my side, the food carefully balanced on my fork and then brought up to my mouth. When I had finally mastered it, I overheard her saying to a friend, "Did you see how nicely she can eat?" But I knew then that I enjoyed my food more when I ate it with my bare hands, and I continued to do so when she wasn't looking. And when my teacher showed us the map, she asked us to study it carefully, because no test we would ever take would be complete without this statement: "Draw a map of England."

I did not know then that the statement "Draw a map of England" was something far worse than a declaration of war, for in fact a flat-out declaration of war would have put me on alert, and again in fact, there was no need for war—I had long ago been conquered. I did not know then that this statement was part of a process that would result in my erasure, not my physical erasure, but my erasure all the same. I did not know then that this statement was meant to make me feel in awe and small whenever I heard the word "England": awe at its existence, small because I was not from it. I did not know very much of anything then—certainly not what a blessing it was that I was unable to draw a map of England correctly.

After that there were many times of seeing England for the first time. I saw England in history. I knew the names of all the kings of England. I knew the names of their children, their wives, their disappointments, their triumphs, the names of people who betrayed them, I knew the dates on which they were born and the dates they died. I knew their conquests and was made to feel glad if I figured in them; I knew their defeats. I knew the details of the year 1066 (the Battle of Hastings, the end of the reign of the Anglo-Saxon kings) before I knew the details of the year 1832 (the year slavery was abolished). It wasn't as bad as I make it sound now; it was worse. I did like so much hearing again and again how Alfred the Great, traveling in disguise, had been left to watch cakes, and because he wasn't used to this the cakes got burned, and Alfred burned his hands pulling them out of the fire, and the woman who had left him to watch the cakes screamed at him. I loved King Alfred. My grandfather was named after him; his son, my uncle, was named after King Alfred; my brother is named after King Alfred. And so there are three people in my family named after a man they have never met, a man who died over ten centuries ago. The first view I got of England then was not unlike the first view received by the person who named my grandfather.

This view, though—the naming of the kings, their deeds, their disappointments—was the vivid view, the forceful view. There were other views, subtler ones, softer, almost not there—but these were the ones that made the most lasting impression on me, these were the ones that made me really feel like nothing. "When morning touched the sky" was one phrase, for no morning touched the sky where I lived. The mornings where I lived came on abruptly, with a shock of heat and loud noises. "Evening approaches" was another, but the evenings where I lived did not approach; in fact, I had no evening—I had night and I had day and they came and went in a mechanical way: on, off; on, off. And then there were gentle mountains and low blue skies and moors over which people took walks for nothing but pleasure, when where I lived a walk was an act of labor, a burden, something only death or the automobile could relieve. And there were things that a small turn of a head could convey—entire worlds, whole lives would depend on this thing, a certain turn of a head. Everyday life could be quite tiring, more tiring than anything I was told not to do. I was told not to gossip, but they did that all the time. And they ate so much food, violating another of those rules they taught me: do not indulge in gluttony. And the foods they ate actually: if only sometime I could eat cold cuts after theater, cold cuts of lamb and mint sauce, and Yorkshire pudding and scones, and clotted cream, and sausages that came from up-country (imagine, "up-country"). And having troubling thoughts at twilight, a good time to have troubling thoughts, apparently; and servants who stole and left in the middle of a crisis, who were born with a limp or some other kind of deformity, not nourished properly in their mother's womb (that last part I figured out for myself; the point was, oh to have an untrustworthy servant); and wonderful cobbled streets onto which solid front doors opened; and people whose eyes were blue and who had fair skins and who smelled only of lavender, or sometimes sweet pea or primrose. And those flowers with those names: delphiniums, foxgloves, tulips, daffodils, floribunda, peonies; in bloom, a striking display, being cut and placed in large glass bowls, crystal, decorating rooms so large twenty families the size of mine could fit in comfortably but used only for passing through. And the weather was so remarkable because the rain fell gently always, only occasionally in deep gusts, and it colored the air various shades of gray, each an appealing shade for a dress to be worn when a portrait was being painted; and when it rained at twilight, wonderful things happened: people bumped into each other unexpectedly and that would lead to all sorts of turns of events—a plot, the mere weather caused plots. I saw that people rushed: they rushed to catch trains, they rushed toward each other and away from each other; they rushed and rushed and rushed. That word: rushed! I did not know what it was to do that. It was too hot to do that, and so I came to envy people who would rush, even though it had no meaning to me to do such a thing. But there they are again. They loved their children; their children were sent to their own rooms as a punishment, rooms larger than my entire house. They were special, everything about them said so, even their clothes; their clothes rustled, swished, soothed. The world was theirs, not mine; everything told me so.

If now as I speak of all this I give the impression of someone on the outside looking in, nose pressed up against a glass window, that is wrong. My nose was pressed up against a glass window all right, but there was an iron vise at the back of my neck forcing my head to stay in place. To avert my gaze was to fall back into something from which I had been rescued, a hole filled with nothing, and that was the word for everything about me, nothing. The reality of my life was conquests, subjugation, humiliation, enforced amnesia. I was forced to forget. Just for instance, this: I lived in a part of St. John's, Antigua, called Ovals. Ovals was made up of five streets, each of them named after a famous English seaman—to be quite frank, an officially sanctioned criminal: Rodney Street (after George Rodney), Nelson Street (after Horatio Nelson), Drake Street (after Francis Drake), Hood Street, and Hawkins Street (after John Hawkins). But John Hawkins was knighted after a trip he made to Africa, opening up a new trade, the slave trade. He was then entitled to wear as his crest a negro bound with a cord. Every single person living on Hawkins Street was descended from a slave. John Hawkins's ship, the one in which he transported the people he had bought and kidnapped, was called the *Jesus*. He later became the treasurer of the Royal Navy and rear admiral.

Again, the reality of my life, the life I led at the time I was being shown these views of England for the first time, for the second time, for the one hundred millionth time, was this: the sun shone with what sometimes seemed to be a deliberate cruelty; we must have done something to deserve that. My dresses did not rustle in the evening air as I strolled to the theater (I had no evening, I had no theater; my dresses were made of a cheap cotton, the weave of which would give way after not too many washings). I got up in the morning, I did my chores (fetched water from the public pipe for my mother, swept the yard), I washed myself, I went to a woman to have my hair combed freshly every day (because before we were allowed into our classroom our teachers would inspect us, and children who had not bathed that day, or had dirt under their fingernails, or whose hair had not been combed anew that day might not be allowed to attend class). I ate that breakfast. I walked to school. At school we gathered in an auditorium and sang a hymn, "All Things Bright and Beautiful," and looking down on us as we sang were portraits of the queen of England and her husband; they wore jewels and medals and they smiled. I was a Brownie. At each meeting we would form a little group around a flagpole, and after raising the union jack, we would say, "I promise to do my best, to do my duty to God and the queen, to help other people every day and obey the scouts' law."

Who were these people and why had I never seen them, I mean really seen them, in the place where they lived. I had never been to England. No one I knew had ever been to England, or I should say, no one I knew had ever been and returned to tell me about it. All the people I knew who had gone to England had stayed there. Sometimes they left behind them their small children, never to see them again. England! I had seen England's representatives. I had seen the governor general at the public grounds at a ceremony celebrating the queen's birthday. I had seen an old princess and I had seen a young princess. They had both been extremely not beautiful, but who of us would have told them that? I had never seen England, really seen it, I had only met a representative, seen a picture, read books, memorized its history. I had never set foot, my own foot, in it.

The space between the idea of something and its reality is always wide and deep and dark. The longer they are kept apart—idea of thing, reality of thing—the wider the width, the deeper the depth, the thicker and darker the darkness. This space starts out empty, there is nothing in it, but it rapidly becomes filled up with obsession or desire or hatred or love—sometimes all of these things, sometimes some of these things, sometimes only one of these things. The existence of the world as I came to know it was a result of this: idea of thing over here, reality of thing way, way over there. There was Christopher Columbus, an unlikable man, an unpleasant man, a liar (and so of course, a thief) surrounded by maps and schemes and plans, and there was the reality on the other side of that width, that depth, that darkness. He became obsessed, he became filled with desire, the hatred came later, love was never a part of it. Eventually, his idea met the longed-for reality. That the idea of something and its reality are often two completely different things is something no one ever remembers; and so when they meet and find that they are not compatible, the weaker of the two, idea or reality, dies. That idea Christopher Columbus had was more powerful than the reality he met and so the reality he met died.

And so finally, when I was a grown-up woman, the mother of two children, the wife of someone, a person who resides in a powerful country that takes up more than its fair share of a continent, the owner of a house with many rooms in it and of two automobiles, with the desire and will (which I very much act upon) to take from the world more than I give back to it, more than I deserve, more than I need, finally then, I saw England, the real England, not a picture, not a painting, not through a story in a book, but England, for the first time. In me, the space between the idea of it and its reality had become filled with hatred, and so when at last I saw it I wanted to take it into my hands and tear it into little pieces and then crumble it up as if it were clay, child's clay. That was impossible, and so I could only indulge in not-favorable opinions.

There were monuments everywhere; they commemorated victories, battles fought between them and the people who lived across the sea from them, all vile people, fought over which of them would have dominion over the people who looked like me. The monuments were useless to them now, people sat on them and ate their lunch. They were like markers on an old useless trail, like a piece of old string tied to a finger to jog the memory, like old decoration in an old house, dirty, useless, in the way. Their skins were so pale, it made them look so fragile, so weak, so ugly. What if I had the power to simply banish them from their land, send boat after boatload of them on a voyage that in fact had no destination, force them to live in a place where the sun's presence was a constant. This would rid them of their pale complexion and make them look more like me, make them look more like the people I love and treasure and hold dear, and more like the people who occupy the near and far reaches of my imagination, my history, my geography, and reduce them and everything they have ever known to figurines as evidence that I was in divine favor, what if all this was in my power? Could I resist it? No one ever has.

And they were rude, they were rude to each other. They didn't like each other very much. They didn't like each other in the way they didn't like me, and it occurred to me that their dislike for me was one of the few things they agreed on. I was on a train in England with a friend, an English woman. Before we were in England she liked me very much. In England she didn't like me at all. She didn't like the claim I said I had on England, she didn't like the views I had of England. I didn't like England, she didn't like England, but she didn't like me not liking it too. She said, "I want to show you my England, I want to show you the England that I know and love." I had told her many times before that I knew England and I didn't want to love it anyway. She no longer lived in England; it was her own country, but it had not been kind to her, so she left. On the train, the conductor was rude to her; she asked something, and he responded in a rude way. She became ashamed. She was ashamed at the way he treated her; she was ashamed at the way he behaved. "This is the new England," she said. But I liked the conductor being rude; his behavior seemed quite appropriate. Earlier this had happened: We had gone to a store to buy a shirt for my husband; it was meant to be a special present, a special shirt to wear on special occasions. This was a store where the Prince of Wales has his shirts made but the shirts sold in this store are beautiful all the same. I found a shirt I thought my husband would like and I wanted to buy him a tie to go with it. When I couldn't decide which one to choose, the salesman showed me a new set. He was very pleased with these, he said, because they bore the crest of the Prince of Wales, and the Prince of Wales had never allowed his crest to decorate an article of clothing before. There was something in the way he said it; his tone was slavish, reverential, awed. It made me feel angry; I wanted to hit him. I didn't do that. I said, my husband and I hate princes, my husband would never wear anything that had a prince's anything on it. My friend stiffened. The salesman stiffened. They both drew themselves in, away from me. My friend told me that the prince was a symbol of her Englishness and I could see that I had caused offense. I looked at her. She was an English person, the sort of English person I used to know at home, the sort who was nobody in England but somebody when they came to live among the people like me. There were many people I could have seen England with; that I was seeing it with this particular person, a person who reminded me of the people who showed me England long ago as I sat in church or at my desk, made me feel silent and afraid, for I wondered if, all these years of our friendship, I had had a friend or had been in the thrall of a racial memory.

I went to Bath—we, my friend and I, did this, but though we were together, I was no longer with her. The landscape was almost as familiar as my own hand, but I had never been in this place before, so how could that be again? And the streets of Bath were familiar, too, but I had never walked on them before. It was all those years of reading, starting with Roman Britain. Why did I have to know about Roman Britain? It was of no real use to me, a person living on a hot, drought-ridden island, and it is of no use to me now, and yet my head is filled with this nonsense, Roman Britain. In Bath, I drank tea in a room I had read about in a novel written in the eighteenth century. In this very same room, young women wearing those dresses that rustled and so on danced and flirted and sometimes disgraced themselves with young men, soldiers, sailors, who were on their way to Bristol or someplace like that, so many places like that where so many adventures, the outcome of which was not good for me, began. Bristol, England. A sentence that began "That night the ship sailed from Bristol, England" would end not so good for me. And then I was driving through the countryside in an English motorcar, on narrow winding roads, and they were so familiar, though I had never been on them before; and through little villages the names of which I somehow knew so well though I had never been there before. And the countryside did have all those hedges and hedges, fields hedged in. I was marveling at all the toil of it, the planting of the hedges to begin with and then the care of it, all that clipping, year after year of clipping, and I wondered at the lives of the people who would have to do this, because wherever I see and feel the hands that hold up the world, I see and feel myself and all the people who look like me. And I said, "Those hedges," and my friend said that someone, a woman named Mrs. Rothchild, worried that the hedges weren't being taken care of properly; the farmers couldn't afford or find the help to keep up the hedges, and often they replaced them with wire fencing. I might have said to that, well if Mrs. Rothchild doesn't like the wire fencing, why doesn't she take care of the hedges herself, but I didn't. And then in those fields that were now hemmed in by wire fencing that a privileged woman didn't like was planted a vile yellow flowering bush that produced an oil, and my friend said that Mrs. Rothchild didn't like this either; it ruined the English countryside, it ruined the traditional look of the English countryside.

It was not at that moment that I wished every sentence, everything I knew, that began with England, would end with "and then it all died; we don't know how, it just all died." At that moment, I was thinking, who are these people who forced me to think of them all the time, who forced me to think that the world I knew was incomplete, or without substance, or did not measure up because it was not England; that I was incomplete, or without substance, and did not measure up because I was not English. Who were these people? The person sitting next to me couldn't give me a clue; no one person could. In any case, if I had said to her, I find England ugly, I hate England; the weather is like a jail sentence, the English are a very ugly people, the food in England is like a jail sentence, the hair of English people is so straight, so dead looking, the English have an unbearable smell so different from the smell of people I know, real people of course, she would have said that I was a person full of prejudice. Apart from the fact that it is I—that is, the people who look like me—who made her aware of the unpleasantness of such a thing, the idea of such a thing, prejudice, she would have been only partly right, sort of right: I may be capable of prejudice, but my prejudices have no weight to them, my prejudices have no force behind them, my prejudices remain opinions, my prejudices remain my personal opinion. And a great feeling of rage and disappointment came over me as I looked at England, my head full of personal opinions that could not have public, my public, approval. The people I come from are powerless to do evil on a grand scale.

The moment I wished every sentence, everything I knew, that began with England would end with "and then it all died, we don't know how, it just all died" was when I saw the white cliffs of Dover. I had sung hymns and recited poems that were about a longing to see the white cliffs of Dover again. At the time I sang the hymns and recited the poems, I could really long to see them again because I had never seen them at all, nor had anyone around me at the time. But there we were, groups of people longing for something we had never seen. And so there they were, the white cliffs, but they were not that pearly majestic thing I used to sing about, that thing that created such a feeling in these people that when they died in the place where I lived they had themselves buried facing a direction that would allow them to see the white cliffs of Dover when they were resurrected, as surely they would be. The white cliffs of Dover, when finally I saw them, were cliffs, but they were not white; you would only call them that if the word "white" meant something special to you; they were dirty and they were steep; they were so steep, the correct height from which all my views of England, starting with the map before me in my classroom and ending with the trip I had just taken, should jump and die and disappear forever.

Biography of a Dress

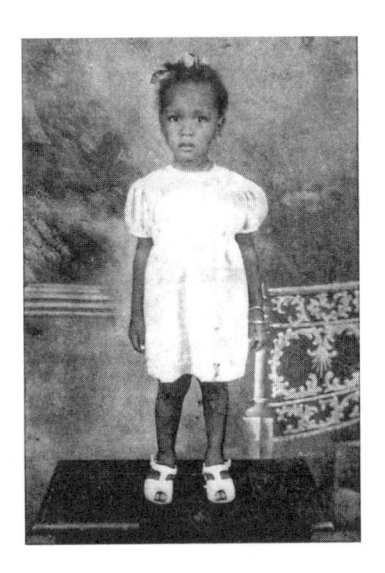

THE DRESS I AM WEARING in this black-and-white photograph, taken when I was two years old, is a yellow dress made of cotton poplin (a fabric with a slightly un-smooth texture first manufactured in the French town of Avignon and brought to England by the Huguenots, but I could not have known that at the time), and it was made for me by my mother. This shade of yellow, the color of my dress that I was wearing when I was two years old, was the same shade of yellow as boiled cornmeal, a food that my mother was always eager for me to eat in one form (as a porridge) or another (as fongie, the starchy part of my midday meal) because it was cheap and therefore easily available (but I did not know that at the time), and because she thought that foods bearing the colors yellow, green, or orange were particularly rich in vitamins and so boiled cornmeal would be particularly good for me. But I was then (not so now) extremely particular about what I would eat, not knowing then (but I do now) of shortages and abundance, having no consciousness of the idea of rich and poor (but I know now that we were poor then), and would eat only boiled beef (which I required my mother to chew for me first and, after she had made it soft, remove it from her mouth and place it in mine), certain kinds of boiled fish (doctor or angel), hard-boiled eggs (from hens, not ducks), poached calf's liver and the milk from cows, and so would not even look at the boiled cornmeal (porridge or fongie). There was not one single thing that I could isolate and say I did not like about the boiled cornmeal (porridge or fongie) because I could not isolate parts of things then (though I can and do now), but whenever I saw this bowl of trembling yellow substance before me I would grow still and silent, I did not cry, that did not make me cry. My mother told me this then (she does not tell me this now, she does not remember this now, she does not remember telling me this now): she knew of a man who had eaten boiled cornmeal at least once a day from the time he was my age then, two years old, and he lived for a very long time, finally dying when he was almost one hundred years old, and when he died he had looked rosy and new, with the springy wrinkles of the newborn, not the slack pleats of skin of the aged; as he lay dead his stomach was cut open, and all his insides were a beautiful shade of yellow, the same shade of yellow as boiled cornmeal. I was powerless then (though not so now) to like or dislike this story; it was beyond me then (though not so now) to understand the span of my lifetime then, two years old, and it was beyond me then (though not so now), the span of time called almost one hundred years old; I did not know then (though I do now) that there was such a thing as an inside to anybody, and that this inside would have a color, and that if the insides were the same shade of yellow as the yellow of boiled cornmeal my mother would want me to know about it.

On a day when it was not raining (that would have been unusual, that would have been out of the ordinary, ruining the fixed form of the day), my mother walked to one of the Harneys' stores (there were many Harneys who owned stores, and they sold the same things, but I did not know then and I do not know now if they were all of the same people) and bought one and a half yards of this yellow cotton poplin to make a dress for me, a dress I would wear to have my picture taken on the day I turned two years old. Inside, the store was cool and dark, and this was a good thing because outside was hot and overly bright. Someone named Harney did not wait on my mother, but someone named Miss Verna did and she was very nice still, so nice that she tickled my cheek as she spoke to my mother, and I reached forward as if to kiss her, but when her cheek met my lips I opened my mouth and bit her hard with my small child's teeth. Her cry of surprise did not pierce the air, but she looked at me hard, as if she knew me very, very well; and later, much later, when I was about twelve years old or so and she was always in and out of the crazy house, I would pass her on the street and throw stones at her, and she would turn and look at me hard, but she did not know who I was, she did not know who anyone was at all, not at all. Miss Verna showed my mother five flat thick bolts of cloth, white, blue (sea), blue (sky), yellow, and pink, and my mother chose the yellow after holding it up against the rich copper color that my hair was then (it is not so now); she paid for it with a one-pound note that had an engraving of the king George the Fifth on it (an ugly man with a cruel, sharp, bony nose, not the kind, soft, fleshy noses I was then used to), and she received change that included crowns, shillings, florins, and farthings.

My mother, carrying me and the just-bought piece of yellow poplin wrapped in coarse brown paper in her arms, walked out of Mr. Harney's store, up the street a few doors away, and into a store called Murdoch's (because the family who owned it were the Murdochs), and there my mother bought two skeins of yellow thread, the kind used for embroidering and a shade of yellow almost identical to the yellow poplin. My mother not only took me with her everywhere she went, she carried me, sometimes in her arms, sometimes on her back; for this errand she carried me in her arms; she did not complain, she never complained (but later she refused to do it anymore and never gave an explanation, at least not one that I can remember now); as usual, she spoke to me and sang to me in French patois (but I did not understand French patois then and I do not now and so I can never know what exactly she said to me then). She walked back to our house on Dickenson Bay Street, stopping often to hold conversations with people (men and women) she knew, speaking to them sometimes in English, sometimes in French; and after they said how beautiful I was (for people would often say that about me then but they do not say that about me now), she would laugh and say that I did not like to be kissed (and I don't know if that was really true then but it is not so now). And that night after we had eaten our supper (boiled fish in a butter-and-lemon-juice sauce) and her husband (who was not my father but I did not know that at the time, I know that now) had gone for a walk (to the jetty), she removed the yellow poplin from its brown wrapper and folded and made creases in it and with scissors made holes (for the arms and neck) and slashes (for an opening in the back and the shoulders); she then placed it along with some ordinary thread (yellow), the thread for embroidering, the scissors and a needle in a basket that she had brought with her from her home in Dominica when she first left it at sixteen years of age.

For days afterward, my mother, after she had finished her usual chores (clothes washing, dish washing, floor scrubbing, bathing me, her only child, feeding me a teaspoon of cod-liver oil), sat on the sill of the doorway, half in the sun, half out of the sun, and sewed together the various parts that would make up altogether my dress of yellow poplin; she gathered and hemmed and made tucks; she was just in the early stages of teaching herself how to make smocking and so was confined to making straight stitches (up-cable, down-cable, outline, stem, chain); the bodice of the dress appeared simple, plain, and the detail and pattern can only be seen close up and in real life, not from far away and not in a photograph; and much later, when she grew in confidence with this craft, the bodice of my dresses became overburdened with the stitches chevron, trellis, diamonds, Vandyke, and species of birds she had never seen (swan) and species of flowers she had never seen (tulip) and species of animals she had never seen (bear) in real life, only in a picture in a book.

My skin was not the color of cream in the process of spoiling, my hair was not the texture of silk and the color of flax, my eyes did not gleam like blue jewels in a crown, the afternoons in which I sat watching my mother make me this dress were not cool, and verdant lawns and pastures and hills and dales did not stretch out before me; but it was the picture of such a girl at two years old—a girl whose skin was the color of cream in the process of spoiling, whose hair was the texture of silk and the color of flax, a girl whose eyes gleamed like blue jewels in a crown, a girl whose afternoons (and mornings and nights) were cool, and before whom stretched verdant lawns and pastures and hills and dales—that my mother saw, a picture on an almanac advertising a particularly fine and scented soap (a soap she could not afford to buy then but I can now), and this picture of this girl wearing a yellow dress with smocking on the front bodice perhaps created in my mother the desire to have a daughter who looked like that or perhaps created the desire in my mother to try and make the daughter she already had look like that. I do not know now and I did not know then. And who was that girl really? (I did not ask then because I could not ask then but I ask now.) And who made her dress? And this girl would have had a mother; did the mother then have some friends, other women, and did they sit together under a tree (or sit somewhere else) and compare strengths of potions used to throw away a child, or weigh the satisfactions to be had from the chaos of revenge or the smooth order of forgiveness; and this girl with skin of cream on its way to spoiling and hair the color of flax, what did her insides look like, what did she eat? (I did not ask then because I could not ask then and I ask now but no one can answer me, really answer me.)

My second birthday was not a major event in anyone's life, certainly not my own (it was not my first and it was not my last, I am now forty-three years old), but my mother, perhaps because of circumstances (I would not have known then and to know now is not a help), perhaps only because of an established custom (but only in her family, other people didn't do this), to mark the occasion of my turning two years old had my ears pierced. One day, at dusk (I would not have called it that then), I was taken to someone's house (a woman from Dominica, a woman who was as dark as my mother was fair, and yet they were so similar that I am sure now as I was then that they shared the same tongue), and two thorns that had been heated in a fire were pierced through my earlobes. I do not now know (and could not have known then) if the pain I experienced resembled in any way the pain my mother experienced while giving birth to me or even if my mother, in having my ears bored in that way, at that time, meant to express hostility or aggression toward me (but without meaning to and without knowing that it was possible to mean to). For days afterward my earlobes were swollen and covered with a golden crust (which might have glistened in the harsh sunlight, but I can only imagine that now), and the pain of my earlobes must have filled up all that made up my entire being then and the pain of my earlobes must have been unbearable, because it was then that was the first time that I separated myself from myself, and I became two people (two small children then, I was two years old), one having the experience, the other observing the one having the experience. And the observer, perhaps because it was an act of my own will (strong then, but stronger now), my first and only real act of self-invention, is the one of the two I most rely on, the one of the two whose voice I believe to be the true voice; and of course it is the observer who cannot be relied on as the final truth to be believed, for the observer has woven between myself and the person who is having an experience a protective membrane, which allows me to see but only feel as much as I can handle at any given moment. And so...

On the day I turned two years old, the twenty-fifth of May 1951, a pair of earrings, small hoops made of gold from British Guiana (it was called that then, it is not called that now), were placed in the bored holes in my earlobes (which by then had healed); a pair of bracelets made of silver from someplace other than British Guiana (and that place too was called one thing then, something else now) was placed one on each wrist; a pair of new shoes bought from Bata's was placed on my feet. That afternoon, I was bathed and powdered, and the dress of yellow poplin, completed, its seams all stitched together with a certainty found only in the natural world (I now realize), was placed over my head, and it is quite possible that this entire act had about it the feeling of being draped in a shroud. My mother, carrying me in her arms (as usual), took me to the studio of a photographer, a man named Mr. Walker, to have my picture taken. As she walked along with me in her arms (not complaining), with the heat of the sun still so overwhelming that it, not gravity, seemed to be the force that kept us pinned to the earth's surface, I placed my lips against one side of her head (the temple) and could feel the rhythm of the blood pulsing through her body; I placed my lips against her throat and could hear her swallow saliva that had collected in her mouth; I placed my face against her neck and inhaled deeply a scent that I could not identify then (how could I, there was nothing to compare it to) and cannot now, because it is not of animal or place or thing, it was (and is) a scent unique to her, and it left a mark of such depth that it eventually became a part of my other senses, and even now (yes, now) that scent is also taste, touch, sight, and sound.

And Mr. Walker lived on Church Street in a house that was mysterious to me (then, not now) because it had a veranda (unlike my own house) and it had many rooms (unlike my own house, but really Mr. Walker's house had only four rooms, my own house had one) and the windows were closed (the windows in my house were always open). He spoke to my mother, I did not understand what they said, they did not share the same tongue. I knew Mr. Walker was a man, but how I knew that I cannot say (now, then, sometime to come). It is possible that because he touched his hair often, smoothing down, caressing, the forcibly straightened strands, and because he admired and said that he admired my dress of yellow poplin with its simple smocking (giving to me a false air of delicacy), and because he admired and said that he admired the plaid taffeta ribbon in my hair, I thought that he perhaps wasn't a man at all, I had never seen a man do or say any of those things, I had then only seen a woman do or say those things. He (Mr. Walker) stood next to a black box which had a curtain at its back (this was his camera but I did not know that at the time, I only know it now) and he asked my mother to stand me on a table, a small table, a table that made me taller, because the scene in the background, against which I was to be photographed, was so vast, it overwhelmed my two-year-old frame, making me seem a mere figurine, not a child at all; and when my mother picked me up, holding me by the armpits with her hands, her thumb accidentally (it could have been deliberate, how could someone who loved me inflict so much pain just in passing?) pressed deeply into my shoulder, and I cried out and then (and still now) looked up at her face and couldn't find any reason in it, and could find no malice in it, only that her eyes were full of something, a feeling that I thought then (and am convinced now) had nothing to do with me; and of course it is possible that just at that moment she had realized that she was exhausted, not physically, but just exhausted by this whole process, celebrating my second birthday, commemorating an event, my birth, that she may not have wished to occur in the first place and may have tried repeatedly to prevent, and then, finally, in trying to find some beauty in it, ended up with a yard and a half of yellow poplin being shaped into a dress, teaching herself smocking and purchasing gold hoops from places whose names never remained the same and silver bracelets from places whose names never remained the same. And Mr. Walker, who was not at all interested in my mother's ups and downs and would never have dreamed of taking in the haphazard mess of her life (but there was nothing so unusual about that, every life, I now know, is a haphazard mess), looked on for a moment as my mother, belying the look in her eyes, said kind and loving words to me in a kind and loving voice, and he then walked over to a looking glass that hung on a wall and squeezed with two of his fingers a lump the size of a pinch of sand that was on his cheek; the lump had a shiny white surface and it broke, emitting a tiny plap sound, and from it came a long ribbon of thick, yellow pus that curled on Mr. Walker's cheek, imitating, almost, the decoration on the birthday cake that awaited me at home, and my birthday cake was decorated with a series of species of flora and fauna my mother had never seen (and still has not seen to this day, she is seventy-three years old).

After that day I never again wore my yellow poplin dress with the smocking my mother had just taught herself to make. It was carefully put aside, saved for me to wear to another special occasion; but by the time another special occasion came (I could say quite clearly then what the special occasion was and can say quite clearly now what the special occasion was but I do not want to), the dress could no longer fit me, I had grown too big for it.

An Antiguan Election Journal

MARCH 1994

The Family Business

AN HOUR OR SO BEFORE an American citizen named Lester Bryant Bird was sworn into office as the third prime minister of the islands of Antigua and Barbuda, his mother came by in a blue motorcar driven by his youngest brother to see him at his home, a house situated on a hill in one of the finest, most exclusive parts of Antigua, a place called Blue Waters. But he was not there. He was out thanking the people of his constituency, St. John's Rural East, who had given him a 2–1 victory over his opponent, an actor by the name of George "Rick" James. The area the new prime minister represents, and has always represented in the seventeen years he has been a member of Parliament, is not one of the finest or most exclusive parts of Antigua. It includes the mental asylum and it includes the poor house, a place that is now respectfully called the Fiennes Institute, but still serves the old purpose of taking in the poor and the destitute who have no one to take care of them. I do not know if that morning while thanking his constituency he included the occupants of the poor house, but I had the day before witnessed them being brought, helped, or pushed in wheelchairs, to the voting booth that was just outside the gate of the institution. It was so agreed that they were solidly for the Antigua Labour Party, the Party of which Lester Bird is leader, that the observer for the opposition, the United People's Party, looked on with amusement; in any case, whatever fraud had been committed to get their vote, it was not the kind of irregularity the observer could do anything about.

That Lester Bird is not a resident of not-so-exclusive St. John's Rural East would not bar him from representing it; a representative does not have to live in the area he is representing. It is one of the ways of governing themselves that Antiguans inherited from their former colonial master, Great Britain. The other, up to now, would seem to be the patriarchal right to run things and pass this right on to a son. Lester Bird succeeded his father as prime minister, who served as the prime minister until ten o'clock of the morning Lester Bird took his oath. The main challenger to Lester Bird was his brother Vere Cornwall Bird, Jr., the first-born son of the former prime minister. Their father, Vere Cornwall Bird, Sr., had been the head of government in Antigua and Barbuda since 1952, as premier (pre-independence from Great Britain) and prime minister, except for one five-year period in the 1970s when the people of Antigua voted for the opposition party; that period now seems to people unreal and it is spoken of with a seriousness that belongs to significant historical events that happened centuries ago.

Lester Bird's patrimony is not in doubt; he is his father's son, he is a Bird. It is his matrimony that is in doubt, for it was his brother, Vere, who first said that perhaps they did not share the same mother. Lester was apparently shaken by that, for he is not his father's favorite son—Vere is that—but he is a Bird, and in a fierce interparty battle with his brother that seemed part Shakespearean, part Tudor dynasty, he won the leadership of the party and then the office of Prime Minister. It was not pleasing to Vere (the father Vere, Sr.—called simply "Bird." Vere, Jr., is Vere; Lester is Lester). And yet, on the day that Lester was to be sworn in as prime minister, Mrs. Bird, who may really be his mother, his aunt, or the former employee of his real mother (the rumors of his matriarchal inheritance are old and ongoing), came to see him, driven by her youngest son. She looked pleased and even happy, the way a mother would look if one of her sons had just been elected to lead his country. And this is not at all the way she used to look when I knew her many, many years ago, when I was a child and her husband was the head of government. They were not living together then; I don't know of anyone my age or younger who has ever seen them together. She occupied herself with a store on South Street that was half haberdashery, half foodstuff, and the attempt at both selling cloth and sewing goods in one half of the store and things to eat in the other was half-hearted; she never had many customers. When I was a seamstress's apprentice, my sewing mistress would only send me to Mrs. Bird's store to buy thread in the ordinary colors of black, white, navy blue, and red, and shirt buttons in the colors white or brown. I never heard anyone ever mention her husband to her. His reputation as a lover of very young girls was quite well known then, and I can remember a day when I must have been about twelve years old, and my mother and I were walking on what was then East Street, and my mother suddenly placing her hands over my eyes and then pushing me to the back of her to shield me from the sight of a girl who seemed not too much older than me getting into the back of the prime minister's car. The prime minister's car was black, the girl was wearing a green dress.

The Opposition

There is a part of the City of St. John's (the capital of Antigua)—the Green Bay and Grays Farm area—that is the exact opposite of the Blue Waters area where Lester Bird lives. It is as close to a slum as one can get on a small island: it is dirty, it is unsafe, it is the poor part of a place that is no longer really poor anymore. In the election of 1989, the Antigua Labour Party won fifteen of the sixteen seats in Parliament. The only seat they did not win was St. John's Rural West, which comprises Green Bay and Grays Farm. In that election, it was well known that almost every candidate representing the ALP, and the ALP itself, was involved with various unsavory characters and events in all sorts of places in the world. And yet the voters in other parts of Antigua overwhelmingly voted for this party and its candidates, as if to show that they approved of the corrupt conduct of their leaders and the tyranny that a party with such a large majority might impose on them. In that election, though, the people of Green Bay/Grays Farm elected the opposition candidate, a man by the name of Baldwin Spencer, who was born and grew up in the area he represents. Spencer has never been accused of or even rumored to be a part of any scandal. He is something Antiguans are not overly familiar with: an honest individual in public life. The election of such a person by the most worse-off constituency seemed laughable to Antiguans, especially when they saw the deliberate social neglect by the government directed toward the residents of St. John's Rural West. It is commonly acknowledged that the people of St. John's Rural West suffer because they had elected to represent them someone not of the governing party; during the recent campaign, they were told by the ALP that if they wanted better social services, they should not re-elect Baldwin Spencer. And yet, they did re-elect him, giving him more votes than any other candidate in Antigua received.

There is a lovely bay called Dieppe Bay and to reach it one had to travel roads that wind through Grays Farm and Green Bay. The ALP government wanted to build a nine-story hotel there, and in so doing they filled in land and built a highway that completely bypasses Grays Farm and Green Bay. The filled-in land and highway have had many unpleasant results for the residents of Grays Farm and Green Bay: water that used to run out to the sea stays with them, and because outsiders who used to travel through parts of the neighborhood on their way to Dieppe Bay no longer do so, there is not reason to keep them up. It is not an uncommon story: in many places the people most qualified to lead from a moral point of view, unfortunately, lead lives of physical squalor.

The Rising Son

The modern history of Antigua (by that I mean the events that began at the end of the fifteenth century) and the modern history of what's called the New World began in criminality, and it is not unreasonable at all to see the influence of this past, beginning with the extermination of native people (the Arawak and Carib), their replacement with the enslaved African people, and the Africans emancipated from slavery not through their own efforts (they tried but the forces against them were always overwhelming), but through the moral conscience and economic convenience of their conquerors.

For about one hundred years after emancipation, Antiguans were neither slaves nor free people, and in their struggle to make themselves one and not the other, they found, in one man, Vere Cornwall Bird, a voice and personality to lead them. He was a very large man, tall (he's shrunk now from old age), with a big voice and a commanding way with words, and his actions always took things to the brink and he won. Until the 1930s, the agricultural land of Antigua, which is to say, most of Antigua then, was owned by people who had never seen Antigua, people who had inherited the land from their slave-owning ancestors and had lived in England off their inheritance in Antigua. This inheritance was usually managed by an overseer, an Englishman hired especially for the job of hiring the descendants of slaves to work very hard cultivating the Antiguan land for a small amount of money. Vere Cornwall Bird was not the first person to try and organize the agricultural workers then, but he was the one who led them and got real results. When an overseer named Moody Stewart threatened to shut the workers out and starve them and their families to death, it was Vere Cornwall Bird who told Stewart that the workers would drink pond water and eat a shrub called the widdy-widdy bush before they would give in. These were strong words, since Antigua does not have an abundance of ponds—in a prolonged drought, the ponds quickly dry up—and the widdy-widdy bush is a tough-stemmed, ugly little bush, not nearly as tender or sweet tasting as many other wild bushes in Antigua. Eventually Stewart gave in. And yet, even in the beginning when Bird was so great and so impressive and in the middle of creating his legendary status as "Father of the Nation," he had apparently been involved in all sorts of corrupt activities: burning houses for the insurance money, stealing from his employers, seducing and impregnating the wives of his colleagues, and taking from the public treasury when he finally got to it. He always seemed so simple in public, beautiful, in a way, in an old-cut suit, old-fashioned shoes, a felt on his head or held in his hand—whatever was appropriate—his head slightly bowed, his hands resting humbly at his side or resting one on top of the other behind his back. But people who know him well say that he loves money, not in the bank, but in the room with him, and he likes to sit and count it, over and over. After so many years in public life, he has left nothing material to commemorate his long presence in Antiguan life, no great or attempted great piece of architecture, no institution of any kind—not an institution of learning, not a health facility, not a playground, not a park—only a legacy of corrupt government and two sons who are deeply involved in the culture of corruption, one the new prime minister. The way Antiguans now picture this man—beautiful and dignified outside, dark and rotten at the core—is a reflection of Antiguan society as a whole.

Antigua has a foreign debt of $400,000,000 U.S. With an official population of 59,000 people it makes each person responsible for $6,780 of it. Baldwin Spencer says that "we have been extremely lucky that the International Bailiff has not moved in." That was just the way he put it. Who exactly holds this debt, nobody knows; the government has not published a proper budget or given a real account of how it is funded in over ten years. Once, apparently, the International Monetary Fund came in and told the old prime minister that there were too many government workers driving too many government-owned vehicles, and to get the economy in proper shape he should fire some of them. He did not fire anyone, and no one lost the use of their government-owned cars. To the few people there who care enough to think about it, it is one of the mysteries of life in Antigua: Why doesn't somebody make this small island pay its debt? Why was the debt allowed to grow so large? How will it be paid anyway?

No one likes to hear anything bad about themselves, especially if what they are hearing is true, unless they are the ones saying it, in which case it doesn't matter at all. The morning after the election, I met Vere Bird, Jr., on the steps of his house, an old house not too far from the St. John's cemetery. I was just passing by when I saw him walking about in his yard and I stopped and introduced myself to him. He was in the process of shaking my hand when he heard my name, and he immediately dropped my hand and told me I should go back to New York and stay there. I felt he hated me. I had never been in the presence of anyone I felt wanted me dead before. I was with a reporter from the Associated Press, and so Vere stopped looking at me when he spoke. He said Antigua had a bad reputation in the world because of people like me and others in the foreign press; he never again looked at me, only calling me "she," and he said that I was an enemy of Antigua, that I did not love Antigua. It was only later, when I was speaking to his brother, Lester, that I was reminded that people who know them say that Lester is smooth and smart, and that Vere, crude and not very smart, always gets the blame for things Lester has really done. Surely Lester Bird must feel the same way about me that Vere does. I have written unflattering things about him, even comparing him to Baby Doc Duvalier, but as we spoke Lester never let on that he had even heard of me or met me before (which he has). If while I am in Antigua I should feel a bullet going through my head, surely among my last thoughts would be, Vere did it.

The brothers, Lester and Vere, had fought over which one of them would succeed the corrupt father. They were not lacking qualifications, Vere especially. He has been involved in so many scandals involving the use of his ministership for illegitimate financial gain that one of them led to an official inquiry by a council to the queen. In the official report, he was accused of being involved with an illegal shipment of arms from Israel to drug dealers in Colombia. The report (published in a two hundred and seven page book called *Guns for Antigua*) recommended that he be barred from holding public office ever again. His father, the prime minister, and the sitting Parliament voted to accept the report and he resigned his ministership but not his seat in the Parliament. Lester is still accused of never making clear which pieces of real estate are his and which he manages for the government, and of benefiting from his associations with known illegal drug dealers and from sales of diplomatic passports. The father wanted Vere, who understands government in the way his father does, passing out patronage jobs to people who never work, doing small favors for them for which they feel eternally grateful, living simply (Vere in his old house), and having a lot of money but doing nothing in particular with it—just to have it is enough. But Vere's way and his father's way is the old way of doing things. Lester is the one who has represented Antigua in foreign places. He hires people who are clever in public relations, an element unknown before in Antiguan politics, he thinks Antigua has an image problem, not a real problem, and he is said to be incredibly disloyal, betraying friends, allies, and members of his own family. In a ceremony that, unknown to the participants, seemed like a scene from a pageant to commemorate an event of colonial times (as viewed from the colonialists' point of view), the father named Lester chairman of the Antigua Labour Party, which meant that he would become the prime minister if that party won the most seats in the election. The ceremony, held in a large tent one evening, was called "The Rising Sun."

The New Overseer

It is said that the Americans (by that, people mean the Central Intelligence Agency) tolerate the behavior of the government of Antigua (and by that, people mean the Bird family and members of the Antigua Labor Party), because Antigua is geographically and strategically important to the Americans. There is an American air base in Antigua and American government airplanes land at all times of the day or night. Once, early this year, a submarine which was assumed to be American could be seen offshore by anyone who could see. It is said that the Americans use Antigua to spy on Cuba, but there are places friendly to the Americans which are closer to Cuba than Antigua. Haiti, or even Florida, for that matter.

The day before the election, I sat in the office of the man who represents American interests in Antigua, a chargé d'affaires named Bryant Salter, who used to be a glamorous figure in American college football. He has been accused, investigated, and cleared of charges involving the sale of visas. Bitter about those accusations,

Salter says that he wishes his state department had defended him more vigorously and thinks that they didn't because of racism. He is an American who looks like most Antiguans because he is of African descent. He is said to be a friend of Lester Bird, he is said to play golf and tennis with him all the time, and it is said that Lester Bird helped him buy land in Antigua. Salter said he has not played golf with Lester Bird in three years, that he does not play tennis—only his wife does—and that he does not own land in Antigua. He said that he is just as much a friend to Lester Bird as he is a friend to opposition leader Baldwin Spencer, and that he doesn't favor one of them over the other. But that in his personal opinion, Lester Bird was the better person to lead Antigua, because he had experience traveling all over the world to meet world leaders and negotiate the loans which have led to any prosperity Antiguans enjoy. In the days leading up to the election, a six-part series of articles, under the heading "Antigua: Corruption, Inc.," had been appearing in the *Virgin Islands Daily News* (a newspaper in St. Thomas). The articles were written by a man named Melvin Claxton, and in them he made the familiar charges of drug trafficking involving members of the government, illegal banking activities, bribery, and theft; none of the charges were new to Antiguans but the paper was sold out every day it was for sale on the island. Salter was bothered by the timing of the articles and the "old news-ness" of the charge. He said that Melvin Claxton was an Antiguan, and that Claxton and his family were opposed to the Birds. I asked him if he really thought that the editor of such an important paper so far away from Antigua would engage one of his reporters and perhaps jeopardize the reporter's family in a vendetta against the independent government of another country. He replied, with the vehemence of someone overly familiar with the incredible, that anything was possible. And I asked him if he thought the sole resource of Antigua, tourism, could continue to support the high standard of living Antiguans enjoy, the highest in the eastern Caribbean, without resorting to loans or the underground economy of drug dealing; he said yes, and gave, as examples of other places that do so, the Cayman Islands and Miami. I did not tell him that the Cayman Islands economy seems to be associated with the same sort of scandals as those of Antigua, drugs and offshore banking, and that Miami, not exactly a drug-free zone, is not an island at all, but part of a country that is among the richest in the world.

On the last day he would serve as prime minister, Bird, the father, did not go into his office. I wanted to see his office, I wanted to see the building, since I was told that it would be torn down and a whole new complex of government offices would soon replace the ones that exist now. In this proposed building of new government offices, one could see the shape of scandals to come: cement scams, building scams, bank scams, as has happened before. I could tell from looking up at the windows of his office from the outside that Bird was not in: the windows were open and curtains were billowing out in the wind. His secretary and his secretary's assistant were in, but they did not know when he would hand in his resignation. Sitting with them just outside the prime minister's private office was an old man who had come to see the prime minister. He needed help in getting back money that he had placed in an offshore bank that had gone bankrupt. The banks are not regulated in a way that would allow anyone with money in them to get their money back if the banks fail, and this man thought that since he was an old ALP supporter, there was something the prime minister could do and retrieve his money for him. It was the sort of scene that used to be quite common when Bird was younger and had real power in Antigua. People from all over the island lined up inside and outside his office, waiting for him to solve any problem they had. He had made his reputation ridding Antigua of the presence of the Overseer, the person left to manage the plantations after emancipation, and once he had rid Antigua of them, he became one himself. It was in that way the man waiting outside his office knew him. I soon recognized the old man: he had lived on the same street that I did when I was a child, and he was one of about three people I knew who had a motorcar. He drove a black Hillman, and it was so rare to have a car go past my house that when he drove to work in the mornings (he worked in the Department of Public Works, I remembered), I would note where I was in my preparation for school. I could tell whether I would be early or late, he was that punctual. When I heard of his plight then, losing all his money in a failed bank, I felt sorry for him, and gave him some of my own. He took it and I realized much later how hard they must have laughed at my easy gullibility. I later learned he was still quite well off.

Lester Bird took the oath of office the very next day after the election in the drawing room of the Government House, the place where the governor general lives. Both the house and the office of governor general are beautiful models of the colonial past, and both are now in a state of decay. The mansion is rotting, the office of governor general is now politically controlled, and the man occupying the office has recently pardoned a minister who was convicted of a crime and sentenced to jail for three months. Both buildings are useful and should be restored, but restoration implies an ease with the past which Antiguans simply do not have. Lester Bird took his oath with his daughters standing next to him. Across the room from him stood the nine other men who had been elected with him from his party; from among them he would choose his cabinet. If they were a familiar bunch, it was because they had served in the same capacity in his father's government. Two of them had been made to give samples of their urine to the American FBI, so they could prove that they were not involved in drug smuggling. They were said to have passed the urine test. Another was one who had only recently been jailed. Two nights before, I had been shown the copy of a deposit made into a bank account of another one of the people he would name to his cabinet; the account was in Miami, the depositor a man who had recently been convicted of drug smuggling. Every one of the men has been suspected of some illicit deed while in office at some time or another.

As Lester Bird gave his inaugural address, the other winners stood still in an unnatural way, as if enlivened by a mortician. Bird's father was absent. Brother Vere, perhaps already aware that Lester would not keep his promise and name him to a cabinet post, was also absent. As he was exiting from the grounds of Government House, he met a group of Vere's angry constituents demanding that Vere be named a member of his cabinet. He managed to pacify them then, and everybody went home.

That afternoon there was a memorial service held for four people, all of European descent, all of them non-Antiguan, who had been murdered on their yacht as it lay anchored off the coast of Barbuda. Their friends spoke of them as people who had worked hard at one thing or another and, in choosing to fulfill dreams of sailing around the world, they were all said to be happy-go-lucky; one of them had even once spent a night in jail for taking a flag down from a pole on a dare. They were sailing off the coast of Barbuda when some boys robbed them and then brutally murdered them. The boys who robbed them passed over the jewelry, taking instead what they really wanted: their credit cards. They did not seem to know that you might not be able to buy very much with the credit cards of people who had been murdered; they only knew that with credit cards you were able to buy almost anything.

In Jane Austen's novel *Mansfield Park*, a family falls apart when its patriarch, who has fallen into the moral abyss of slave-owning, is called away to take care of problems on his plantation. That plantation is in Antigua, and though the world of Antigua and its slaves is treated almost as an excuse to write the novel, to me the only thing that really matters is what happens to Lord Bertram (the patriarch) when he leaves Mansfield Park and is in Antigua. What does he see, what does he do? *Mansfield Park* is a work of fiction. I know all too well what really happened to the descendants of the slaves. Once freed, they proceeded to create for themselves their own moral abyss.

Christmas Pictures from a Warm Climate

I FIRST CAME TO KNOW CHRISTMAS, like so many other things in my life, through a picture. There was the picture of Christmas on Christmas cards, the picture of Christmas on my Sunday school Bible cards, and the picture of Christmas in books. These pictures bore no resemblance to the experience of Christmas that I had for a very logical reason: Christmas was invented by people who had nothing in common with people like me. The Christmas of the Christmas card pictures was filled with people wearing velvet coats and frocks trimmed with silk ribbons. They held aloft in their arms white packages tied up with silver and green ribbons, the kind of ribbons that I would have been very happy to have tied in my pleasantly unsmoothed hair; if the people in these Christmas cards were kind, they would have made up a box of all the things they had no use for, and among the treasures in the box would be those discarded ribbons.

In these cards, people had red lips, their tongues and their tonsils were not visible, and they walked along with wide-open mouths from which emerged musical notes. They were set in an extraordinary scene that did not convey any discomfort: surrounded by many feet of snow, a blizzard in the distance behind them, a thick shower of snow on the near figures, a snowman so solid that he might have been a fixture on the surface of the sun itself. Nothing marred the velvet, nothing marred the satin; the notes never fell to the ground overwhelmed by frigidity. The wrapped presents remained forever a source of surprise and excitement.

My Sunday school Bible cards of Christmas portrayed the birth of Jesus. It was a picture of poverty and humility, but I, who was poor, found it as distant as the scene on the Christmas card, because I knew the outcome. He eventually would rule the world, and I was to remain poor and humble.

Christmas, then, for me was filled with confusion. I did not have riches; the velvet and satin would have been all wrong for my climate; there could be no snow, I lived in the tropics. My poverty had its roots in an incredible injustice, the enslavement of my ancestors, and such a consciousness can only breed rebellion, not humility.

I cannot remember one present I received for Christmas when I was a child except for a white shirt that had the words JINGLE BELLS written on its front; sometime after Christmas had passed, I felt uncomfortable wearing it. That was strange—I was too poor to be aware of fashion, I should have only been glad to have something to wear.

The present I remember wanting most was a doll made in England, called a Pedigree doll. That must have been its brand name, Pedigree. It is only now that I understand the humor in it. In any case my parents could not afford the doll, and I used to go and look at it prominently displayed in a toy-store window on High Street and wish and wish for it. It looked like any of the stupid dolls I can now afford to buy my daughter: a short crop of yellow nylon hair, eyes that open and close, and it could sit up all by itself.

Words are superior to a picture because words can make a picture; a picture is just by itself—it frustrates; it will remain itself no matter what you do, no matter what you say; it will only offer likenesses, comparisons.

Ten years after I left home, I received word that my father had died. This news came to me only two days before Christmas, and I fell into a sadness that surprised me and made me feel a great scorn for myself. I no longer liked my mother and father; I loved them, but in such a relationship, parent and child, love is not enough. And yet the loss of my father, the fact that I would never see him again, cast such a pall over me that this thing I had come to look forward to with some joy—I had come to like Christmas because the atmosphere I now lived in approximated the one of the Christmas cards from my childhood—became a nightmare.

I was at a funeral all alone. I was living by myself in New York and had not seen my family for many years. I could not have said the words "My father died" to someone, because I did not know anyone well enough for them to really understand; no one I knew had known my father. I was living in the land of snow, but it no sooner fell to the ground than it became dirty, and no one wore velvet and satin, for to wear it in the way of the Christmas cards was no longer in fashion.

By the time I heard about my father's death that Christmas, he had been dead and buried months before. His death and Christmas became fixed in my mind. I wanted to see his grave, and when I returned home, I asked to be shown the place in the graveyard where he had been buried. But his illness and death had left such a trauma in our family (he had been ill for a long time, and when he died he left my mother penniless, something she only understood when, attempting to pay for his burial, she went to the places where he kept money and found them all empty) that none of them had visited his grave from the time he was put in it.

One day, many years later, I persuaded my mother to go with me to the cemetery to show me the grave. We walked up and down looking for the spot, but there had never been so much as a marker at his gravesite and she could not remember anything special in the landscape—a tree, a rock—near where he had been buried. We walked up and down the parched ground, a searing hot sun beating down on us, large lizards rustling about among the dried-up grass and fallen leaves. Lizards are usually shy of people, but suddenly a large one ran up to my mother and leapt up the front of her skirt and started to climb toward her bosom. This frightened me and I almost started to scream, but my mother shook the lizard off her as if it were an everyday occurrence, only saying that she hoped it wasn't one of those people, meaning the dead, come to ask her to join them.

When this happened, it was not Christmas—which is a Victorian invention, and not at all suited to a tropical climate.

Introduction to *The Best American Essays, 1995*

A N ESSAY! The fixed form or the fixed category of any kind, any definition at all, fills me with such despair that I feel compelled to do or be its opposite. And if I cannot do its opposite, if I can in fact complete the task that is the fixed form, or fill the fixed category, I then deny it, I then decline to participate at all. Is this a complex view? But I believe I have stated it simply: anything that I might do, anything that I might be, I cannot bear to be enclosed by, I cannot bear to have its meaning applied to me.

    The Essay: and this is not a form of literary expression unfamiliar to me. I can remember being introduced to it. It was the opinions and observations of people I did not know, and their opinions and observations bore no relationship to my life as I lived it then. But even now, especially now, I do not find anything peculiar or wrong about this; after all, the opinions and observations of people you do not know are the most interesting, and even the most important, for your own opinions and observations can only, ultimately, fix

---

1995. Introduction to *The Best American Essays, 1995*, ed. Jamaica Kincaid. Boston: Houghton Mifflin. xii–xv.

you, categorize you—the very thing that leads me to dissent or denial.

To choose a good essay, then, from among a number of essays is something I am quite able to do. A good essay for me is an essay that pleases me. And this isn't to say that pleasing myself is my sole aspiration in this world, but how else can I make a judgment about anything, including an essay?

I must have been taught the principles of the essay, for surely it must have such a thing, principles; that is, a certain integrity that must not be violated. I do not remember them. I remember the principles involved in writing a letter. I was taught them. A letter has six parts: the sender's address should be written in the upper right-hand corner of the paper, underneath that should be the date, on the next line but over on the left should be the name and address of the recipient of the letter, underneath that should be the greeting or salutation, then comes the body of the letter, and last is the yours truly, the closing. *What are the principles involved in writing a letter?* would have been a question asked of me many times as a part of an exam, and passing the exam itself was a way for other people to know whether I was worth the effort being expended on me and whether I should be given access to certain parts of the world. An example of my letter-writing ability had to be demonstrated: a letter to an imaginary friend living in another part of the colonial empire.

An essay too has principles: you state, you build on your statement, you sum up. How awful that sounds to me now, how dry, how impossible. I could not see it then, but I can see it now: this definition was meant to be a restriction, and it worked very well; for how could I express any truth about myself or anything I might know in the form of state, build, and sum up when everything about me and everything I knew existed in a state of rage, rage, and more rage. I came into being in the colonial situation. It does not lend itself to any literary situation that is in existence. Not to me, anyway.

The examples of this literary form, the essay, that were shown to me when I was being taught its principles were written by men of substantial standing in their societies, men who had the time to contemplate an idea, who knew that their opinions might influence events in their day. It wasn't difficult to notice that unethical men, living in times of ethical scarcity, were preoccupied with ethics and not as they might practice ethical behavior but as an exercise in contemplation. And so too with the idea of freedom. They, these men, seemed to have thought hard and long before writing volumes on the idea of freedom, that state of being not a slave, while surrounded by people who were enslaved, or dependent on the labor of people who were enslaved. On being given these essays to study and then to imitate not the content, only the style, I did not have these thoughts. I had a feeling when reading them: I felt angry, I felt sad, I felt I could never have command over words, I felt I would never have an idea, I felt no matter how big I got, I would always remain small.

I did not know then how really useful it would become to have read the thoughts of Francis Bacon, how his ideas, the language he used, would be one of the many sources from which I come, and so without it a part of me could not exist. The phrase "capable of perpetual renovation" appears in Bacon's essay "The Advancement of Learning." He was referring then to the revolution in knowledge occurring in his time. When I first read it many years ago, this idea of "perpetual renovation," I did not grasp any meaning in it that would apply to me. I suspect that Francis Bacon did not know that someone like me would find comfort in it. But it must be this perpetual renovation that leads me to say that if there is a form to the essay, if there is a fixed way to execute it, that way does not satisfy me now, not its form, not its luxurious content.

The luxurious content: And why should I call "The Advancement of Learning" luxurious? Sitting in a room that is one of many in a large house, as a citizen of a prosperous country, which is to say a country whose actions in the world have been successful and so they are the best and correct ones, I now understand the meaning of contemplation: it is to think about something related to you or related to something far removed from you but its resolution is not urgent to you, its resolution is not like a thorn in the side of your body whose removal would offer an obvious contrast. Someone for whom learning, the world of knowledge, is such an unquestioned existence can speak of its possibilities, its depths, its unlimitedness; someone for whom existence means existing physically from day to day might find summing up the world through the use of the imagination, summoning up the world solely through the mind, a luxury, an enviable act out of the ordinary and so therefore to be dismissed. Just for instance, as I am writing this, I have come across a quote by a man who lived to be one hundred years old and at that grew tired of living and so he starved himself to death. He said, "Death is either a transition or an awakening. In either case it is to be welcomed, like every other aspect of the life process." But I am forty-six years of age and I don't see death in that way at all: my own death now would be among the last things I would welcome: living is urgent, not to be taken for granted. Desiring its opposite, death, is a luxury.

The essays I selected here have no visible theme, again they only pleased me, which is to say that I loved reading them and had that childish pleasure while reading them that everything else apart from reading was labor (and labor is quite different from work, one being forced, the other a source of realization; I say this not with any universal certainty, it is only my opinion). "Burl's," the essay by Bernard Cooper about a boy discovering his homosexuality, was the most familiar and yet the strangest. I know what it is like to discover who you really are, or really might be; on the other hand, I am not yet homosexual (I put it this way because I don't like to close the door on anything). The essays are mostly by writers I have always admired—Edna O'Brien, Cynthia Ozick, Harold

Brodkey, William H. Gass, Henry Louis Gates, Joseph Brodsky, Elaine Scarry, Edward Hoagland, James A. McPherson—writers whose voices I am familiar with in a pleasing way and so I suspect wanted to hear yet again. But then there were writers whose prose I had never read before and was thrilled to read for the first time—Josephine Foo—and writers whose work I knew only through their poems so I was not familiar with them in this form (the essay) at all—Maxine Kumin, Charles Simic.

Ideally, the essays are supposed to be arranged in alphabetical order, to show that I do not prefer one over the other, for that would no doubt cause some hurt feelings, and why should people who have done nothing except write something that I like have their feelings hurt? They are arranged alphabetically then, except I chose to begin with the essay on Marcus Aurelius by Joseph Brodsky and end with an essay on the end of the century (which makes me feel as if I have come to the end of a large landmass) by Elaine Scarry. I chose to do this because Marcus Aurelius reminds me of my earliest memories of learning, for as a child in a school I had to memorize the history of the Romans and their influence on Britain, and because at the very end of the century I hope to be alive, and if I am not, I believe poetry, the work of it (not the labor, it is not labor, I believe so), will be.

As I write this, it is the middle of the night, it is hot, the curtains are drawn open in the room in which I write. A moth so large banged up against the mesh window screen that it caused the screen to make a shuddering sound. It was attracted to the light from my lamp. The great essay about the moth has been written and I can see no room for renovation.

The Little Revenge from the Periphery

WHAT IS AMERICA TO ME? This is America to me.

It begins this way: I was about nine and living in Dominica with my mother's family because I was so jealous of my brothers' being born that my mother was afraid I would kill them (I had dropped one brother on his head; it had been an accident). My mother's family lived in the village of Mahaut, but the school I attended was in the village, five miles away, called Massacre (it had a bloody history and that was how it had gotten its name, Massacre). One morning at school—it might have been before recess, it might have been after—we were sitting on the ground at our teacher's feet. She was sitting on a chair in the shade of a large, old tamarind tree, reading to us, only instead of reading to us a poem about England, she was reading a news report from *Time* magazine, a magazine we had never heard of. The news report was about a man named George Wallace who lived in a place called Alabama, and Alabama was quite near a river named

1997, Spring. "The Little Revenge from the Periphery." *Transition*. Iss. 73: 68–73.

Mississippi, and this man named George Wallace, who was from a place called Alabama that was not far from the Mississippi, had violent and coarse feelings about people who looked more or less like me and my schoolmates and our teacher, but who only looked more or less like us—they were not us, because for one thing they lived in Alabama, near the Mississippi, and they knew someone named George Wallace. We did not know people like George Wallace who were filled up with such violent and coarse feelings. At the end of our teacher's reading, we and she fell silent; we were stunned and frightened. What to do in a world like that, with a man like that? Our teacher said aloud, "What to do in a world like that, with a man like that?" There must have been a breeze; it would have caused the leaves on the trees to make a rustling sound; most likely a lizard was running up and down the trunk of the tamarind tree; most likely one of us was being bitten right then by an ant of one kind or another. What to do in a world like that, with a man like that? We were silent. But by then my mind had already been firmly formed by the thing known as the "British Empire," and so I knew that people who lived in places near rivers with funny-sounding names like Zambezi or Amazon or Mississippi (and not proper-sounding names like Thames, for instance) were savages, and so George Wallace of Alabama, a place near the Mississippi, was a savage and so the answer to what to do in a world like that, with a man like that, was very simple: we should send him some Bibles. I placed my brown arm in the air. "Miss Miss," I said (we never called her "Miss"; she was Miss Miss), "I know what we should do. We should send this man some Bibles. I think we should take up some money and send him some missionaries and some Bibles." My idea was a good one, my teacher and my classmates agreed; we did not mention that we had no money to spare for missionaries or Bibles, but that didn't matter, we had the thought of it and that was good enough.

This is my first real memory of America. That my first real

memory, my first emotional attachment, should involve noticing the country's relationship to its citizens of African descent does not now surprise me. Here is what I can see: America does not exist without this group of people. No one would want to come to America if these people were not present, because without them, there would be no benchmark against which to measure oneself. African Americans were born wearing the equivalent of the yellow Star of David, and they wear it in perpetuity. What would this place, America, be without them?

America begins with the Declaration of Independence, the most important clue to the character of Americans as a people. It is true what everybody says: it is a remarkable document, seeming to be divinely inspired, and no one who reads it can fail to be moved by it. But who really needs this document, the Declaration of Independence?

There is a painting in Philadelphia of the men who signed it. These men are relaxed; they are enjoying the activity of thinking, the luxury of it. They have the time to examine this thing called their conscience and to act on it. They need not feel compromised because they do not need to compromise. They are wonderful to look at. Some keep their hair in an unkempt style (Jefferson, Washington), and others keep their hair well groomed (Franklin). Their clothes are pressed, their shoes polished; nothing about their appearance is shameful. Can they buy as much as they like? Can they cross the street in a manner that they would like? Can their children cleave to their breast until death, or until the children simply grow up and leave home? The answer is yes. They can do whatever they want. The fact is, there isn't anything we can do today that they could not do then, and we consider ourselves free people. We consider ourselves such an example of free people-ness that we kill other people in the world if we find they can't agree to our present idea of free people-ness. So who needs this document, which proclaims, "We hold these truths to be self-evident that all men are created equal, that they are endowed by their creator with unalienable rights, that among these are Life, Liberty, and the pursuit of Happiness"? Who needs this document? Is it these men in the painting (which itself is enshrined in a temple devoted to this sacred moment in the ongoing invention of the American narrative) who need these passionately felt sentiments, or is it the people whom you cannot see, the people absent from the painting, the people who made the signers of this document ready to sign it, the people who made their coffee and made their beds and made their clothes nicely pressed and made their hair appear well groomed or in a state of studied dishevelment? Who needs this document? And if I ask obsessively, it is because I am obsessed with this question. Who needs this document? The people sitting around the table, with their nice hair, their well-pressed suits, their nice warm homes, their supine wives, their even more supine concubines, their ability to cause suffering and to alleviate suffering, or the people whom you cannot see, the people who made the physical, material existence of the people sitting around the table possible? The people outside the picture could not decide on the style of their hair, they could not buy clothes that fit some idea that they had of their own personality, for they could not have such a thing, a personality, an idea of themselves unique to them (and I can imagine someone reading this will know of some individual example, but an individual example will not do).

The solemnity of this occasion, the signing of this missive to the Toy Tyrant George III, must have seemed humorous to the person who had just styled Ben's and George's hair. He or she might have broken into sidesplitting laughter at the thought of these people being regarded as the Founding Fathers, for surely these people (the ones in the picture, the ones whose signatures follow the missive to the Toy Tyrant) would have seemed as nothing so much as ventriloquists, the Founding Father Ventriloquists, for their powerful feelings about their situation bore no resemblance to reality. The

Declaration of Independence was not about them; it was about the people who were in their midst, it was about the people they held in bondage, it was about the existence of their slaves. And though they loved having people subject to their economic needs and other whims, they understood all too well the feelings a subject people might have toward their subjection. It was Jefferson, who could only take every opinion he held to its extreme (this was a problem: his stance on one issue contradicted his stance on another), who wrote in a draft of the Declaration of Independence:

> He has waged cruel war against human nature itself, violating its most sacred rights of life and liberty in the persons of a distant people who never offended him, captivating and carrying them into slavery in another hemisphere, or to incur miserable death in their transportation thither. This piratical warfare, the opprobrium of infidel powers, is the warfare of the Christian King of Great Britain. Determined to keep open a market where MEN should be bought and sold, he has prostituted his negative for suppressing every legislative attempt to prohibit or restrain this execrable commerce; and that this assemblage of horrors might want no fact of distinguished die, he is now exciting these very people to rise in arms among us, and to purchase that liberty of which he deprived them, by murdering the people on whom he also obtruded them; thus paying off former crimes committed against the Liberties of one people, with the crimes which he urges them to commit against the Lives of another.

This paragraph is not to be found in the Declaration of Independence or in schoolbooks. I can so well imagine the situation: his fellow ventriloquists, when coming upon this paragraph, took him into a room, a room in which they could not hear their own consciences, and said to him, "Tom, Tom, are you nuts? The one good thing King George has done—made the seas safe for the slave trade, which makes our high-minded insights into the subjugation of others and our feelings of goodwill toward each other possible—you are calling a crime." And this: "Tom, you can't be left alone in a room with words. You get so carried away."

That the Declaration of Independence is so contradictory should come as no surprise, however, since its author, Thomas Jefferson, was himself a definition of contradiction. He was a man who loved the intimacy of the small landscape of Virginia while plotting to know the large landmass that was the United States. He was a man obsessed with the idea of freedom while surrounded by people who were not free. He insisted on the superiority of something called "white people" while wholly dependent on something called "black people." He had a garden and he had a farm—those things are not so much opposed to each other as they are just different: one is about necessity (the farm), the other is about how it looks and how the way it looks makes you feel (the garden). He invents the American language; to look at America is to look at him, and to look at him is to look at what he was not: he was a free man, not a slave; he was a white man, not a black man.

America is not so much a country as it is an idea, and that must be why so many people are drawn to it, the idea of it, the idea that you might be free of your past, free of the traditions that kept you in your own tradition—that is the idea of it: freedom from your very own self. But freedom from yourself and your own traditions is fine . . . for ten seconds. Past that is insanity. Everyone in every place needs a boundary; in America the boundary is the phrase "I am not black." No wonder then that the people who are black are obsessed with identity. Having given every other bit of riffraff who enters the American narrative one—"I am not black, I am something else. The black is something Other"—they find themselves in this strange position of making other people real. Such an arduous task.

Ordinarily, the color of your skin is not a spiritual experience;

ordinarily the color of your skin just offers protection from too much exposure to the sun. For the African in America, this is not so. The color of skin determines everything—where you will live and, then again, how you will live. The color of your skin is the national religion of America, and the African in our midst is its prophet and priest. How embittering, then, not to be just an ordinary congregant in ordinary worship—in other words, a disgruntled person from a certain neighborhood of Milwaukee or Chicago or Queens or Pittsburgh.

What if social status in American society were based on nothing else but time of arrival? By now, the very top of American society would be thoroughly integrated, if not majority African American. And instead of Jesse Jackson having to defend every ridiculous idea he has against some equally ridiculous counter-idea, his ridiculous ideas would be the ones by which we all had to live. For example, I do not like affirmative action, but only as it might apply to me; if I suspect that I were the victim of this idea, I believe I would appreciate the element of kindness in it and say, "Thank you ever so much. How nice," and politely reject this favor. But affirmative action seems appropriate to many people whose ancestors were brought here centuries ago, and so who am I, someone who just got off the boat yesterday, someone coming from another bleak crevice of the world, to tell them otherwise.

America is a Nation, a Country, made by a People. But the Nation, the Country, is one thing, and its People are another. The Nation, the Country, is white; the People are black. If it were only a Nation, if it were only a Country, it would be like everyplace else in the world; it is its People that make it interesting, it is its People that make the rest of the world pay attention to it.

Introduction to *Generations of Women*

I HAVE A MOTHER and I know her now and she had a mother and she used to know her mother; her mother is now dead. I have a daughter and she has a mother and I am that, her mother. I knew that woman, my mother's mother; I know her more deeply and more fully than if I had spent every day of my childhood life with her. I spent every day of my childhood life with my own mother and I know my own mother better than I will know anyone else. This is so.

My mother's mother was from Dominica. I know this about her, I know she was from Dominica. Who was her mother, I do not know, and I did not wonder who her mother was—that is, who was my grandmother's mother—until just now. That my grandmother could have had a mother was unthinkable to me; to believe such a thing, that my own grandmother could have had a mother also, would have meant that I would have had to think of my grandmother as a child, helpless and vulnerable to the whims of someone

---

1998. Introduction to *Generations of Women: In Their Own Words*, by Mariana Cook. San Francisco: Chronicle Books. 9–11.

more powerful than herself. There could be no one more powerful than my mother's mother; my mother was afraid of her mother, so much so that she could not bear to even live on the same island with her very own mother.

For a long time, nine years (but that is a very long time in a child's mind), I was an only child. I was the only child my mother and father had together; I was the only child descended from my grandmother; her other daughter, my mother's sister, my aunt Mary, could not have children; her son, my mother's brother, had died. I loved being an only child. I concentrated all my attention on myself, I treasured myself, no hurt directed at me was too small to go unnoticed by me. If I felt lonely that would not have been a small hurt, that would have been a big hurt. I was lonely. I took care of this in a way that even now I find useful. I imagined things.

I was sent to Dominica to visit my grandmother. It was not an ordinary visit, I had been sent to stay with her and my mother's sister because after nine years my mother had given birth to another child, my brother, and when he was a baby and I was nine years old, I dropped him and he landed on his head but I did not mean to actually do that, I only wished to do that, I did not mean to actually do that. There was a moment when I dropped him on his head and the next moment I was on a boat to Dominica to stay with my grandmother. Dominica is an island far away from the place where I was from, I had never been apart from my mother before, in any case a large body of water had never separated us before. It was on that journey to visit my grandmother, my mother's own mother, that I invented a cousin, a girl named Gillian who lived in Trinidad.

When I saw Dominica for the first time, it was a Sunday morning, and it was raining. I could not have been the first person in the world to see Dominica on a Sunday morning when it was raining. I was on a boat that would bring to my mother letters from her family, it was on that same boat that the reply she made to them was carried back. The *M. V. Rippon* was a substantial thread in the fabric of my little life then, it was the solid thing that moved between my mother, who was a big part of me, and her mother, who was a bigger part of her. I loved my mother then, I did not yet hate her; she hated her mother then, she had loved her own mother a long time ago.

Nothing is ever the same as you think it will be. When I saw Dominica for the first time it was a huge mound of green, a more huge mound of realness than I had ever thought a huge mound could be, and mist, though not fog, for fog is not a tropical phenomenon, no matter what a person who is scientifically familiar with fog might say. I had never seen a landscape like this, not even in literature, for it turned out that a landscape like that had never inspired literature; it had inspired other things, but the written word as I had come to know it was not a part of this scenery.

When I first saw the woman who began the world as I knew it then, my mother's own mother, I was full of sorrow for myself, for more than anything in the world, I missed her daughter, who was my own mother. I could not see my mother in her and so I could not see myself in her; I tried, because my mother would look at various parts of my body—my instep, my second toe longer than my big toe, my hands, the shape of my head, the slight curve in my back, the long narrow shape of my physical frame then—and would say how much I reminded her of her own mother, how much like her own mother I looked, but when I saw this woman, my mother's mother, I did not think of myself at all. I only missed the person that I was from directly, the person in whose body I had lain curled up, breathing through her lungs, living through her blood. It was seeing my mother's mother for the first time that made me feel pity for my own mother for the first time, but that must have been because I was feeling sorry for my own self, realizing how sad I was to be apart from my mother and so feeling that my mother was sorry to be apart from her mother also. Sometime between then and now I used to know with certainty what my own mother thought of her mother; but at this very moment I have no confidence at all in that certainty, the certainty of what my mother feels about her own mother; to recall what I used to know, to put it into words, is not something I am unable to do, it is only that to do it fills me with despair.

My grandmother, for that is what my own mother's mother was, my grandmother, had long ago ceased to like her own life, I knew that then and I can put it into words now, it does not fill me with despair to say that, but she did not want to abandon this, her life. When she was almost still young, she had lost her only son, he died of a disease that is now curable, and from then on she wore only black. My mother when she was almost a really old woman lost her youngest son to a disease for which there is not yet a cure. My mother did not become grief-stricken over this, for by the time it occurred, the course of her own life had been already set, my mother had never let her disappointments or sorrows matter too much to her. I cannot imagine my own life without either of my children now that I have them, and when they were first born I would stand over them when they were asleep and weep and weep at how sad they would be if I were to suddenly die of a disease, curable or not; but that must have been because of the thought when I was a child of not ever seeing my mother again, not for the reason that she migrated to another earthly domain but because I was afraid that she had died while giving birth to her other children or while suffering an attack of one of her terrible headaches. One headache in particular was brought on when to her face I wished her dead because she would not allow me to attend the Mayfair and see some girls who were much older than me dance around the Maypole. I loved those girls.

Where did my mother's mother come from? Who was her mother? Did she miss her, her own mother? In that house in Dominica my own mother's mother and I slept in the same bed. In that bed I clung to her and she clung to me. She did not bathe very often and the smells from her not-very-often-washed body were an overwhelming stink that would cause me to fall into a deep sleep, and in my sleep I almost always dreamed of my own mother. In my dreams my own mother smelled of roses, and this was odd for I was not so familiar with roses that the smell of them was readily available to me.

To sleep with my grandmother, to walk alongside her or a little behind her, to sit with her, to stand still with her, just to be near her in any position at all did not seem strange to me. Her presence was a comfort because I missed the person she most reminded me of, her own daughter; the very sight of her, the very presence of her, was a torment because she so reminded me of the person I missed most in the world, her very own daughter, my mother. And if my mother used to look at me and say that I reminded her of her mother, because of the way my instep was shaped or because of the way my hands were shaped, my grandmother did not ever look at me and say that I reminded her of her own daughter. I loved my grandmother then, she is a mystery to me now. She has been dead for a long time.

The light in Dominica was so different from what I had been used to; it was never harsh, it was never unsparing in its brightness, I could not see everything. Each morning, no matter the name of the day, she would wake me up just after she awoke herself, and it was at that time of the morning when the day was fresh, when the day was just being born. She dressed herself quickly; she wore white drawers made of coarse cotton and a black dress made from a finer cotton, but not so fine a cotton that a Sunday dress or a church dress could be made from it. Her only son had been dead for many years then, but she still wore black as if she would never be free of mourning. From the time she woke me up, I then would do everything she had done, only I was three breaths behind; that is, she awoke three breaths before me, I got out of our bed three breaths after her, I followed her out through the small rooms of her house, she unbarred the door, and we were outside in the cool air. The air was always cool, and inside the coolness were small drops of moisture, the moisture stung our cheeks but not in a way to suggest discomfort, only in a way to suggest that even in such a small thing, drops of moisture trapped inside some cool air, a myriad of sensations could exist, such a myriad that merely contemplating just them, I am temporarily incapacitated.

She would then retrieve an old earthenware jar from which she would remove some cured coffee beans and then she would roast them, pound them in a mortar. And when the beans were reduced to a state of coarse powder they were boiled, separated from the water with a coarse piece of cloth used as a strainer; the water, now transformed into the beverage of coffee, a thick, black strange medicinelike potion, was then poured into tiny enamel cups that were decorated with a flora to which we had no intimate connection or even mild acquaintance (had never even seen it in a book, for instance). We drank the coffee stooped over the fire that had just boiled the water that made the coffee, a fire that had been made from wood she and I had brought from a place in the mountains, a place far away, and we had brought this wood strapped to the back of a donkey. I then was indifferent to the feelings of the donkeys, but I am not indifferent now; to contemplate their lot now is useless, but I do it all the same, for even what is useless I have come to see is useful.

The taste of the coffee then was new to me, it was a taste I had not even imagined; the taste of coffee crossed the border of my likes and dislikes. When drinking coffee my grandmother and I would lean into each other. This is not something I am now imagining, this something I am now remembering. As I leaned into her I could smell all the old smells that I had become so familiar with from the night of sleeping next to her, and then the new one of the coffee as it clung to the moist fissures that made up the landscape that was the inside of her mouth; some of the teeth in the back of her mouth were missing, some of the others had holes in them, two teeth in the front bottom row were jammed tightly together and this made them slightly askew, as if the person putting them in had grown tired just at this point, as if the foundation on which they stood had grown weak just at this point. This very flaw in the arrangement of my grandmother's teeth appears in the arrangement of my mother's teeth and it appears in the arrangement of my own teeth. It does not appear in the arrangement of my daughter's teeth.

The presence of my mother's mother reminded me of my own mother's absence, and all the more I wanted to be with my mother again. My mother spoke of her mother constantly, her mother never spoke of her at all; I now speak of my mother constantly, from what I am told, by my mother's other children, my mother never speaks of me at all; I bear my daughter in mind all the time, it would sadden me if she thought of me or spoke of me constantly. My past and my future are undimmed as I purposely place the delicate wick that is life, my life, between the two flames.

"What to say?" These words, what to say, would rush out of the mouth of my own mother and her mother when they were at an age, as old as I am now, to take in that everything, every event, every place, could evoke ten thousand different sensations, ten thousand different feelings, and each of them in deep contradiction, a contradiction that mere acts of violence could not resolve; the contradictions were as old as they were, the contradictions were as old as I am now.

Introduction to *My Favorite Plant*

I AM AMAZED at such a thing: that I would have asked writers who have a garden, writers whom I admire who do not have a garden but have a passion or a memory of some kind about flowers, writers who are gardeners and write about it with all its ups and downs, its disappointments, its rewards, and who are attached to the garden with a blindness, plus a jumble of feelings that mere language (as far as I can see) seems inadequate to express, or to define an attachment that is so ordinary: to a plant, loved especially for something endemic to it (it cannot help its situation: it loves the wet, it loves the dry, it reminds the person seeing it of a wave or a waterfall or some event that contains so personal an experience such as: when my mother would not allow me to do something I particularly wanted to do, and in my misery I noticed that the frangipani tree was in bloom).

I know gardeners well (or at least I think I do, for I am a gar-

---

1998. Introduction to *My Favorite Plant: Writers and Gardeners on the Plants They Love*, ed. Jamaica Kincaid. New York: Farrar, Straus and Giroux. xiii–xix.

dener, too, but I experience it as an act of utter futility, I shall never have the garden I have in my mind, but that for me is the joy of it; certain things can never be realized and so all the more reason to attempt them). I know their fickleness, I know their weakness for wanting in their own gardens the thing they have never seen before, or never possessed before, or saw in a garden (their friends') something which they do not have and would like to have (though what they really like and envy—especially that, envy—is the entire garden they are seeing, but as a disguise they focus on just one thing: the Mexican poppies, the giant butterbur, the extremely plump blooms of white, purple, black, pink, green hellebores emerging from the cold, damp, and brown earth).

I was not surprised that everyone I asked had something definite that they liked. Gardeners (or just plain simple writers who write about the garden) always have something they like intensely and in particular, right at the moment you engage them in the reality of the borders they cultivate, the space in the garden they occupy; at any moment, they like in particular this, or they like in particular that. Nothing in front of them (that is, in the borders they cultivate, the space in the garden they occupy) is repulsive and fills them with hatred, or this thing would not be in front of them. They only love, and they only love in the moment; when the moment has passed they love the memory of the moment, they love the memory of that particular plant or that particular bloom, but the plant of the bloom itself, they have moved on from; they have left it behind for something else, something new, especially something from far away, and from so far away, a place they will never live (occupy, cultivate; the Himalayas, just for an example).

Of all the benefits that come from having endured childhood (for it is something to which we must submit, no matter how beautiful we find it, no matter how enjoyable it has been) certainly among them will be the garden and the desire to be involved with gardening. A gardener's grandmother will have grown such and such a rose, and the smell of that rose at dusk (for flowers always seem to be most smelling at the end of the day, as if that, smelling, was the last thing to do before going to sleep), when the gardener was a child and walking in that grandmother's footsteps as she went about her business in her garden—the memory of that smell of the rose combined with the memory of that smell of the grandmother's skirt will forever inform and influence the life of the gardener, inside or outside the garden itself. And so in a conversation with such a person (a gardener), a sentence, a thought that goes something like this—"You know when I was such and such an age, I went to the market for a reason that is no longer of any particular interest to me, but it was there I saw for the first time something that I have never and can never forget"—floats out into the clear air, and the person from whom these words or this thought emanates is standing in front of you all bare and trembly, full of feeling, full of memory. Memory is a gardener's real palette; memory as it summons up the past, memory as it shapes the present, memory as it dictates the future.

This book, this anthology, this collection of essays that you (a reader) hold in your hands is meant to be like a garden, a garden that I might make, for everything in it, every flower, every tree, every whatever enclosed here, everything mentioned has made a claim on my memory and passion at some moment in my life as a gardener. I have never been able to grow *Meconopsis betonicifolia* with success (it sits there, a green rosette of leaves, looking at me with no bloom. I look back at it myself, without a pleasing countenance), but the picture of it that I have in my mind, a picture made up of memory (I saw it some time ago), a picture made up of "to come" (the future, which is the opposite of remembering), is so intense that whatever happens between me and this plant will never satisfy the picture I have of it (the past remembered, the past to come). I first saw it (*Meconopsis betonicifolia*) in Wayne Winterrowd's garden (a garden he shares with that other garden eminence

Joe Eck), and I shall never see this plant (in flower or not, in the wild or cultivated) again without thinking of him (of them, really—he and Joe Eck) and saying to myself, It shall never look quite like this (the way I saw it in their garden), for in their garden it was itself and beyond comparison (whatever that should amount to right now, whatever that might ultimately turn out to be), and I will always want it to look that way, growing comfortably in the mountains of Vermont, so far away from the place to which it is endemic, so far away from the place in which it was natural, unnoticed, and so going about its own peculiar ways of perpetuating itself (perennial, biannual, monocarpic or not).

What I mean to say in the end is that this book, this collection of essays, looks to me like a landscape, an enclosure, a garden I would create, if I could. The ideal garden that I would make begins with Wayne (Winterrowd) and ends with Elaine (Scarry). I first came to the garden with practicality in mind, a real beginning which would lead to a real end: where to get this, how to grow that. Where to get this was always nearby, a nursery never too far away; how to grow that led me to acquire volume upon volume, books all with the same advice (likes shade, does not tolerate lime, needs slaking), but in the end I came to know how to grow the things I like to grow through looking—at other people's gardens. I imagine they acquired knowledge of such things in much the same way—looking and looking at somebody else's garden.

But about this book again: I have tried to arrange these essays and poems (and excerpts from gardeners, be they in the wild like Frank Kingdon Ward in the foothills of the Himalayas, or at home like Katharine S. White on a farm in Maine) in such a way as to give the illusion of a garden, a garden I would like (*sometimes, only sometimes, feelings about a garden will change, too*), a garden of words and images made of words, and flowers turned into words, and the words in turn making the flower, the plant, the bean (Maxine Kumin) visible. I loved reading all the pieces in here. I was amazed by and grateful for the generosity of the contributors, but then gardeners will give wholeheartedly and bigheartedly; that is why they are allowed to covet. At the end of it (this book), I hope the reader will have some satisfaction—not complete satisfaction, only some satisfaction. A garden, no matter how good it is, must never completely satisfy. The world as we know it, after all, began in a very good garden, a completely satisfying garden—Paradise—but after a while the owner and the occupants wanted more.

Introduction to *Poetics of Place*

THIS IS THE WAY the land is: up, down, straight across, undulating, an overcrowding that causes misshapenness (and the beauty of that is admired, but the patience to see it take shape is unbearable). To gaze on the land, to see the land for a great length of time will inspire the belief that the land has made us, has shaped us in a way that is only good; to gaze upon the land has made us, has shaped us in a way that is only good; to gaze upon the land, to see the land for a great length of time seems to inspire in us the desire to change the land, to make it into a shape that pleases us, to see it in a way that pleases us.

At the beginning I could not see (the first picture: Parc de Sceaux, France) and then in the end all that I had seen then lay beyond and through a window (Hidcote, England). In between those two (the beginning and the end) were many scenes: scenes of punishing order, scenes that glorify the exact, scenes of chaos playing with a notion of the understandable arrangement (Damme,

---

1998. Introduction to *Poetics of Place*, photographs by Lynn Geesaman. New York: Umbrage Editions.

Belgium), scenes of abandonment (Palatine Hill, Italy), scenes of emptiness (Ostia Antica, Italy), scenes of loneliness (Parc de Caradeuc, France). There are no people in these scenes, only replicas of people (Godinton Park, England), no people at all.

What do people do? I could ask, What do we do? but the "we" seems too presumptuous on my part, I cannot speak for anybody other than myself, I do not wish to speak for anybody but myself; what do people who live within these landscapes (Italy, France, Belgium, Germany, the United States, England) do when they find themselves surrounded by the impartiality of nature (whatever that may be), with nature's disregard for the beautiful in stature, its disregard for the beautiful of any kind? What do people do? For there are all the frightening forests of trees, the implacable mass of stone shaped into mountains, the willful rush of water in rill, in stream, in river, ending in the sea itself. What do people do when we see these things? What can we say?

Certainly nothing new! For the forest would be so much better understood if we had planted it ourselves; the forest is ours if we had planted each tree ourselves; the forest is ours certainly when we have given it a name (Eden, Paradise, on and so on). And we make the forest ours when we can call each thing in it by name: this is some pine, though not all pines are the same; this is an oak, though not all oaks are the same, some oaks are different from others; this is a beech, it will grow straight up, it will spread, it will have purple leaves, it will have green leaves. And so on and on and on. The forest explained, the forest named, the forest made desirable, the forest desired and then rejected, the forest discarded, the forest in the end remaining just itself, the forest!

And what do I mean when I say this? Just what do I mean exactly? The landscape seen for the first time is never absolutely friendly, the landscape seen for the hundredth time is not friendly. When is the landscape friendly? A gate will make it so, an entrance or its opposite (a barrier to entering) made by human hand, will make it so. When is the landscape friendly?

When some flowers familiar through scent or through shape (sight) will make it so; the landscape is friendly when it yields nourishment, when it can sustain a generation and then another and then even so, another; and the generation who profits most is the generation that turns against it, the landscape; for familiarity breeds love and it is love, in all its ups and downs, that breeds contempt.

And we love what it is that lies before us, the land, the water, the sky, and all the many ways in which the elements arrange themselves, and we are helpless before this arrangement, and we are without hope as we observe and then regard (that, regard, seems something internal) this arrangement of land, of water, of sky, and we try, oh how we try, to rearrange all that we see before us, all that lies at our feet. And we make the water gather when its natural movement is a flow, and we pass through the mountain when it means to make us go no further or at any rate around, not through, and even the veil that is the sky, even that is penetrable.

What is the land then? What is the landscape? Is the landscape the earth and the things (the trees, the bodies of water) that it supports? Does the landscape begin and end and begin again at the horizon, and the horizon, is that the place where the land meets the sky as far as the eye can see? And what lies between that? It might go without saying (in the end it goes without saying), that the horizon is only the horizon because I (we) say so ("that is the horizon!").

And within the horizon, that is, between the space where I (we) stand and here the land meets the sky, is there a creature (a moth) with white wings decorated with black spots; is there a creature (a mammal) whose body is covered with hair, and beneath the hair a thin covering (skin) and beneath the thin covering an orderly arrangement that can be named but even so remains mysterious; and is there a creature whose body used to be covered with hair but now the hair appears in a fixed place and the hair is thin (and this is a mammal again, the mammals are everywhere, the mammals are most important to me, I am one of them) and the hair curls up tightly or sometimes just lies flat against the surface; and is there a creature, only this time covered in scales and sometimes it carries poison in its tongue and sometimes the sharp flick of its tongue is harmless; and again is there a creature of only feathers for a covering and sometimes the feathers are all of one color (gray, black) or a combination of colors (black all over with red or yellow on the breast; blue in one place, another shade of blue in another place; a deep gray that is almost black; a gray so slight it is almost gray; and so on and so on).

The color black and the color white are not ultimately the colors of the imagination; the colors black and white are so useful, they are the colors of work, the colors black and white are the best way for the harshness of reality (and the real is always so harsh if only because it is its true self); in the beginning, the one to which we are, for good and bad attached, the words are black written on paper which is white. The words in black against an impartial blank space that is white summon up fear (but that fear is love, or attached to love whatever in the world that turns out to be) and that fear is attached to love, that fear is seared to love. And so all the things that we must love (we cannot help ourselves, we love the words in black as they appear on the blank, white paper), memories of places we once knew actually, once knew the way we still knew our fingers (though my own fingernail was caught in the force of the slam of a door and the whole thing had to be removed and now it grows back in a way, crooked, and I wonder if it means something and should I see a fortune teller, someone who is familiar with the cosmic arrangement of the hands in general), memories of places we have experienced through this strangeness, the black words on white paper.

The colors black and the colors white, combined, contrasted, isolated from each other, are what make up things just before they come into being and they are the colors that make up things just before they slowly vanish into something else (I do not know the name for that). Nothing, really!

Leaves are green, we can see that; the barks of the trees are brown or mottled silver and green and brown (I am seeing a *Stewartia monodelphia*, or a *Stewartia koreana*); the leaves on the ground are decaying and decay has its own integrity, independent of color; the flowing stream reflects the young trees with their slim trunks, a long alley of trees has in its middle a gate ornamental, decorative, that would not deter or frustrate a small child (a mammal) who could only creep, it would not deter even a rabbit (a mammal).

To gaze on the land, to see the land for a great deal of time, inspires the belief that the land has made us. In the beginning, nothing can be seen; in the middle there are many things to be seen; in the end there is nothing again, everything vanished.

Looking at Giverny

A WALK THROUGH MONET'S ELUSIVE LANDSCAPE

WHAT WOULD THE GARDEN BE without the paintings? Would I be standing in it (the garden, Claude Monet's garden at Giverny), looking at the leaf-green arches on which were trained roses (American Pillar, Dainty Bess, Paul's Scarlet Rambler) and *Clematis montana* Rubens, looking at the beds of opium poppies, Oriental poppies, looking at a sweep of bearded iris (they had just passed bloom), looking at dottings of fat peonies (plants only, they had just passed bloom), and looking at roses again, this time standardized, in bloom in that way of the paintings (the real made to shimmer as if it will vanish from itself, the real made to seem so nearby and at the same time so far away)?

It was in June, I was standing looking at the Solanum Optical Illusion (Monet himself grew the species *Solanum retonii*, but "S. Optical Illusion" is what I saw on a label placed next to this plant) and the hollyhock *zebrina* (they were in bloom in all their simple straightforwardness, their uncomplicated mauve-colored petals streaked with lines of purple, and this color purple seemed innocent of doubt); looking at the other kind of hollyhock, *rosea*, which were only in bud, so I could not surreptitiously filch their seed pods; looking at the yellow flowering thalictrum and the poppies again (only this time they were field poppies, *Papaver rhoeas*, and they were in a small area to the side of the arches of roses, but you can't count on them being there from year to year, for all the poppies self-sow wherever they want).

The garden at Giverny that he (Monet) made is alive in the paintings.

I was looking at all these things, but I had their counterparts in Monet's paintings on my mind. I had missed the lawn full of blooming daffodils and fritillarias; they came in the spring. And all this was only the main part of the garden, separate from the water garden, famous for the water lilies, the wisteria growing over the Japanese bridge, the Hoschedé girls in a boat.

And would the water garden be the same without the paintings? On the day (days) I saw it, the water garden—that is, the pond with lilies growing in it—the Hoschedé girls were not standing in a boat on the pond, for they had been dead for a very long time, and if I expected them to appear, standing in the boat, it is only because the pond itself looked so familiar, like the paintings, shimmering (that is sight), enigmatic (that is feeling, or what you say about feeling when you mean many things) and new (which is what you say about something you have no words for yet, good or bad, accept or reject: "It's new!")—yes, yes, so familiar from the paintings.

And would the water garden be the same without the paintings?

But when I saw the water garden itself (the real thing, the thing that Monet himself had first made and the thing that has become only a memory of what he had made after he was no longer there to care about it, he had been dead by then), it had been restored and looked without doubt as the thing Monet had made, a small body of water manipulated by him, its direction coming from a natural source, a nearby stream. On that day I saw it, the pond, the Hoschedé girls (all three of them) were not in a boat looking so real that when they were seen in that particular painting (*The Boat at Giverny*) they would then define reality. The Hoschedé girls were not there, for they had long been dead also, and in fact there were no girls in a boat on the pond, only a woman, and she was in a boat and holding a long-handled sieve, skimming debris from the surface of the pond. The pond itself (and this still is on the day that I saw it) was in some flux, water was coming in or water was going out, I could not really tell (and I did not really want to know). The water lilies were lying on their sides, their roots exposed to clear air, but on seeing them that way I immediately put them back in the arrangement I am most familiar seeing them in, the paintings, sitting in the water that is the canvas with all their beginnings and all their ends hidden from me.

The wisteria growing over the Japanese bridge was so familiar to me (again), and how very unprepared I was to see that its trunk had rotted out and was hollow and looked ravaged, and ravaged is not what Monet brings up in anyone looking at anything associated with him (even to see the painting he made of Camille, his wife before Alice, dead, she does not look ravaged, only dead, as if to be dead were only another way to exist). But to see these things—the wisteria, the bridge, the Japanese bridge, the water lilies, the pond itself (especially the pond, for here the pond looks like a canvas)—is to be suddenly in a whirl of feelings. For here is the real thing, the real material thing—wisteria, water lily, pond, Japanese bridge—in its proper setting, a made-up landscape in Giverny, made up by the gardener Claude Monet. And yet I see these scenes now because I had seen them the day before in a museum (the Musée d'Orsay) and the day before that in another museum (the Musée Marmottan) and many days and many nights (while lying in bed) before that, in books, and it is the impression of them (wisteria, water lily, pond, Japanese bridge) that I had seen in these other ways before (the paintings in the museums, the reproductions in the books) that gave them a life, a meaning outside of the ordinary.

A garden will die with its owner, a garden will die with the death of the person who made it. I had this realization one day while walking around in the great (and even worthwhile) effort that is Sissinghurst, the garden made by Vita Sackville-West and her husband, Harold Nicholson. Sissinghurst is extraordinary: it has all the impersonal beauty of a park (small), yet each part of it has the intimacy of a garden—a garden you could imagine creating yourself if only you were so capable. And then again to see how a garden will die with the gardener you have only to look at Monet's friend and patron Gustave Caillebotte. The garden he made at Petit Gennevilliers no longer exists; the garden in Yerres, where he grew up, the one depicted in some of his paintings, is mostly in disarray. When I saw the potagerie, the scene that is the painting *Yerres, in the Kitchen Garden, Gardeners Watering the Plants* was now a dilapidated forest of weeds: a cat that looked as if it belonged to no one stared crossly at me; a large tin drum stood just where you might expect to see a gardener, barefoot and carrying two watering cans. The Yerres river itself no longer seemed wide and deep and mysteriously shimmering (as in *Boater Pulling in His Périssoire*, *Banks of the Yerres*, or *Bathers, Banks of the Yerres*), it was now only ordinarily meandering, dirty, like any old memory.

And so would the garden, Giverny, in which I was standing one day in early June, mean so much to me and to all the other people traipsing around without the paintings? The painting *The Artist's Garden at Giverny* is in a museum in Connecticut, the painting *The Flowering Arches* is in a museum in Arizona, the painting *The Japanese Footbridge* is in a museum in Houston, *Water Lilies* are everywhere. On seeing them, these paintings, either in the setting of a museum or reproduced in a book, this gardener can't help but long to see the place they came from, the place that held the roses growing up arches, the pond in which the lilies grew, the great big path (called the Grande Allée) that led from the front door of the house and divided the garden into two, the weeping willow, the Japanese bridge, the gladiolas (they were not yet in bloom when I was there), the peonies (they were past bloom when I was there), the dahlias (they were not yet in bloom when I was there).

That very same garden that he (Monet) made does not exist; that garden died, too, the way gardens do when their creators and sustainers disappear. And yet the garden at Giverny that he (Monet) made is alive in the paintings, and the person seeing the paintings (and that would be anyone, really) can't help but wonder where they came from, what the things in the painting were really like in their vegetable and animal (physical) form. In the narrative that we are in (the Western one), the word comes before the picture; the word makes us long for a picture, but the word is never enough for the thing just seen—the picture!

The garden that Monet made has been restored so that when we now look at it, there is no discrepancy, it is just the way we remembered it (but this must be the paintings), it is just the way it should be. As I was standing there in June (nearby were tray upon tray of argemone seedlings about to be planted out in a bedding), a man holding a camera (and he was the very definition of confidence) said to me, "Monet knew exactly what he was doing." I did not say to him that people who know exactly what they are doing always end up with exactly what they are doing.

The house at Giverny in which he (Monet) lived has also been restored. It can be seen, a tour of the house and garden is available. As I was going through the rooms of the house—the yellow dining room, the blue kitchen, the bedrooms with the beds all properly made up, the drawing room with prints of scenes and people from Japan—I hurried, I rushed through. I felt as if at any moment now the occupant, the owner (Monet, whoever it might be) would soon return and I would be caught looking into someone's private life. I would be caught in a place I was not really meant to be.

Those Words That Echo... Echo... Echo Through Life

How do I write? Why do I write? What do I write? This is what I am writing: I am writing *Mr. Potter*. It begins in this way; this is its first sentence: "Mr. Potter was my father, my father's name was Mr. Potter." So much went into that one sentence; much happened before I settled on those eleven words.

Walking up and down in the little room in which I write, sitting down and then getting up out of the chair that is in the little room in which I write, I wanted to go to the bathroom. In the bathroom Mr. Potter vanished from my mind; I examined the tiles on the floor in front of me and found them ugly, worn out.

I looked at the faucet and the sink in front of me, but not too closely; I did not examine those. I flushed the toilet and I thought: Will the plumbing now just back up? Does the septic need pumping? Should I call Mr. A. Aaron? But Mr. A. Aaron's name is not that at all. His real name is something quite far from that. His real

1999, June 7. "Those Words That Echo... Echo... Echo Through Life." *The New York Times*: E1–E2.

name is something like Mr. Christian or Mr. Zenith, though I cannot remember exactly. He only calls himself A. Aaron so he can be the first listing in the telephone book under the heading "Septic Tanks & Systems—Cleaning." I come back and look at Mr. Potter.

"Mr. Potter," I write, and I put clothes on him, even though I do not see him naked, for he was my father, and just now he is not yet dead. He is a young man, and I am not yet born. Oh, I believe I am seeing him as a little boy; as a little boy he has clothes, but he has not shoes. I do not place him in shoes until he is—I have not decided when exactly I shall allow him to wear shoes.

And then after many days of this and that and back and forth, I wrote, with a certainty that I did not necessarily intend to last, "Mr. Potter was my father, my father's name was Mr. Potter." And Mr. Potter remained my father, and Mr. Potter remained my father's name for a long time, even up to now.

And then? I grew tired of that sentence and those eleven words just sitting there all alone followed by all that blank space. I grew sad at seeing that sentence and those eleven words just sitting there followed by nothing, nothing, and nothing again. After many days it frightened me to see nothing but that one sentence and those eleven words and nothing, nothing, and nothing again came after them. "Say something," I said to Mr. Potter. To myself I had nothing to say.

Speaking no longer to Mr. Potter, speaking no longer to myself in regard to Mr. Potter, I got up at five o'clock in the morning and at half-past five o'clock went running with my friend Meg and a man named Dennis Murray; he builds houses of every kind in the city of Bennington in the state of Vermont.

"My father is dead," I said to Dennis one morning as we were just past the Mahar funeral parlor on Main Street. I never make an effort to speak before the funeral parlor. I despise death and consider it a humiliation and in any case much overdone and so plan never to do it myself and plan never to have anything at all to do with it, for it is so contagious. I have noticed that when you know people who die, you catch it and end up dead, too.

"My father is dead," I said to Dennis, but he could not hear me for he was far ahead. He runs at a faster pace than I do, and he thought I was agreeing with something he had just said about the weekend he had just spent hiking into the woods and spending the night and fishing with a friend whose name I cannot remember and catching many trout and cooking them and eating them and going to sleep in a tent while there was a great downpour of rain outside and waking up the next morning and having the best pancakes and fishing again and doing everything again and all of it as perfect as it had been before and then coming home to his wife who loves him very much.

And the perfect narrative of Dennis's life, uninterrupted by any feelings of approaching and then leaving behind the Mahar funeral parlor, did not make me envious or make me grieve that Mr. Potter's life remained frozen in the vault that was his name and the vault of being only my father.

The days then rapidly grew thick into all darkness with only small spaces of light (that is autumn) and then remained solidly all darkness with only small patches of light (that is winter), and then the darkness slowly thinned out (that is spring), but the light was never as overwhelming in its way as the darkness was overwhelmingly dark in its way (that is summer). So, too, was the night dark except for when the moon was full and the day bright with light, except for when clouds blocked out the sun. And Mr. Potter remained my father, and my father's name remained Mr. Potter for a very long time.

One day when I seemed uncertain about which foot to put first, the one in front of the other, my husband said to me, "Mrs. S., Mrs. S., how are you doing?" and "Are you O.K.?" The first letter in his family's chosen name is S. Our children go to school every day on a great big bus that was painted yellow and driven by a woman named Verta. A man named Mr. Sweet came and picked up our rubbish.

In the American way we have much rubbish, and Mr. Sweet is hard of hearing. Saying to him, as I feel I must if I see him, I must say to him, "Hallo, Mr. Sweet." And since he cannot hear me, he is deaf, he looks at me and then holds his ear forward, cupping it in the palm of his hand, as if it were a receptacle, for he wants it to receive the sounds that I am making.

"What?" says Mr. Sweet. "Hallo," I say again, and Mr. Sweet is then very nice and sincerely so, and he asks if I could pay him for the eight weeks he has picked up the rubbish without being paid.

"But no," I say to him, and then I explain that I am not allowed to write checks because I never put the debits and balances in their proper columns, and I make a mess of the household accounts. Mr. Sweet says, "Yep, yep," and then Mr. Sweet says he will see me next week. Mr. Sweet does not know about Mr. Potter, not in the way of my writing about him, not in the way of Mr. Potter as a real person.

And one day, after all sorts of ups and downs and many travails that are interesting, especially to me, Mr. Potter was driving a motorcar and dressing in a way imitative of men who had enormous amounts of money. And of course Mr. Potter was right to imitate the wardrobe of men who had enormous amounts of money, for without the existence of Mr. Potter and people like him, working very hard and being paid a mere pittance, there can be no enormous amounts of money. And I am Mr. Potter's daughter, so I know this.

But that "and one day" left me bereft and exhausted and feeling empty; and that "and one day" is just what I want when in the process of encountering a certain aspect of my world.

And then that one day, that one day after Mr. Potter's life advanced and exploded on the page, I had to have my lunch, but I could not eat too much of anything, not even plain green leaves.

I could only eat very small amounts of anything, for I wanted to fit into my nice blue (tilting to lavender) silk taffeta skirt, a skirt that has box pleats. And I so love my nice blue (tilting to lavender) silk taffeta skirt with the box pleats and will not eat too much of anything, even just plain green leaves, for I look very beautiful in it. I look most beautiful in it when I am in a room all by myself, just alone with only my reflection, no one at all there to observe me.

In the early afternoon, just after I have eaten my lunch, I look at Mr. Potter, in my own way, a way I am imagining, a way that is most certainly true and real. (His name really was Roderick Potter; he really was my father.) He cannot look back at me unless I make him do so, and I shall never make him do so.

The telephone rings, and I do not answer it. The telephone rings, and I do not answer it. The telephone rings, I answer it, and on the other end is someone employed by one of my many creditors asking me to satisfy my debt. I promise to do so in a given time, but I have no money. I like having no money. I do not like having no money. I only like to have contempt for people who have a great deal of money and are unhappy even so, or are happy with money in a way that I find contemptible.

Driving past a sign that says YIELD, driving past the house where a dentist lives, driving past the house where the chiropractor I see from time to time lives, swiftly I pass by a sloping moist field that in spring is filled up with marsh marigolds. Swiftly I go past the home for delinquent children. Swiftly I go to await my children getting off the bus with Verta.

My children will soon get off the school bus, the one painted a harsh yellow, and it is driven by Verta. "Mr. Shoul," I say to myself, for I am all alone in the car having driven so swiftly. "Mr. Shoul," I say, for I now can see that I have saddled Mr. Potter with this personality, Mr. Shoul. And Mr. Shoul is a merchant, an ordinary merchant, specializing in nothing particular; he sells anything. Mr. Shoul sells everything. Mr. Shoul might sell Mr. Potter; on the other hand he might draw the line at selling Mr. Potter. And I have saddled Mr. Potter with Mr. Shoul.

Mr. Potter does not know the world. He is produced by the world, but he is not familiar with the world. He does not know its parameters. Mr. Potter was my father, my father's name was Mr. Potter. My children pour out of the bus. My daughter (she is fourteen) hurls an insult at my son (he is ten). His small self (the self that is not seen) crumbles to the ground; I rush to pick his self that is not seen but has fallen to the ground and bring it back together again with his self that I can see.

I look at her, my daughter. What should I do? For her selves (one or two or three or more) are not all in one bundle, tied up together, either.

"Mr. Shoul," I say to myself, for I am at the bus stop and can tell no one what I am really thinking. "Mr. Shoul," I say. What to tell Mr. Potter about Mr. Shoul, where to begin?

"Mr. Shoul!" I shout at Mr. Potter, but Mr. Potter cannot hear me. I have left him at home on the page, the white page, the clean white page, all alone with Mr. Shoul. "Mr. Shoul," I will write, "Mr. Shoul," I will tell Mr. Potter, "Mr. Shoul comes from Lebanon."

Islander Once, Now a Voyager

A WRITER'S JOURNEY

UNTIL I WAS NINETEEN YEARS OLD and, by then, living in New York (which once again celebrates itself as book country this weekend), I had never read a book of serious literature written in the twentieth century and I had never read a book of serious literature written by someone who was not English and by that I do not mean someone from Britain. I mean literature written by someone from that place known as England. This wasn't the fault of anyone in particular. No one made a special effort to keep me from Virginia Woolf or E. M. Forster. It is just that I spent the first sixteen years of my life on an island in the Caribbean Sea that was a British colony. To us the British Empire was the entire alphabet and in it we were not more than the dot over the common letter i.

I grew up in this place in the 1950s. The British Empire had come to a well-deserved halt in the late 1940s but nobody had bothered to tell us. And so we celebrated Queen Victoria's birthday

2000, Sept. 22. "Islander Once, Now Voyager." *The New York Times*: E29, E40.

during whose reign the empire was at its apogee; and we kept up with the world as shown to us by Thomas Hardy and Charles Dickens and Jane Austen and John Keats and William Shakespeare, not for their sole literary value, not because the books by these authors might be the best books in all the world worth reading, but because it was the world of the people who held such intimate dominion over us, a world in which trouble and pain were the ideals of trouble and pain, such different trouble and pain from our own, which were messy and everlasting, never going away like the ones in the books would do when we closed the covers.

And so at nineteen, if I had been asked why I had not ever read the thing called serious literature written in the twentieth century, I would have had to say that no one wrote books with that quality anymore; that kind of serious literature had been a fashion and, after Dickens, there was nothing; that kind of thing was no longer done.

But then at nineteen I was living as a servant with a family in New York City and the woman at the head of the household was a feminist and because of that she was not unsympathetic to my predicament in the world—I was female and poor. This woman was female but most of all she was privileged and her privileges included reading real literature and this literature led her to believe that her existence was not enchanted. It was this woman who gave me as a present some books by Woolf, and lent me *The Second Sex* by Simone de Beauvoir and *Mastering the Art of French Cooking* by Julia Child, Louisette Bertholle, and Simone Beck.

It must have been the powerful anger I then had (and have now and hope to have to the end of a very long life) as someone female and poor—but above all female—that led my employer to give me *The Second Sex*, but when I read it I did not feel grateful that someone (Beauvoir or the female head of the household in which I was a servant) had made valid or confirmed the things I knew already about being female. I only became even more angry that people I had thought to be in a position superior to mine could only tell me about the misery I already knew; they could not tell me how to alleviate it.

I read *The Second Sex*, putting it aside to walk some small children through Central Park so they could get some fresh air, putting it aside so I could wash their clothes and cook their dinner. When I finished reading the book I put it away and never looked at it again, not up to now. I recommend it to women, especially if they are at the age I was when I first read it, but I will never read it again.

Not so *Mastering the Art of French Cooking*. The book itself was big and thick, oversize for a book. I had never seen a book full of recipes before. My mother was a very good cook of West Indian food and even English food. Everybody loved her cooking and found it delicious and told her so; but all the food she cooked she seemed to know how to make into something worth eating just by looking at it. I never saw her consult a book. I cannot now even remember what made me so in love with a mere cookbook then, for no dish in it was familiar. There is a recipe in it for mayonnaise and when I first saw this, a recipe for mayonnaise, I was so surprised. To me then, mayonnaise was something that could only come in a bottle from England.

On very, very special occasions, we would have a dish, a salad of canned peas, canned sliced carrots, and canned sliced beets, and how pleased we were with ourselves to be having things from a tin instead of the very same things just growing outside our house. My mother was very good at growing everything, flowers for ornaments or vegetables for feeding our family, but we were not the first or the last to have become convinced that the sweat of our brow was repulsive.

It was many years after I first came to know *Mastering the Art of French Cooking* that I made mayonnaise. The first thing I made from this book was Bavarois a l'Orange—its subtitle was Orange Bavarian Cream—a cold dessert. It was such a triumph, and everyone told me so and they were not being kind, for even I could tell that it was very good.

Not so very long after that I was working at a magazine that was at the corner of 12th Street and Fifth Avenue, and next door to my job was a bookstore but it carried only old books. This job was such a good example of how ill-suited I am to be under anyone's thumb. The head of my department was a very nice man before lunch; I was a very competent employee before lunch. At lunchtime he went to a restaurant next door to the office and this restaurant had an enormous bar and I went home to my apartment, which was only two blocks from where I worked and I smoked marijuana. When he came back from lunch he was an angry person; when I came back from lunch I was stupendously incompetent.

This angry person, the man in charge of my department, was not entirely unfamiliar to me, for by then I had read much American literature. In the old bookstore next door I had found the complete works (complete up to then) of Ernest Hemingway, the complete works (complete up to then) of F. Scott Fitzgerald, the complete works (complete up to then) of John O'Hara. If only life could be so seamless, I said to myself. But life is so seamless, if only I would agree to accept its seamlessness, is another thing I said to myself.

When I was twenty-five years old I began to write for a magazine whose address was 25 West 43rd Street. I lived then at 449 West 22nd Street and sometimes I would walk the mile or so to my office and sometimes I would take the subway. New York then seems so innocent to me now. But how can that be? For I can remember one very hot day in a crowded train, having a very nice chat with a man standing next to me, and I happened to look down and saw that he was sexually aroused and was rubbing himself up against me. When in fear and shame I looked at him, he laughed in my face and wormed his way into another car.

The writer George Trow introduced me to the editor of the

magazine that was at 25 West 43rd Street, and it was George Trow who introduced me to Ian (Sandy) Frazier. George thought that Sandy, who had graduated from Harvard University, and I, who had spent two seconds at a strange college in New Hampshire, were ill read. George was six years older than I and eight years older than Sandy, and on top of that we thought he was a great writer (then and now) and would read everything he wrote with awe and wonderment at how he had done it, how did he write the thing we had just read.

When he implied that we were almost illiterate because of the things we had not read, we were not insulted, we were quite pleased. He made Sandy read all seven volumes of *Remembrance of Things Past*; it took Sandy two years to do this. He bought for me a copy of *Fowler's Modern English Usage* and he told me that I should read it from beginning to end. I stopped at the end of U.

While reading all of Proust, Sandy was also reading and committing to memory *Ninety-Two in the Shade*, the novel by Thomas McGuane. While reading Fowler's guide I was also reading a biography of Lytton Strachey. But Sandy had decided to make me his audience for the novel he had memorized, and when I showed only a small interest in Thomas McGuane because I was so absorbed by the life of Strachey, he decided to read about Strachey also. Sandy was then and still is now an honorable and just version of that thing no one wants to be anymore: an American white man; and so after he read about Strachey and his friends, Sandy wrote a funny piece called "The Bloomsbury Group Live at the Apollo."

When I was three and a half years old my mother taught me to read, for she was a compulsive reader and I was always interrupting her when she was concentrating on her reading and she thought that if I knew how to read, I would be so absorbed by reading, the way she was, that I would leave her alone. That became true. I became so absorbed by reading that I did leave my mother alone to do her own reading, but once I knew how to read I loved it so much that I read everything in front of me. I read the Bible and for my seventh birthday my mother gave me a copy of the *Concise Oxford English Dictionary*. Since I had nothing else but the Bible to read, I also read the dictionary. How I loved it. But somehow, somewhere, I lost it, and as if to make up for that loss, I am forever buying a dictionary and comparing definitions and meanings.

That particular world of my particular childhood placed me in the world of books. In that particular world of my particular childhood I was poor and female and that latter vulnerability made my family not think twice about sending me out into the world where I would work and my earnings would support them. In New York I found books and I made a living writing them. This was not something anybody had counted on.

Sowers and Reapers

WHY MUST PEOPLE INSIST that the garden is a place of rest and repose, a place to forget the cares of the world, a place in which to distance yourself from the painful responsibility that comes with being a human being?

The day after I spoke to a group of people at the Garden Conservancy's tenth-anniversary celebration, in Charleston, South Carolina, an American man named Frank Cabot, the chairman and founder of the organization and a very rich man, who has spent some of his money creating a spectacular garden in the surprisingly hospitable climate of eastern Canada, told me that he was sorry I had been invited, that he was utterly offended by what I had said and the occasion I had used to say it, for I had done something unforgivable—I had introduced race and politics into the garden.

There were three of us on a panel, and our topic was "My Favorite Garden." One of the speakers said that his favorite was Hidcote Manor, in England, created by an American Anglophile named Lawrence Johnston. (A very nice climbing yellow rose, which is sometimes available through the Wayside Gardens catalogue, is named after him.) There are at least a thousand gardens in every corner of the world, but especially in England, that should come before Hidcote as a choice for favorite garden. The garden of the filmmaker Derek Jarman, who succumbed to AIDS in 1994, is a particularly good example. Dramatically set in the shadow of a nuclear power station in Dungeness, Kent, surrounding a one-story house that has been painted black, this garden, when I saw it, was abloom with poppies in brilliant shades and with *Crambe maritima* (sea kale) and pathways lined with pebbles, the kind found at the seashore, and all sorts of worn-down objects that looked as if they were the remains of a long-ago shipwreck just found. When you see it for the first time, it so defies what you expect that this thought really will occur to you: Now, what is a garden? And, at the same time, you will be filled with pleasure and inspiration.

Another man spoke of a garden he was designing in Chicago which would include a re-creation of a quadripartite garden made by prisoners in Auschwitz. (This way of organizing a garden is quite common, and it has a history that begins with Genesis 2:10—"A river issues from Eden to water the garden, and it then divides and becomes four branches.") The garden in Auschwitz was created over many years and by many people, all of whom were facing death, and it gave me a sharp pang to realize that, while waiting to be brutally murdered, some people had made a garden.

I had prepared a talk in which I was going to say that my favorite garden is the Garden of Eden, because every time I see a garden that I love it becomes my favorite garden until I see another garden that I love and completely forget the garden that so dominated my affections a short time before; and also because this garden, Eden, is described in the fewest words I have ever seen used to describe a garden, and yet how unforgettable and vivid the description remains: "And from the ground the Lord God caused to grow every tree that was pleasing to the sight and good for food, with the tree of life in the middle of the garden, and the tree of knowledge of good and bad."

But after that man spoke of the Holocaust garden, a nice speech on Eden was no longer possible.

I heard myself telling my audience that I had been surprised to see, on the way into my hotel, in the little park across the way, a statue of John Caldwell Calhoun, that inventor of the rhetoric of states' rights and the evil encoded in it, who was elected vice president of the United States twice. I remarked on how hard it must be for the black citizens of Charleston to pass each day by the statue of a man who hated them, cast in a heroic pose. And then I wondered if anyone in the audience had seen the Holocaust memorial right next to the statue of John Caldwell Calhoun: a strange cryptlike, criblike structure, another commemoration of some of the people who were murdered by the Germans. Then I said that John Caldwell Calhoun was not altogether so far removed from Adolf Hitler; that these two men seem to be more in the same universe than not.

It was all this and more that I said that made Frank Cabot angry at me, but not long after his outburst I joined a group of attendees to the conference who were going off to tour and have dinner at Middleton Place, the famous plantation. Middleton is a popular destination for Americans who are interested in gardens, garden history, or a whiff of the sweet stench that makes up so much of American history. It is, on the one hand, a series of beautiful rooms in the garden sense: there is a part for roses only, there is a part for azaleas, there is a part for camellias, and so on and so on. The most spectacular part of the garden is a grassy terrace made by human hands, and on the slope of the terrace are small and perfectly regular risings, so that when seen from below they look like stiff pleats in a skirt that has just been disturbed by a faint breeze. At the foot of the terrace are two small lakes that have been fashioned to look like a butterfly stilled by chloroform. It is all very beautiful, even slightly awesome; and then there is the awfulness, for those gardens and that terrace and those lakes were made by slaves. The water from the river adjacent to the plantation was channeled to flood the rice fields, and this was done by slaves, who had brought their rice-cultivation skills with them from Africa. For, as far as I know, there are no rice fields in England, Scotland, Ireland, or Wales. I was feeling quite sad about all this when I came upon a big rubble of bricks. It was all that remained of the main house on the plantation in the wake of the strategy, conceived by that ingenious pyromaniac and great general from the North, William Tecumseh Sherman, which had helped to bring the traitorous South to its knees. As I walked toward a tent to have a dinner of black-eyed peas and rice, ribs and chicken and sweet potatoes, a dinner that I think of as the cuisine of black people from the American South, and where I would hear the Lester Lanin orchestra accompany a white man imitating the voice of Louis Armstrong as he sang songs made famous by Louis Armstrong, I ran into Mr. Frank Cabot, and I kept from him a fact that I happen to know: Arthur Middleton, of Middleton plantation, was one of the signers of the Declaration of Independence.

Nowhere is the relationship between the world and the garden better documented than in Thomas Jefferson's "Garden and Farm Books," obsessively detailed accounts of his domestic life. People like to say that Jefferson is an enigma, that he was a man of contradictions, as if those things could not be said of just about anybody. But you have only to read anything he wrote, and you will find the true man, Thomas Jefferson, who is always so unwittingly transparent, always most revealing when confident that he has covered his tracks. He tried to write an autobiography, but he stopped before he had written a hundred pages. In it he states that he was born, that his father's name was Peter, that he wrote the Declaration of Independence, that he went to France and witnessed the French Revolution. The whole thing reads as if it were composed by one of the many marble busts of him which decorate the vestibules of government buildings. The Jefferson to be found in the autobiography is the unwittingly transparent Jefferson. The Jefferson who is confident that he has covered his tracks is to be found in the "Garden and Farm Books." The first entry in the "Garden" book is so beautiful, and so simple a statement: "1766. Shadwell Mar. 30. Purple hyacinth begins to bloom." It goes on: "Apr. 6. Narcissus and Puckoon open. [Apr.] 13. Puckoon Bowers fallen. [Apr.] 16. a bluish colored, funnel-formed flower in lowgrounds in bloom." (This must have been *Mertensia virginica*.) The entries continue in this way for years, until 1824: the peas are sown, the asparagus planted, the fruit trees planted, the vegetables reaped. Each entry reads as if it were a single line removed from a poem: something should come before, and something should come after. And what should come before and after is to be found in the "Farm" book, and it comes in the form of a list of names: Ursula, George, Jupiter, Davy, Minerva, Caesar, and Jamy; and the Hemingses, Beverly, Betty, Peter, John, and Sally. (Why is it that people who readily agree that Jefferson owned Sally Hemings cannot believe that he slept with her?) It is they who sowed the peas, dug the trenches, and filled them with manure. It is they who planted and harvested the corn. And when Jefferson makes this entry in his "Garden" book, on April 8, 1794—"our first dish of Asparagus"—it is they who have made it possible for him to enjoy asparagus. None of these names appear in the "Garden" book; the garden is free of their presence, but they turn up in the "Farm" book, and in painful, but valuable-to-know, detail. Little Beverly Hemings, Jefferson's son by Sally, must have been a very small boy the year that he was allotted one and a half yards of wool. One year, John Hemings, Sally's uncle, received, along with Sally's mother, seven yards of linen, five yards of blue wool, and a pair of shoes. On and on it goes: the garden emerging from the farm, the garden unable to exist without the farm, the garden kept apart from the farm, race and politics kept out of the garden.

But, you know, the garden Jefferson made at Monticello is not really very good. You don't see it and think, Now, there is something I would like to do. It is not beautiful in the way that the garden George Washington's slaves made at Mount Vernon is beautiful. (I owe this new appreciation of Mount Vernon to Mac Griswold and her excellent book *Washington's Gardens at Mount Vernon: Landscape of the Inner Man*.) There is hardly anything featured in the garden at Monticello that makes you want to rush home, subdue a few people, and re-create it. And the reason might be that Jefferson was less interested in the garden than in the marvelous things grown there. Each year, I order packets of something he grew, *Dolichos lablab*, purple hyacinth beans, something no garden should be without. What is beautiful about Monticello is the views, whether you are looking out from the house or looking at it from far away. Jefferson did not so much make a garden as a landscape. The explanation for this may be very simple: his father was a surveyor. This might also explain why he is responsible for some of the great vistas we know—the American West.

Not long after I returned from Charleston, a small amount of money that I had not expected came my way. In my ongoing conversation with my garden, I had for a very long time wanted to build a wall to add to its shape and character. So I immediately called Ron Pembroke, the maker of the most excellent landscapes in the area where I live. My house is situated on a little rise, a knoll, and I find the way it looks from many angles in the general landscape to be very pleasing, and so I had firmly in mind just the kind of wall I wanted. But Ron Pembroke, after walking me up and down and back and forth with a measuring tape in his hand, and taking me in his truck to see the other walls he had built, convinced me that my design was really quite ugly and that his was beautiful and superior.

And so began the building of two hundred-foot-long walls, one above the other, separated by a terrace eight feet wide. One day, four men arrived in the yard, and they were accompanied by big pieces of machinery, including, of course, an earthmover. The men began to rearrange the slope that fell away from the house, and by the end of the day my nice house looked as if it were the only thing left standing after a particularly disastrous natural event. The construction of the walls went on. Day after day, four men, whose names were Jared Clawson, Dan, Tony, and John, came and dug trenches and pounded stakes into the ground after they had looked through a surveyor's instrument many times. One day, truckloads of coarsely pummeled gray stone were deposited in the driveway and carefully laid at the bottom of the trenches. Another day, truckloads of a beautiful gray, blue, yellowish, and glistening stone were delivered and left on the lawn. This stone came from a quarry in Goshen, Massachusetts, Ron Pembroke told me. It is the stone he prefers to use when he builds walls, and it is more expensive than other kinds of stone, but it does display his work to best advantage. My two walls, he said, would most likely require a hundred tons of stone.

The walls started to take shape, at first almost mysteriously. The four men began by placing stones atop one another, in a staggered arrangement, so that always one stone was resting on top of two. In the beginning, each stone they picked up seemed to be just the perfect one needed. But then things began to get more difficult. Sometimes a stone would be carried to the wall with great effort, and after being pounded into place, it would not look quite right to Tony and Dan and John and Jared Clawson.

And did I say that all this was being done in the autumn? I do not know if that is the ideal time to build a wall, but I was so happy to see my walls being made that I became very possessive of the time spent on them and wanted the four men to be building only my walls. I didn't begrudge them lunchtime or time taken to smoke a cigarette, but why did they have to stop working when the day was at an end, and why did the day have to come to an end, for that matter? How I loved to watch those men work, especially the man named Jared Clawson. It was he who built the stairs that made it possible to walk from the lower wall to the eight-foot-wide terrace, and then up to the level ground of a patio, which was made flush with the top of the upper wall. And the stairs were difficult to make, or so it seemed to me, for it took Jared Clawson ten days to make them.

One day, it was finished. The walls were built, and they looked fantastic. My friend Paige had given me twelve bottles of champagne, a present for my twentieth wedding anniversary. I loved the taste of this champagne so much that I gave a bottle to each of the men who had helped build my walls. How glad was my spirit when, at the end of all this, Ron Pembroke presented me with a bill, and I in turn gave him a check for the complete amount, and there was nothing between us but complete respect and admiration and no feeling of the injustice of it all, no disgust directed toward me and my nice house, beautifully set off by those dramatic walls, for he had his own house and his own wall and his own spouse and his own anniversary.

At the foot of the lower wall, I have planted five hundred daffodils, ranging in shade from bright yellow to creamy white. In the terrace separating the lower and the upper walls, I have planted two hundred *Tulipa* "Mrs. J. T. Scheepers," which is perhaps my favorite tulip in the world. In the four beds on either side of the patio, I have planted two hundred *Tulipa* "Blue Diamond," a hundred *Tulipa* "Angelique," and only fifty of *Tulipa* "Black Hero" because they were so expensive. Towering above these hundreds of bulbs, I planted the magnolias "Woodsman" and "Elizabeth" and "Miss Honeybee"; and then *Magnolia zenii* and *Magnolia denudata*. At the beginning of the woodland, which I can see from a certain angle if I am standing on the upper wall, I planted a hundred *Fritillaria meleagris* and fifty each of *Galanthus elwesii* and *Galanthus nivalis*.

Ron Pembroke refilled the trenches with a rich topsoil, a mixture of composted organic material and riverbank soil, but I did not see one earthworm wriggling around in it, and this made me worry, for I have such a reverence for earthworms, whose presence signifies that the soil is good. Their anxious, iridescent, wriggly form, when confronted with broad daylight, is very reassuring. We may be made from dust (the dust of the garden, I presume), but it is not to dust that we immediately return; first, we join the worms.

The garden is not a place to lose your cares; the garden is not a place of rest and repose. Even God did not find it so.

Her Best Friend Provokes Her to Write About Her Garden

I USED TO WRITE in a small, cramped room off the kitchen in my house and because I faced north, I got no sun at all. I did have a good view of my then unfenced-in vegetable garden and while sitting at my desk trying to write, I witnessed a great deal of the murder and mayhem that will occur anyplace things are cultivated. There was a flock of sparrows chasing and screaming at a hawk that had raided their nest. There was the fox lying in wait for and eventually catching a rabbit. There was the racket the crows would set up every time the fox emerged from his lair and I could not tell if that enmity was long-standing, based in instinct, or a result of a recent action of the fox. Eventually, they drove the fox out of his nearby home and that is how I came to be plagued once more by rabbits. There was a row of carefully planted beans that disappeared into the fat mouth of a woodchuck as he meandered by, seemingly without having anything particular on his mind.

2002, May. "Her Best Friend Provokes Her to Write About Her Garden." *Architectural Digest*. Vol. 59, iss. 5: 74–76.

Just outside the window through which I could see all these things was a patch of ground over which I devoted a lot of time, fretting. What to plant in it? That patch of ground was exposed to only morning sun and it was the last patch to be rid of snow and ice at the end of winter. What should I plant in it?

Then, as is true now, I had a friend named Sandy, my best friend in the whole world. We talk just about every day and sometimes more than just once in a day. We talk about the very big things happening in the world and we talk about things that are of interest to us with the certain knowledge that everyone else, including the people who love us deeply—especially the people who love us deeply—would find these things unbelievably boring. We seem to agree on everything, and when we disagree, we agree that we disagree and the disagreeing is just as much fun as agreeing. This agreeing and agreeing to disagree is sometimes annoying to our other friends and one of them called us a folie à deux and this moniker was so painful and apt, we made a joke of it and now refer to it frequently.

The fretful-making space just outside the window of the room in which I wrote soon became the only thing I could talk about to my friend. I would imagine the shape it should take, I would imagine the things I would plant in that shape, I eventually began to talk of the plants not only in their common names but also in their proper Latin names. My friend Sandy, after a while, objected strongly when I said that perhaps I should let the *Convallaria majalis*, which had so firmly established itself in that place, stay and continue to extend its reach in its world and beyond. First he grew very fierce and made me promise that I would never learn the Latin names of any plants, because it sounded so pretentious. I promised and then went right on learning the Latin names of plants so that now I hardly know the common names of anything, but I never told him I had done so. Second, he said, he was really tired of listening to me talk about the garden, and he said, why didn't I just go on and write about the garden and get the whole thing off my chest and not talk so much about it. In any case, he said, he wanted to talk about himself, not listen to me talk about something he had no interest in whatsoever.

How easy and wonderful it is that a little playful admonishment from your best friend can change your life! For until then, I wrote, in the form of fiction or nonfiction, about myself, my mother, the place where I had grown up, myself and my mother again. But the minute my friend said, why don't you just write about it, I thought, why don't I just write about it. But how should I do it? Should I just say I put some seeds in the ground and then waited for them to come up? I had done that, placed some seeds in the ground and waited for them to come up. They did not come up.

In the years since I had become a gardener, I read about the garden from the point of view of important people in the world of gardening and landscape design and also from accounts of Explorers and Conquerors. It is from these latter two that I came to see the garden as being so often an essential part of that thing called history. And so as I became familiar with Gertrude Jekyll and Victoria Sackville-West, and the journal that Christopher Columbus kept of his first voyage; the "Garden and Farm Books" of Thomas Jefferson; *The Travels of William Bartram*, an account of a trip this colonial American made botanizing through the South; the accounts of plant hunting in Asia by Ernest H. Wilson and Frank Kingdon-Ward; and the literature to be found in seed and plant catalogues, the pleasure I found in these books, so long locked up in me, was released and found its answering echo in: "Why don't you just write about it." It was that very moment that I began to write about the garden.

Now, writing about the garden, thinking about what I will write about the garden, is so natural an occurrence, so normal. It has its own realm. It begins with reading catalogues, ordering from them, worrying about how I will pay for the things I have ordered, fretting about how things are getting on when I have put them in the ground, eating them, decorating a room with them, finding the proper words to make them come to life again when they are no longer in my sight.

The room in which I now write faces south and I look out on ground constantly bathed in sunlight. I look out on the wetlands. Because of federal and state laws, I am not allowed to change it, I am not allowed to do anything but look at it. I believe I can write about it, I believe there is not a law against that.

Splendor in the Glass

HARVARD'S MUSEUM OF NATURAL HISTORY STORES FLOWERS
MORE REAL THAN REAL

THERE ARE SOME TREASURES permanently stored in display cases in the Museum of Natural History at Harvard, and these treasures are flowers made of glass. They are called the Glass Flowers, with just that amount of plain certainty, as if they constituted a genus onto themselves, and in a way they do.

Their existence began in the late nineteenth century in the glass workshop of Leopold and Rudolf Blaschka, a team of father-and-son artisans who lived and worked near Dresden, Germany. Until then, the Blaschkas had been involved in producing replicas of invertebrates who inhabit the sea, for museums. The study of the natural world was done through observing things that had been first dead and then preserved from decay. Imagine, then, the frustration of a scientist, or the curious-minded, who needed to look at their chosen world in its many stages of realization, but instead could only find it dried up and lacking any kind of vitality. It was the genius of a man named George Lincoln Goodale, a professor of botany at Harvard in the late nineteenth century, to travel to Germany and ask the Blaschkas to make replicas of some of the inhabitants of the vegetable kingdom. What he wanted was to show not just the various parts of plants—flowers and their reproductive organs, leaves, stalks, and so on—but the diseases that might afflict them. And he wanted them not only for decoration, but as teaching tools. A student of botany could see as clearly as if it had just been picked from the American roadside, where it grows naturally, a branch of *Aster novae-angliae*. And perhaps most wonderful of all, the student need not worry about the specimen wilting and perishing, for it was made of glass, beautiful glass.

Altogether, in the nineteenth century, the earth and the things that existed on its surface were of the utmost interest to certain people and some of the ways they pursued this interest are painful to recall. And that is partly why trying to understand the world of the vegetable kingdom portrayed so artfully in glass is a pleasure.

To see the flowers now made of glass, lying down on their sides, in their display cabinets, so accurate, so pristine, so without blemish, is to be in a state of wonderment. For in the end, they do not look like perfect flowers on the stems of perfect branches adorned with perfect leaves growing from perfect plants. They look real enough but as if the real is from another realm.

I came to know of this place, this realm of the flowers made of glass, because one day a friend said to me that we should have coffee together and then go see the glass flowers. The glass flowers! I said out loud, and the glass flowers! I said to myself. The museum, where the glass flowers are on constant display, has had its small share of unpleasantness; the bones of Native Americans have been housed there, for instance, and so some people think twice before they rush off to view things kept in it. But the glass flowers are there to, in a small way, make amends.

Among the first of the glass renderings to greet a visitor are members of the *Rosaceae* family: apples, strawberries, and peaches. There is a large branch of an apple tree thick with fully opened blossoms and young leaves. The branch is knobby and blackish, glistening as if covered with dew, looking so real with freshness and as if it is about to be offered to the person viewing it for some innocent and heroic deed. Not far from that and continuing in the same family is a rendering of the strawberry (*Fragaria vesca*). It is displayed on a branch with leaves and in three different stages of fruiting: the small, young fruit nestled in the sepals of the now passed flower, the ripening fruit and then the ripe strawberry waiting to be picked. There is another rendering of the strawberry, only fruits this time, and they are coated with a cottonlike substance, looking just the way strawberries look when you have not eaten them soon enough or have left them in the fridge too long.

But the vegetable Kingdom of Glass goes on. It goes into the Grasses and suddenly the thing you eat with enjoyment (that would be rice or a slice of bread) or the thing you walk on while having pleasant thoughts (that would be the lawn) are shown to be the same and yet different when encased in this glass. Or their reproductive mechanism can be seen in detail from many different angles: transverse or longitudinal, for instance. I only really understood the true beauty of stamen and pistil and pollen and petal after seeing them rendered in glass. This true beauty, of course, eventually led me into a state of dissatisfaction. The glass flowers and their many stages of being are in a state of perfection stilled. It is always a gardener's wish to have perfection and then to have it forever. It is also within the gardener's temperament to first desire forever and then to do everything possible to dismantle and smash forever. If the flowers encased in cabinets stored in the museum make up a garden, they are not the exception to this latter sentiment. Though it seems as if they will last forever, every cabinet bears a legend warning of their fragility. The people taking care of them give assurance that they will last forever. But as every gardener knows, forever is as long as a day.

To see the flowers of glass is to be in a state of wonderment.

The Garden the Year Just Passed

OH, HOW THE ENEMIES of the contented gardener prospered in the gardening year just passed. One glorious summer's day last July, Meg Woolmington was having a conversation with two of her three daughters (Bliss and Caroline) in a room that overlooks a vegetable and flower garden that she has made with her husband, Rob, when suddenly they heard the loud close-by bang! of a shotgun going off. They leapt out of their seats just like the way it is portrayed in a cartoon (the Bumsteads of *Blondie* in particular) in shock and fear. Eventually they were amused and loving when they realized that the frightening noise of the gun was because their husband and father had been trying once again to rid his garden of an enemy, a woodchuck, and such uncharacteristic action, resorting to removing the shotgun from its hidden place in the house and then waiting in a room for the culprit that had been decimating the fruits of the variously and carefully tended crops, was an expression of frustration on his

2002, Summer. "The Garden the Year Just Passed." *Callaloo*. Vol. 25, iss. 3: 785–89.

part. Rob had planted rows and rows and rows of many things: broccoli, tomatoes, lettuce, brussels sprouts, and so on, and each day he came home from his office in Manchester, Vermont, where he is a lawyer, longing to view his domain of specialized vegetables flourishing before him, as he had imagined it flourishing in his absence. But each time he saw his garden at the end of the day, it was less than what he had seen the day before; and it was not less in a sickly, withering way, as if suffering from some bacteria or fungus. It was less, just plain less than before, as if someone or something had come with a set of fine, sharp jagged-edged scissors and just trimmed away with pleasure. Every gardener in my part of the world knows what the garden looks like when a woodchuck has been in it, and not long after Rob first noticed his garden's decline, he came home one day to find a woodchuck leisurely walking along a row of something that had just begun to grow up. He did the usual screaming and chasing the woodchuck out of his garden and the woodchuck ran off so fast for a fat, big, lumbering thing and Rob knew that would never be the end of things so he went out and bought a Havahart trap, that ridiculous contraption that allows you to catch the animal that has destroyed your garden and release it someplace else, far away.

The Havahart trap is such a nice idea for nice people. I own two of them. I do not like them. What I would really like is a home gardener's version of that seemingly useful hydrogen bomb called the Daisy Cutter or a home gardener's version of a land mine in the shape of a butterfly. And this is why: After Rob bought his Havahart trap, he dutifully filled it up with tempting green leaves and set it out in his garden, where a woodchuck dutifully wandered into it and was caught. He felt so triumphant as he drove the woodchuck deep into the woods, far away from any place where there might be cultivated crops. For a few days his garden seemed to be thriving and then it was not. A woodchuck was eating the flowers and vegetables again. The trap was set out, the woodchuck was caught and released far away up into the mountains, away from areas of cultivation, after a few days new shoots began to appear on the eaten plants and then shortly after that they began to disappear, as if something was eating them, and something *was* eating them. A woodchuck.

Before Rob resorted to staking out a position in a room in his house with him holding a shotgun, he once again placed the trapped woodchuck in the trunk of his car and drove it around and around the village, hoping to confuse the woodchuck and make it think that Rob had driven to a distant place that was very tricky to get to. The place was a lake in our village, where he released it at the deepest and widest stretch. He thought that the woodchuck would swim over to the other side of the lake and the effort would make him so exhausted and befuddled he would not be able to make his way back to Rob's garden, for by that time Rob had decided that it was the same woodchuck that kept coming back to his garden. When he released the woodchuck, it cleverly did not swim across the lake but swam downstream along the bank, and feeling safely out of Rob's reach, it then leapt out and waddled swiftly away. For a few days after that, Rob's garden again thrived and then promptly again began its decline. He retained a deep belief in the live-and-let-live ideal of the Havahart trap (I once called it a pantywaist contraption), and it was with some regret that he had to admit the woodchuck did not share any kindly thoughts toward him; for in fact there are many delicious wild crops to be found all in the fields: dandelions, crest, and all sorts of broadleaf succulents that would have been perfectly tasty for a woodchuck.

How I sympathized with Rob and his garden trouble. Years ago, I paid a man a large sum of money to enclose my vegetable garden with wire fencing that started four feet belowground and was five feet high starting at ground level; I used to watch from my own bedroom window a carnival of rabbits, woodchucks, raccoons, and from time to time deer parade through my rows of vegetables eating everything that appeared in front of their noses. The rabbits in particular multiplied and sometimes they were so many, gamboling about the lawn or everywhere else outside, that I became afraid of them if only because they were so many and I am not a rabbit. But then a family of foxes moved in. I used to be able to see them as they crisscrossed the wetlands, the lawn, the road, perfecting a physical coordination that deserves the highest accolade somewhere. Two seasons went by before I understood the relationship between regular sightings of foxes and infrequent sightings of rabbits. One day, I heard much screeching, so much, that I thought I should call somebody. I did not call anybody and the murdering yells and screams subsided. Shortly after there were not many rabbits on the lawn cavorting. There were no rabbits at all, to be truthful.

The issue of the four-legged, fur-covered mammal marauders was forever on my mind. In a part of the garden where, depending on the time of season, the fragrance from the *Viburnum carlesii* or *Lilium "Casa Blanca"* is overwhelming, the smell of the presence of a skunk dominated. I never actually saw it with my own eyes, I only could smell its presence. I was fretting away to Jared Clawson, the man who with great care made the elegant stairs that connect the two terraces and walls in my garden, telling him of Rob's encounter with the woodchuck, the invisible skunk that haunts my garden, and he, after nodding in sympathy, told me of Mr. Pembroke's (Dick, our local representative in the lower House of Vermont, not Ron, his son, whom I also regard as Mr. Pembroke) experience with a mammal as pest: Mr. Pembroke plants fields of corn, "Silver Queen" and other delicious varieties like that, for the sole purpose of being eaten by human beings during the pleasurable summer months, as opposed to corn grown for the sole purpose of being eaten by other mammals (cows for instance). A dinner of Mr. Pembroke's corn, which comes to me by way of Jared, for he works for Mr. Pembroke and when I make a purchase of corn, Jared kindly brings it to me, freshly picked, is one of the best things of summer. When I saw Jared that day, he was making real some transaction between Mr. Pembroke and myself, perhaps it was a delivery of mulch, perhaps it was tending the wetland, perhaps it was making sure the newly planted trees were thriving, I can't remember exactly, but when I saw him, I immediately launched into the problem with Rob and his family and the woodchuck and Jared listened and nodded in sympathy and then told me of an adventure Mr. Pembroke had with another four-footed, fur-covered mammal, a racoon. One growing season, a summer, Mr. Pembroke was plagued with rows of disappearing corn. He accurately judged it to be a large rodent and he set out a Havahart trap, for Mr. Pembroke is such a good man. He caught the rodent, a racoon, and he dutifully took it far away from any other domesticated environs and set it free. Not too many days went by and the mammal pest appeared again in the same form, a racoon, and Mr. Pembroke set his trap, caught the malice, and released it in a manner he judged proper and thought that was that. But this process, of trapping and releasing, repeated itself so many times that Mr. Pembroke began to feel suspicious. He said to himself, what if it is the same individual returning to his home in my cornfield after I have released him, no matter how far away I have done so? My Pembroke then embraced the brilliant idea of marking the detested racoon. A can of spray paint in the color orange seems always to be constantly present in the company of people who work in modifying the landscape, and Mr. Pembroke is in the business generally of doing that. When he caught his racoon in the silly Havahart trap, just as a joke, just for curiosity, he sprayed its hind area a strong and bright patch of orange. He did his usual, releasing it far away from his cornfields, and as usual, he enjoyed a small amount of communal pride, because he had not participated in the obvious: kill the thing that is an annoyance to you right away because you can. Very soon after all this, Mr. Pembroke caught in his reliable Havahart another pest, a racoon. To satisfy his curiosity, he examined its hind. Yes, yes, and yes again, there was not so faintly at all, the mark of the orange paint.

When Jared finished telling me this story of Mr. Pembroke's kindheartedness backfiring, he laughed and I laughed too; but I was really thinking of what fun it would be to confirm Rob's fears to him. It was clear to me that he kept catching and releasing the same woodchuck, over and over again. I am sure of it even right now. I then remembered Rob's experience some years ago with another rodent. He used to take great pride in growing his tomatoes from seed and I remember him spending a small sum of money on starter growing kits ordered from Gardener's Supply, a company that sells garden implements to the home gardener in Burlington, Vermont. One year, just as his tomato plants had grown stout with health, he noticed that something was eating them, they were growing shorter and shorter, just the way they would do if they were outside and being attacked by a woodchuck or something like that. Oh, too soon, he realized that this maliciousness was being perpetrated by a rat. How well I remember the indignation and rage with which he set off to buy rat traps and then patrolled the family communal space, where the tomato plants were growing on a windowsill. I don't remember how it was all resolved, but Rob now buys his tomato plants from Andrew Knafel, who owns an organic farm, the Clearbrook Farm, down the road and quite nearby us.

I do not really know how much my story of Mr. Pembroke and the painted racoon added to Rob's fury at his failure to rid his garden of its nemesis, but it was not so long after that he interrupted the rest of his family's tranquility one nice afternoon.

My amusement and interest in Rob's travails with the marauding four-legged mammal in the garden was because I have had my own problems with them in my garden for years and years now. Sometimes, with their sudden, unexpected movements they shatter me out of a daydream I have been enjoying; sometimes I am surprised by something they have eaten, something that I did not think I should protect from them, the black hollyhocks, for instance. I had placed the black hollyhocks in the holding bed, along with some *Belamcanda* I had grown from seeds I ordered from Thomas Jefferson's garden, Monticello. The woodchuck had eaten the hollyhocks but not the blackberry lily (*Belamcanda chinensis*). Of course, this led to much fretting. And then I noticed that there was a large hole, tunnellike, leading from the holding bed heading toward the vegetable garden. Immediately I knew what this meant: the malice of the woodchucks had been extended; my vegetable garden, which had been carefully hemmed in by a well-made fence, was now about to be attacked. After feeling shocked, after feeling angry, I said to myself, Oh well, and I placed a Havahart trap next to the opening of the hole and went about my ways. Of course I thought of going to Whitman's, a store in my village that sells everything having to do with the well-being of livestock and this includes the demise of the enemies of people who take care of livestock. A woodchuck or a racoon or even a rabbit can be an enemy to people who take care of livestock. So many times, over the years, I have gone to Whitman's and bought a smoke bomb and come home and lit it, then thrown it into the hole of some pest and then run away, for the smoke went not into the hole but toward me and seemed to follow me inside my house. And so I no longer buy these smoke bombs, I no longer do anything but talk about my pests, listen to other people talk about their pests, and position the silly Peter, Paul and Mary–like Havahart trap here and there in my garden.

It is so that by halfway through September, more or less, I had forgotten about pests in the garden and any other problem regarding the garden. For by then, the world that I had come to live in was in tatters. Well, the world wasn't actually in tatters, certainly the rest of the world as it would appear to the Associated Press or

Reuters was not in tatters; that world was just as it had always been; things going wrong, things going in a disastrous direction, here and there. But the world that I lived in was in tatters. Just for instance, the sky above me, here in Vermont where I live, was empty of airplanes. I was looking up at a primordial sky, a sky that seemed determinedly innocent of the many goings-on below it. The sky had a hard, steel-like quality to it, and a constant blue, that eventually grew terrifying for it was so unchanging. No frost had yet come and so the dahlias, "Thomas Edison," "Barbarossa," "Kelvin Floodlight," "Lilac Time," all of them so strong and violent in color (maroon, red, yellow, purple) were blooming with an almost sickening exuberance. They really are overdone, the dinner plate dahlias, and I ought to know better when I order them, but I seem to never believe they will outdo their image in the catalogues from which I order them (Dutch Gardens). And the collection of *Hibiscus moscheotos* ("Kopper King," "Fireball," "Fantasia") bred by the Fleming Brothers of Lincoln, Nebraska. Also producing copiously underneath this primordial sky were the ever-bearing golden raspberries, and there was an unusual strangeness to picking bowlful after bowlful of them and then sitting down on the ground to eat them and look up to see and hear the empty, silent sky. And then again to know that skies were silent and empty because something terrible had happened.

It was once, when going to pick some of those delicious golden raspberries (and they have the best flavor of any raspberry I have eaten, as if the texture and taste of fresh cream had been bred into them to begin with) that I came upon the Havahart trap I had placed at the mouth of the tunnel that was being dug underneath my vegetable garden. There was something in it, something that looked like the collar of an old coat, or a much worn, now lost hat. I knew immediately what it really was and so called Jared Clawson to get rid of it for me. That is the trouble I find with killing things: What should I do with them afterward? Of course the good thing about killing things that are causing you trouble, in the garden anyway, is that they can't come back, they can't find their way back to take up their old nest and continue to keep you in a constant state of vexation. The very bad thing about killing things that are causing you trouble, again in the garden anyway, is that killing isn't at all funny. There are no funny stories of dying in the garden. When things die in the garden, only stories of lamentation come from them.

The Lure of the Poppy

SO VIVACIOUS, with its freshly laid egg-yolk-yellow petals, four of them, sitting in a little saucer-shaped sepal, open-faced in the sun, fluted closed in the shade, blooming on a thin stem above finely cut bluish-greenish leaves. How humble and pleasing it looks when found, one or two, in an unexpected spot in the garden, a place where you never dreamed of placing it. And how staggeringly beautiful it can be when seen massed on a chalky cliff or in a sun-drenched meadow or along the side of the road or in somebody's garden. In the places it likes, dry and sunny, it is among the easiest of annuals to grow. It is the state flower of California, and flower and state are so well suited to each other that I can almost make the case that the nature of this flower has shaped the character of the state.

Its proper name is *Eschscholzia californica*, and it was named by a German naturalist of French descent, Adelbert von Chamisso, for his friend, a Russian doctor of French descent named Johann

2002, Dec. "The Lure of the Poppy." *Architectural Digest.* Vol. 59, iss. 12: 138–42.

Friedrich von Eschscholtz. Chamisso was one of the scientists on a Russian-sponsored expedition that hoped to find a subarctic route across North America. The world by this time (early nineteenth century) had been very well traversed and claimed over and over again by many European explorers. James Cook, who captained a voyage around the world and who established the custom of taking scientists and artists with him on his journeys, had long been dead. Meriwether Lewis and William Clark had already made the trip from east to west on the North American continent, and not long after that Lewis killed himself.

If on seeing the California poppy the burdens of Chamisso's journey became lighter, he does not say. His account of this trip, documented in a book called *A Voyage Around the World with the Romanzov Exploring Expedition in the Years 1815–1818 in the Brig Rurik, Captain Otto von Kotzebue*, is one of the most quarrelsome of its kind that I have ever read (my edition is edited and translated by Henry Kratz). Everyone and every situation seem to offer him some irritation, except for "my faithful Eschscholtz," with whom he was "in complete harmony" and with whom "I always studied, observed, and collected." How almost completely perfect, then, that he should commemorate this satisfactory friendship with this friendly flower.

And it is a friendly flower in every way. In the first place, a packet usually costs less than two dollars, and that packet will contain about three hundred seeds, which is about the amount found in a few of the seedpods formed after the flower has bloomed. It is these seedpods, capsule-shaped, that cause some people to pause when contemplating this poppy's generosity. For when ripe, they explode, scatter the seeds every which way, and the California poppy does best where it seeds itself. Like most members of the family *Papaveraceae*, it isn't especially happy to be transplanted. In Vermont, where I live, they begin to show up in the places where I have deliberately placed them and in places where I least expect them, blooming sometime after midsummer. From then on I have them until a deep hard frost wipes them out.

When I first saw them growing in a part of their natural habitat in some hills above Los Angeles, the sight of such beauty overwhelmed me, and I could not imagine bringing them into the garden, taming them by working their carefreeness into a garden scheme. Some flowers are like that. When you see them in the wild, you feel for one reason or another that they ought to stay there. Goldenrod (*Solidago canadensis*) is such a flower. Some others, the minute you lay eyes on them, you begin to hatch all sorts of deceitful plots to place them in your garden. The latter happened to me when I first laid eyes on a climbing monkshood (*Aconitum hemsleyanum*) in western China; fortunately, my traveling companion, a botanist and nurseryman, quickly told me that I could purchase it from his plant catalogue. And so for many years in my gardening life my garden remained free of one of my favorite poppies. Then one day, when I was visiting the garden the late filmmaker Derek Jarman made at his house, which stands directly in the shade of a nuclear power plant in Dungeness, England, I saw them joyously growing in bunches among sea kale (*Crambe maritima*), opium poppies (*Papaver somniferum*), and marigolds. The garden is unusual in this way: its main feature is the house, a small one-story structure that is painted black, and the windows are trimmed with a yellow that on a paint chart would be called cadmium yellow but is in fact quite close to the yellow of the California poppy. I left that garden with a new feeling about plants in the garden. It was not unlike being a writer and reading a book that had been written in a way you had not thought of before.

I returned to my own garden with an almost excessive embrace of the California poppy. I planted it in its species form and then in its various cultivars: "Ballerina Mixed," "Red Chief," and "Purple Violet." The cultivars never came back, but the true species shows up again and again in the unexpected places with such regularity that I think any advice on how to use it ought to begin and end with "unexpected places" and leave it at that.

In a book he wrote about his garden, the garden where I found the California poppy, Jarman wrote this: "Paradise haunts gardens, and it haunts mine." This thought brings me back to Chamisso. Explorers and naturalists are in search of a paradise, not a hell. Sometimes a flower is just a flower, and sometimes a flower is full of something else. When the migrant Chamisso saw the California poppy, he thought of his friend and fellow migrant Eschscholtz. When I saw the California poppy in Jarman's garden, immediately on coming home, I started to grow it. I live in Vermont, but I am not native to it, I am a migrant living there. The ease with which this plant grows in its native habitat or a place that duplicates its native habitat and the open-faced welcome of its blossoms seem all so much a definition of California itself.

Gardening

REGARDING THE GARDEN: whether I am in doubt, whether I am certain, when I am overly pleased with the arrangement of the disaster lying on the ground in front of me, when I am made sad by my ignorance which led to the disaster lying on the ground in front of me, I turn to a book. A book about the garden is a gardener's best friend. Another gardener is not a gardener's best friend. Another gardener is very complicated. Other gardeners have all sorts of opinions about your garden, about their garden, about somebody else's garden, and they are not afraid to voice them. And then again, another gardener in your garden, this whole relationship will be brimming over with feelings. They love yellow flowers so very much, you love blue flowers so very much; you both then try to love red flowers only a little. On it goes, so exhausting. Not so with my best garden friend, the garden book.

There are thousands of garden books. Some of them are devoted to the practical, some of them are just to demonstrate the sheer joy to be had in one aspect of the garden (the water garden, the garden that demands almost no water, the large garden that has only a few plants, the patio garden in which an entire catalogue of plants thrive), some hold the thoughts and experiences of gardeners or people who just love the garden. But even so there are never enough books and there never can be, at least for someone like me. For let's suppose I have a mixed border of acid-loving shrubs, will I be satisfied with one or two volumes devoted to it? No. Yet another book on the acid-loving mixed shrub border will say the same thing as the others and yet not so at all. The world of the garden book is made up of the radically same and the radically different at once.

As I write this, before me, lying at my feet, are many books about the garden. It is spring but the brutal winter just past lingers. I am looking out a window through which I should see a sloping hillside dotted with crocus in flower. I see no such thing. Instead, I see stretch after stretch of barren (no crocus) green. I can only imagine that the crocuses are blooming in the stomachs of the small furry mammals who ate them. I have a book that tells me how to avoid this catastrophe, I have a book or six. One day I will acquire yet another book telling me how to do this and at the moment I do I will forget about the others.

Just look at how eager and earnest I go over five of the books that I have lying in front of me. They are five books devoted to color, four of them focused on flowers and leaves and one on bark—that is, tree bark. I go over them as if I had never heard of the ideas before. Color is not an obsession for a gardener, color in the garden is the garden for most of us gardeners. The architecture of the garden is another stage of evolution which some of us (this gardener is Exhibit A) will never reach. Color is all there is. And so *Colour in Your Garden* (Frances Lincoln/Antique Collectors' Club, paper, $29.25), by Penelope Hobhouse, will give pleasure to gardeners who already understand the concept of "clear yellows" even as they will soon sag with the weight of inferiority produced by a picture accurately described: "a sea of Meconopsis grandis floods a woodland glade between evergreen shrubs." This is a good book, for it confirms and also vindicates your hard-earned convictions. And it also offers a challenge, but of the most delicate kind: no harm will come to the world if some gardener in the state of Vermont decides to make a sea of *Meconopsis grandis* do anything. Kind and good too is *The Gardener's Palette: Creating Color in the Garden* (Contemporary Books, $29.95), by Sydney Eddison. It has a chapter subheaded "Harmonies," and an accompanying illustration of maroon and red tulips, and Eddison says: "The easiest harmonies to put together are pairs of adjacent colors. There is always a sense of rightness about them." So true, I say, as if I will recognize adjacent colors when I see them, but most of the plants mentioned were ones I knew very well and the ways to use them would satisfy me, if only I could take instructions. But it also shows you how the really great gardeners have done a thing or two. I loved the illustration of a Lynden Miller border: a combination of variegated miscanthus, berberis, phlox, echinacea, and cotinus. I recommend Sue Fisher's *Garden Colour* (Hamlyn/Sterling, $19.95) to anyone who is afraid of the authenticity and authority of Penelope Hobhouse. It is full of wonderful suggestions and has an unsettling way of making the familiar seem new ("bamboo creates a junglelike background in an exotic foliage planting"). But of the color books I have to save my most heated enthusiasm for *Color in the Garden: Planting with Color in the Contemporary Garden* (Soma, paper, $24.95), by Nori and Sandra Pope, the two gardeners who revived Hadspen Garden in Somerset, England. Here is one of their declarations: "Yellow flowers do not form any complex clashes with their own leaves." This book has been the single thing to keep me occupied on some of the most dismal days of the extended winter. The pictures are beautiful, showing to perfection the way the Popes used showy plants in the garden. They are bold. Look at the way they use the red rose "Altissimo" and the practically black-leaved but red-in-flower dahlia "Bishop of Llandaff" against a red brick wall. Or at this, my favorite combination:

the lime-green yellow of euphorbia "Polychroma" and lime-green yellow tulip called "Spring Green." I once visited Hadspen House, and I remember walking down the alleys of borders with combinations of flowers (Eric Smith, the hybridizer of the blue-leaved hosta "Halcyon," had been a gardener there many years before and since I feel a special sympathy for him, that was the reason I visited Hadspen Garden) that were a joy to see. Nothing matched in a way that I understood. The yellows clashed and then finally conceded that their common qualities were exceptional and so therefore cause to unify. It was in this garden that I first saw *Papaver orientale* "Patty's Plum" and the yellow-leaved *Dicentra spectabilis* "Goldheart" (though not growing together). Both plants originated in this garden that was revived by the Popes.

As for *Tree Bark: A Color Guide* (Timber, $39.95), by Hugues Vaucher, here is a book that is so much like its subject, for trees are easily taken for granted. But I found myself returning to its many color illustrations to see trunks of trees that were not at all familiar: the craggy, deep-fissured trunk of *Phillyrea latifolia*, the fist-size bulges that make up the trunk of *Erythrina carnea*, the accordion-like wrinkling of *Leucadendron argenteum*, as if the trunk had successfully prevented the tree from slowly collapsing on itself.

Perhaps even more than wanting to manipulate the color of the plants growing in a garden, a gardener wants to manipulate the space allotted to the garden. *The Well-Designed Mixed Garden: Building Beds and Borders with Trees, Shrubs, Perennials, Annuals, and Bulbs* (Timber, $39.95), by Tracy DiSabato-Aust, is a good one to start with or to continue with if you already have some plans. It has all sorts of charts and diagrams and pictures; and a listing of plants by their "design characteristics," which is probably a useful thing. But this is a hefty book and so might be hard to take out to the site of all those places that need its help. Two other very good ones on the designing-the-space issue are *Front Yard Gardens: Growing More Than Grass* (Firefly, $35; paper, $24.95), by Liz

Primeau, and *Natural Gardening in Small Spaces* (Timber, $29.95), by Noël Kingsbury. It is harder to garden in a small space than a bigger space, or so it appears to me, but they make me think I am wrong. And then before I leave the space of the garden, here is one other way of approaching it, that way of looking at the garden as you might look at a house, from the point of view of the architecture of the garden. I suppose because I don't have the pocketbook and taste to go with this approach, I shy away from it. But Janet Waymark's *Modern Garden Design: Innovation Since 1900* (Thames and Hudson, $40) and *Architecture in the Garden* (Random House, $39.95), by James van Sweden with Thomas Christopher, are two books worth looking at, if for no other reason than this: within the realm of the garden, modernism is architecture and architecture is modernism and these two things make everything gray. It's a very pleasant kind of gray, mind you, and certainly a gray that the color-obsessed have not yet figured out.

Some other books about the garden in which I shall find refuge from the garden itself?

Here is *Palms Won't Grow Here and Other Myths: Warm-Climate Plants for Cooler Areas* (Timber, $27.95), by David A. Francko. I like the idea of this book for I have had a *Franklinia alatamaha* for seven years now and it seems to have survived even the brutality that was winter just past. I live in a cold zone 5. I cannot grow crape myrtle, no matter what this author says. I have tried because I love its mottled bark and I love stumbling upon it in the writing of William Bartram. But I cannot grow it here. This book insists I can. I could almost believe it. To demonstrate the point it insists on making, the cover illustration is of some fan palm fronds (*Trachycarpus fortunei*) covered with snow. It is practically a commandment that a gardener who lives on top of the North Pole will long to grow bananas and that a gardener who lives in a place where bananas are endemic will long to have an Alpine scree. All of which is to say that the general idea of this book is correct but only in your dreams.

And here also is *A Brief History of Thyme: And Other Herbs* (Grove, paper, $14.95), by Miranda Seymour, and *The Herb Garden* (Frances Lincoln/Antique Collectors' Club, paper, $19.95), by Sarah Garland, both slender volumes but robust with information; *Weeds in My Garden: Observations on Some Misunderstood Plants* (Timber, $22.95), by Charles B. Heiser, is a reminder that some of the misunderstood plants in the world have turned out to be herbs. *Gathering Moss: A Natural and Cultural History of Mosses* (Oregon State University, paper, $17.95), by Robin Wall Kimmerer, is an interesting account, both personal and exact, of an area of the vegetable kingdom that I often do not even notice. This book, with its passionate emphasis on something often most successfully appreciated by viewing through a microscope, made me look at the great Penelope Hobhouse's *Story of Gardening* (DK Publishing, $40). It is on a grand scale, as is everything associated with this grand and very good gardener, and she is a good antidote to moss. And when reading this book, I think again, garden book or garden friend? Among the very good friends would be William Cobbett. *The American Gardener* (Modern Library, paper, $11.95), written in the early nineteenth century, is being republished as part of a series of worthy books about the garden, edited by Michael Pollan. Cobbett's writing is important in garden literature: he writes so well; he is full of still relevant advice on how to do all sorts of things. This book has an introduction by the American garden writer and essayist Verlyn Klinkenborg, who writes editorials for *The New York Times*, briefly sketching out the political and personal turmoil of Cobbett's life. Apparently he went from radical right to radical left and remained so—that is, radical left—for the rest of his life. Such a gardener as William Cobbett is exactly the kind of gardening friend I would like to be with in my garden. Such a person would be better than a book. But that he comes at this time, only in a book, is enough happiness.

Living History in Vermont

VERMONT, NESTLED AS IT IS between the harsh granite prominence that is New Hampshire and the history and wealth of New York and Massachusetts, often becomes known to us through its endless rows of gently high green hills, open pastures populated with just the right number of cows, covered bridges, and inhabitants whose good nature is a constant. Yet it has its own distinct heroic historical moments.

In 1770 it fought to separate itself from New Hampshire and New York, whose two governors sought jurisdiction over it. In 1777 it declared itself independent of them. It was the first state to join the Union after the original thirteen and it was the first state to ban slavery outright in its constitution. It played an important part in the history of the Underground Railroad. And in our Civil War, fighting on the right side, the side of the Union, it lost more citizens than any other state in the Union.

Not too much is made of these great accomplishments. Yes,

2003, June. "Living History in Vermont." *Architectural Digest*. Vol. 60, iss. 6: 80–86.

every year there is a parade in Bennington, the third-largest city in Vermont, with a population of 15,700, to celebrate the Battle of Bennington, an important victory in the Revolutionary War. But that would seem to be about all there is. Vermont behaves like the very good person who does the very good thing—anonymously.

It is often in the small, the personal, and the domestic that Vermont takes note of itself. There is, for instance, in the town of Manchester Center, the North Shire Museum and History Center. This entity is made up of a set of seven different structures built in the eighteenth and nineteenth centuries, each of them a reminder of a Vermont that is past and yet is strangely familiar. There is Oliver Rice House, and his barn, a tavern, and the tavern's two barns, another barn called the Weir Wheelwright and Blacksmith Shop, and yet another called the Parker Cole Barn. So many barns, indeed, but among the thrilling sights to behold on a beautiful sunny day in Vermont is a barn, painted red or not, sitting in the middle of a newly mowed field of green grass.

In this little museum, though, it is Oliver Rice House that is of particular interest. Oliver Rice was born circa 1730 in Hardwick, Massachusetts, but in that way so typical of Americans, he moved from the place he was born to someplace else, where he would find his real and true self and live his real and true life. He moved to Bennington, got married, built himself a house on a large piece of property, and made a farm there. That house—big and saltbox-like in architectural style—stood there for over two hundred years. One day, in another quite typical American way, it was found to be standing directly in the path of a proposed highway and so it was dismantled board by board and tenderly taken to Manchester Center, where it was reassembled and restored to look the way it had when first built and lived in by Oliver Rice.

To see the house now, the details of its usefulness revived but only for display, is to be reminded that American style does not come from the top. Rice is only an aristocrat in retrospect, he is only an aristocrat when compared to a slave.

Perhaps the best way to see the rest of the buildings is to imagine yourself Oliver Rice, a farmer not just in northern New England, but in Vermont. A barn would be a necessity, a visit to the blacksmith shop would be needed from time to time, and a tavern is always very important.

The Northshire, as that area of Vermont is called, an area just directly north of Bennington and not too much farther than that, is among the most pleasing areas of a very pleasing-to-look-at state. On certain days, and they are not rare, it is among the most beautiful places in which to find yourself alive.

How thrilling it can be to find yourself in a place among things that remind you of some of the difficulties involved in being a human being and, at the same time, some of its pleasures. The North Shire Museum and History Center captures this feeling exactly.

Desert Blooms

Is it not so that most gardeners, on making a garden, are influenced by the narrative in Genesis on the creation story and in particular the creation of the Garden of Eden? How else to explain the godlike authority with which any gardener approaches the Garden itself?

Here is an Eden I had never seen before, Lotusland, a garden in Santa Barbara, California, made by the opera singer Ganna Walska. She married much better than she sang (a Russian nobleman, the chairman of International Harvester, a neurologist, a physicist), and at the end of each marriage she was richer than before. In 1941 she bought a house and former nursery in Montecito and turned it into the place now called Lotusland.

No part of this garden suggests the tamed and subdued, the peace and rest, so often associated with the cultivated landscape. Not even the Japanese part of the garden, not even again the water garden.

The garden is planted mostly with plants that give an impression of bristles and thrusts: cacti, euphorbias, aloes, cycads, ferns, succulents. The principle "If one is good, many times that is better" is the only one that operates here. And when applied to cacti, euphorbias, cycads, succulents, the garden seems menacing in a make-believe way.

Put to particular ingenious use is *Euphorbia ingens*, a euphorbia with a thick, treelike trunk that is over ten feet high when mature, and from its top fall coiling "leaves," down to the ground where it continues to grow in a sort of crawl, a green barbed snake with the substance of a cactus. Ingenious too is the way some dragon trees (*Dracaena draco*) are planted, close together like in a forest, their blue aloelike leaves brandished as if on guard.

It is nothing but exciting in each part of this garden and each part is so complete in itself that wherever you are in it, the other parts are memories. The Japanese garden has water, of course; the water garden has water lilies, of course; the aloe garden has a pool surrounded by seashells, some small enough to appear natural, some so large that they might be man-made or they may have been made by the very same forces that commanded the dragon tree into being.

The vision of this garden is no doubt Madame Walska's, as she came to be called, but she had some collaborators. The son of a nurseryman who once owned the property helped her originally. Later two men, Charles Glass and Robert Foster, helped her with the aloe garden and the cacti. When she died in 1984, she might have looked out on all of it with satisfaction, certain that her vision of this Eden was complete and fixed. But if a garden, so dependent on its maker's love and devotion, dies with the gardener, it will sometimes be lucky and find new lovers to make it come alive again.

So it is with Lotusland. A new area has been added to it. Splendidly designed by the landscaper Eric Nagelmann, it is meant to be a replica of the hot and high desert. Though it is only three-quarters of an acre or so in size, it immediately feels desolate and dry and easy to be lost in. In keeping with its designated terrain, it is planted with the members of the vegetable kingdom that like to store up carefully their moisture—the cactus family.

Nagelmann has used the space ingeniously, making four separate winding paths that gradually go upward and then all end on a plateau a short distance later. All the while this short journey has the feel of an isolated canyon. Large rocks are carefully placed so that they seem to be jutting out from some large hidden surface; smaller rocks look as if they have just suddenly become displaced. In all this the tricks the desert can play on the imagination are not missing either. On a calm sunny day in December, the heat bouncing off the stony surface of the garden, I became certain that I heard the rattling of a reptile and the breathing of a preying mammal. It was all supremely wonderful, shivery-making, inspiring, among the feelings to be had in a great garden.

Jumby Bay

HERE IS A WAY TO GO HOME AGAIN: take a vacation in a place that is within sight of the place where you grew up. I grew up on the island of Antigua, a place that is famous for attracting people who want to go there and do just that: take a vacation. But since it is my home, my ancestral home at that, it holds for me an array of emotions, none of them leading me to relax or to forget. Yet, loving that place as much as I do, its natural beauty, it seems to me, unsurpassed by any other island in that area of the world, I long to go there.

A number of small islets are strewn off the shores of Antigua. One of them, called Long Island by Christopher Columbus as he sailed by in 1493, hosts the resort Jumby Bay. I spent four perfect vacation days there, sitting on a white-sand beach looking at the series of low-lying mounds that make up the island of Antigua. In back of me were some beautiful bungalows, roomy and luxurious inside. I stayed in one of them and marveled at the fact that it was much bigger than the house in which I grew up.

2004, Aug. "Jumby Bay." *Architectural Digest*. Vol. 61, iss. 8: 180–84.

So much of places like Jumby Bay is about trying to reconcile the past with the present, trying to make the past, which is almost always horrible, stay there in the past, while making the present enjoyable. Many years ago Jumby Bay, then called Long Island, used to be a sugar plantation. No real evidence of the slaves who made the plantation possible remains, but that they were there is not at all denied. The relic of the sugar mill, which they worked, is still there. The great house, which sheltered the people who owned them, has been refurbished and is a wonderful place to have a delicious formal dinner. The sugar fields themselves are now big, open pastureland of tall grasses, beautiful to behold, especially when seen early in the morning still damp with dew.

If the sugar fields are now just open pasture, something of the island that existed before Christopher Columbus, the ritual of the hawksbill turtle nesting, still occurs. On a small stretch of beach, situated on the Atlantic Ocean and one of the three that dot the tiny island, is where the females of this species of turtle come every year from July to November to nest. Needless to say, this ancient creature is rare and so not taxing the poor earth's resources. Not far from where the turtles nest is the home of Peter Swann, the man who is president of the corporation that owns the island of Jumby Bay and the hotel itself. His house is one of twenty or so homes that are on the island. It is a house of incredible loveliness and natural beauty. When inside, you feel as if you are outside, sheltered in a grove of wood and leaves. A swimming pool practically, just almost, spills out onto the beach, but it never does so. And this is how that marvelous turtle survives, by living next to Peter Swann. I can remember well that when I was a child, my family and other people we knew lived for turtle season. In particular, I was encouraged to eat turtle egg soup because I was so sickly.

Such a place as Jumby Bay needs a wonderful host, and it has one. His name is Peter Bowling, and one day I went with him around the island just to have a look. That can be done anyway—a guest can get up and walk around early in the morning before that infernal sun, which is good for warming the air but hard on any kind of human skin, gets going. But I wanted to see the island with someone who lives there all the time and loves it passionately. We drove around on narrow cemented pathways—for there are no roads—in a golf cart. Never out of view were the surreally glittering surfaces of the Atlantic Ocean or the Caribbean Sea. A nice breeze rustled through the many different plantings of bougainvillea (hedged or growing freely), palm trees, and all the other plants that will prosper in a tropical atmosphere. The island then looked paradisiacal, as if in all the world it alone had been spared knowledge of and familiarity with all the bad things that can and have happened in this exceptional world we live in.

Introduction to *The Best American Travel Writing, 2005*

THE TRAVEL WRITER: She is not a refugee. Refugees don't do that, write travel narratives. No, they don't. It is the Travel Writer who does that. The Travel Writer is a dignified refugee, but a dignified refugee is no refugee at all. A refugee is usually fleeing the place where the Travel Writer is going to enjoy herself—but later, for the Travel Writer tends to enjoy traveling most when not doing so at all, when sitting at home comfortably and reflecting on the journey that has been taken.

The Travel Writer doesn't get up one morning and throw a dart at a map of the world, a map that is just lying on the floor at her feet, and decide to journey to the place exactly where the dart lands. Not so at all. These journeys that the Travel Writer makes begin with a broken heart sometimes, a tender heart fractured, its sweet matter bejeweled with the sharp slivers of a special pain. Or these journeys that the Travel Writer makes begin in curiosity but not of the

---

2005. Introduction to *The Best American Travel Writing, 2005*, ed. Jamaica Kincaid. Boston: Houghton Mifflin.

Joseph Dalton Hooker kind (Imperial Acts of Conquests) or of the Lewis and Clark kind (Imperial Acts of Conquests) or of the William Wells Brown kind (an African American slave who freed himself and then traveled in Europe and wrote about it). No, not that kind of curiosity but another kind, a curiosity that comes from a supreme contentment, comfort, and satisfaction with your place in the world and this benevolent situation, so perfect and so just, it should be universally distributed, it should be endemic to individual human existence, and would lead an unexpected anyone to go somewhere and write about it. In this case, everyone who goes anywhere and notices her surroundings and finds them of interest will be a Travel Writer.

This person I have been describing, the Travel Writer, almost certainly is myself. And also this person I have been describing reflects the writers of these essays in this anthology. Especially because I have selected these essays, I see the writers and their motives in much the same way I see my own. I will not be disturbed when they object, I will only continue to see them in this way.

At the beginning of the travel narrative is much confusion, for even though when sitting down to write, to give an account of what has recently transpired, the outcome is known, has been a success; the Travel Writer must begin at the beginning. The beginning is a cauldron of anxiety (the passport is lost, the visa might be denied, the funds to finance the journey are late in coming, a child comes down with a childhood disease). Things all work out, she is on the boat or the airplane or the train. Or he is in the restaurant, eating something that is delicious (that would be William Least Heat-Moon?), but even so there is no respite. For the traveler (who will eventually become the Travel Writer) is in a state of displacement, not in the here of the familiar (home), not in the there of destination (a place that has been made familiar by imagining being in it in the first place). That time between the here that is truly familiar and the here that has come through imagining, and therefore forcibly made familiar, is dangerous, for the possibility of loss of every kind is so real. Yet the Travel Writer, travel narrator, will persist. Nothing can stop her, only death, the unexpected failure of the human body, the airplane falls out of the sky, the ship sinks, the train bolts from its rails and falls headlong into the deepest part of the river. She eventually arrives at her destination; she begins to collect the experience that will constitute the work of the Travel Writer. She gathers herself up, a vulnerable bundle of a human being, a mass of nerves, and she begins.

The first time I traveled anywhere, I was not yet a writer, but I can now see that I must have been in the process of becoming one. I was nine years old and had been the only child in my family until then, when, suddenly it seemed to me, my first brother was born. My mother no longer paid any attention to me; she seemed to care only about my new brother. One day, I was asked to hold him and he fell out of my arms. My mother said that I had dropped him, and as a punishment, she sent me off to live with her sister and her parents, all of whom she hated. They lived in Dominica, an island, one night's distance by steamer boat away. The boat I sailed on was called *M. V. Rippon*, and it traveled up and down the British Caribbean with a cargo of people, goods, and letters. No one I knew personally had ever sailed on it, but it often brought to our home angry exchanges of letters from my mother's family. And sometimes it also brought to us packages of cocoa, cured coffee beans, castor oil, unusually large grapefruits, almonds, and dasheen, all of these things my mother's family grew on their plantation. The angry letters and the produce came from the same place and from the same people.

It was to this place and these people that my mother sent me as a punishment for dropping my new and first brother on his head. The *M. V. Rippon*, which had until then been so mysterious, a great big, black hulk, with a band of deep red running all around its upper part, appearing every two weeks, resting in a deep part offshore from Rat Island for a day or two and then disappearing for another two weeks, soon became so well known to me that I have never forgotten it. My mother took me on board, abandoned me in a cabin that I was to share with another passenger, a woman she and I did not know, and then left. Even before the *Rippon* set sail my stomach began to heave. It never stopped; my stomach heaved all night. My nine-year-old self thought I would die, of course, but I didn't. After eternity (and I did not experience this as an eternity; I experienced it as the thing itself, Eternity), it was morning and I looked out through a porthole and saw a massive green height in front of me. It was Dominica. Slowly the *Rippon* pulled into port. It was raining, and it was raining as if it had been doing so for a long time and planned to continue doing so for even longer than that. All the passengers got off the boat. I could not. There was no one to greet me. In my nine years I had never known this feeling, a feeling with which I am now, at fifty-six, quite familiar: displacement, the feeling that I had lost my memory because what I could remember had no meaning right then; I could not apply it to anything in front of me; I did not know who I was. I remembered that I was my mother's daughter, but between that and the place I was then, the jetty in Roseau, Dominica, that person had been lost or modified or transformed, and there was nothing and no one on the jetty in Roseau, Dominica, to help me be myself again, the daughter of my mother.

I believe it was the captain of the *Rippon*, or someone like that, someone in charge of things, who got a car with a driver to take me to the village of Mahaut, which was where my mother grew up and where her family still lived. But the voyage from the jetty in Roseau to the village of Mahaut was as difficult a journey in its way as had been the voyage from Antigua to Dominica. This new landscape of an everlasting green, broken up into lighter green and darker green, was not even in my imagination. I had never read a description of it. Perhaps I had read about it and thought it not believable. Perhaps my mother had told me about it, for she told me so many things about her childhood and this place in which she grew up, but such a detail as this, the way the land lay, the look of things, did not make an impression, not a lasting, memorable one. In any case, I had thought that mountains were something in my geography book, not something in real life. I had thought that constant rainfall was something in a chapter of unusual natural occurrences, not something everyday. My mother did not tell me that in her growing up, it rained nine months of the entire year. It explained much about her, but I could not have put it into words then; I didn't know her really then. And then the roads were winding but in a dangerous way. They wound around the sides of the mountain, sharply. On one side of the road was the side of the mountain, which went up to a height that I did not know existed, for Antigua is a flat island with some hills here and there; on the other side of the road was always a precipice, a sharp deep drop to the bottom. My aunt, my mother's sister, was made lame while riding a bicycle on one of these roads, and she went around a sharp turn incorrectly and fell into one of these precipices on the road between Roseau and Mahaut when she was young. I arrived at the house, the home where my mother grew up. Her sister had not been opening her letters for a while now (this is a tradition that I have kept up, not opening letters from people with whom I am having a quarrel) and so had no idea that my mother had decided to send me to live with her family. She had never seen me in real life; she only knew of me through my mother's letters. I almost attended her wedding, but then my family couldn't afford to send me to it. She seemed glad to see me. But I didn't like her, my aunt, for she didn't like my mother. I immediately began to plan to leave. My stay with them, my mother's family, was open-ended. I think it was meant to last until I grew up, and no longer wanted to see my little brother dead.

By the time I got to Mahaut, I had forgotten that I wanted him dead. I only wanted to go home to my mother.

I went to school in Mahaut. I learned how to walk in the rain. In Antigua, it rained so infrequently that when such a thing did happen, rain, the streets became empty of people. It was as if we didn't know how to exist normally with such a thing as rain. People would say, I wanted to do such and such a thing, but I couldn't because it was raining, and such a statement was always met with incredible sympathy and understanding. We did nothing, when it was raining, in Antigua. In Dominica, the rain falling was the same as the sun shining; it was all met with indifference. I learned how to use a cutlass. I learned the meaning of the word *homesickness*. At the end of each day, when the sun was about to drop suddenly into the depths beneath the horizon and the onset of the blackest of nights would dramatically come on, I did not think I would lose my mind; I did not think I would die. I thought I would live in this way, in this blackness, this place, where in the dark everything lost its shape even when you touched it and could run your hands over its contours, forever, that night would never end.

From the beginning, I began to think of ways to get out of this place. But I could not find a solution. There was nothing wrong. My mother's father was of no interest to me, but my mother's mother was very special. She quarreled with the rest of her family and so never had anything to do with them. She cooked her own food and ate it all by herself. After a while, I liked her so much that I was allowed to be with her all the time. I would squat with her over a fire as she roasted coffee beans and then ground them and then made us little cups of coffee that had a small mound of sugar at the bottom of the cup. I liked her green figs with flying fish cooked in coconut milk better than I liked my mother's. She and I even slept in the same bed. That was the wonderful part. Still, I wanted to go home; I wanted to go back to my mother.

I wrote to my mother the usual sorts of letters: How are you? I am well. I miss you very much. But in my school notebook, the one that had a picture of the Queen of England and her husband on the cover, I wrote another kind of letter, and these had some very harsh and untrue things about my daily life as I lived it with my mother's family. In that notebook, I wrote that my aunt hated me and often beat me harshly. I wrote that she sent me to bed without my dinner. I wrote that she did not allow me to bathe properly, leaving my private parts unclean, and that my unwashed body smelled in a way that made my classmates avoid me. I wrote those things over and over again in that notebook, but after I wrote them down, I would tear out the page from the book, fold it up, and hide it under a large stone outside near the hedge of periwinkle that grew in the garden. I did not mean for these letters to be found; I did not mean that anyone else should read them. All the same—inevitably, no doubt—my aunt found them and after she read them became ablaze with anger, and my mother and I became one to her, a despicable duo to be banished forever from her presence, and she placed me on the *M. V. Rippon* the next time it was due back in Dominica to make a voyage to Antigua.

No detail of my return to Antigua is clear to me now; I only wanted to arrive there. I did, of course, and found my mother even more lost to me than before. She had given birth to another son, my second brother, and she loved me even less, as she loved my brothers even more. It was at eleven years of age that I began to wish for the journey out that led to my life now. I did not know then that it would be possible; I most certainly did not know of the sharp turns and deep precipices that existed and continue to exist to this day.

And what of the essays here? Every one of them reminds me of two of the many sentiments attached to the travel narrative: curiosity and displacement. None of them are about a night's stay in a nice hotel anywhere; none of them chronicle a day at a beach. They were not chosen to say something about the state of American travel writing; they were chosen because I simply liked them. And I chose these travel narratives: John McPhee's "Tight-Assed River," Ian Frazier's "Route 3," Jim Harrison's "A Really Big Lunch," Thomas Keneally's "Romancing the Abyss," Bucky McMahon's "Adrift," Robert Young Pelton's "Into the Land of bin Laden," Tom Ireland's "My Thai Girlfriends," Peter Hessler's "Kindergarten," Kira Salak's "The Vision Seekers," Timothy Bascom's "A Vocabulary for My Senses," Torn Bissell's "War Wounds," Charles Martin Kearney's "Maps and Dreaming," Seth Stevenson's "Trying Really Hard to Like India," William E. Blundell's "My Florida," and Pam Houston's "The Vertigo Girls Do the East Tonto Trail," and the rest of the entire table of contents, for they all hold an idea that is so central to my own understanding of the world I have inherited. These essays stimulate my curiosity; they underline my sense of my displacement.

How I like that, the feeling of being out of place. And again, what of the essays here? Reading John McPhee's "Tight-Assed River" and Ian Frazier's "Route 3" again and again, for the pleasure of the writing itself, and this pleasure is a sort of journey too. For as I read these two essays, I kept saying to myself, how did he do that, in wonder at the beauty of the sentences. And then there is the deliciously funny "Trying Really Hard to Like India" by Seth Stevenson and the truly hilarious "The Vision Seekers" by Kira Salak. I will stop here.

But before I do, here is this: Not so long ago, I was in Nepal, walking about in the foothills around Makalu and Kanchenjunga, collecting seeds for my flower garden. The journey was full of the usual difficulties: avoiding being killed by Maoist guerrillas, avoiding being killed by the constantly shifting landscape. I was not killed by anything, and I also collected the seeds of many different plant specimens. While there, I liked being in that place, and I liked what I was doing. I returned home and to this day, the memory of it pleases me.

Read these essays, close the book, sit back, and just wait, but you won't have to wait for too long.

Formal Meets Folly

THE WORDS *DESIGN* AND *ARCHITECTURE* are not comfortably anchored together in the garden; for in the end a garden is made, not designed or built; a garden is always made. But then something that is made has a maker and that word, *maker*, is fraught with contradictions: The lowliest among us make things for us (the bed, the food we eat), the highest among us (a divine being) makes us. No wonder, then, that when a garden, in all its glory, is brought into being, its creator (another fraught word) dallies with the words *designer* and *architect*. These words, *design* (designer) and *architecture* (architect), raise the individual involved in the garden above the servant and at the same time protect him or her from being omniscient.

I was thinking all this while looking at a garden on the eastern coast of Florida, designed (as he would prefer) and made (as I see it) by Mario Nievera for Theodore and Ruth Baum. On a day that any of us would deem ideal (there was not a cloud in the sky, and its blueness had a benign sovereignty), he showed it to me.

2005, Nov. "Formal Meets Folly." *Architectural Digest*. Vol. 62, iss. 11: 114–21.

It is a spectacular garden, situated on the edge of an isthmus, that looks out toward a lagoon overgrown with mangrove, seaside grape, and palm trees. It begins with some severity—a low, severely clipped hedge of box. And this traditional arrangement never fails to please, which is why it is so often imitated, but in this garden, the box hedge is used as a basic ingredient. For in front of it is an equally severely clipped hedge of *Hibiscus rosa-sinensis* "White Wing," whose pure white petals and red-eye center are dazzling against the clipped green box. A sweet-smelling jasmine vine has been made to form a set of squares, making eighteen "windows," against a wall. At the feet of columns of climbing *Clerodendron* are fat-stemmed and blooming fists of *Begonia odorata* "Alba."

Walking into the heart of the garden itself (where a swimming pool, its sides and bottom dark-plastered, looks more like a reflecting pool), having passed four stout *Calophyllum*, that wonderful tropical evergreen, used as accents, is to find *Dombeya* "Seminole Pink," with its hydrangea-like flowers, dispersed here and there, sparingly and so, therefore, unforgettable. The long canes of some bougainvillea have been trained to rush up and cover columns that are the support of a pergola; the pergola itself serves as a line of demarcation, for beyond it is a more formal arrangement, and beyond this formal arrangement is the view of the lagoon.

Here the contrast between the garden, as we make it, and garden, as natural circumstances will it, is dazzling and really worthy to contemplate: in the borders are the tender shrub ruellia and the hybrid tea, *Rosa* "Cary Grant," grown in clay pots that have been suppressed in the ground. The sweet-smelling and white flowering gardenias prosper near a parterre made of hardy boxwood. In the near distance is the lagoon, shallow water hugging sand barriers, on which are growing all the things that love such an environment, and doing so with abandon. A natural force has made the lagoon. A beautiful garden in Palm Beach, Florida, was made by Mario Nievera.

Foreword to Ian Frazier's *Gone to New York*

TO WRITE AN INTRODUCTION to a collection of essays written by my dearest friend in all the still-sphere-shaped world, I have to write about our youth and what he was like when I first met him, as he was just arriving in New York and hired by *The New Yorker* as a Talk writer.

In the spring of 1973, I met Sandy outside a movie theater on Eighth Avenue where the movie *Thomasine & Bushrod* was being shown for the first time to a general audience. George W. S. Trow, then an established writer for *The New Yorker*, introduced us. George was the most fascinating person we had ever met. He knew all sorts of wonderful things about New York and all sorts of people, some of whom were not so wonderful. We, Sandy and I, became George's younger siblings almost immediately. He thought we were pretty smart but ignorant, and he was always doing his best to educate and civilize us. He introduced me to Jacqueline Onassis and he introduced Sandy to Mrs. Vreeland. We didn't like

---

2006. Foreword to *Gone to New York: Adventures in the City*, by Ian Frazier. New York: Picador. ix–xvii.

either of them. He made us read Proust. Sandy read all six volumes, I stopped where I always stop: at volume three. He took Sandy to a store that sold good-quality men's clothing and bought him a beige poplin summer suit. Once, when Sandy was feeling gloomy, George jokingly asked him if he wanted to go to Payne Whitney and have a soothing entrée. Sandy, thinking Payne Whitney was a restaurant, said yes. George said, "Oh dear." George started an anti-rudeness campaign that came to an end when one day, on the subway, after he corrected someone's behavior, he got punched in the eye.

That afternoon outside the theater showing *Thomasine & Bushrod* where I first met Sandy, he was wearing a coat made of green cloth. The coat looked like something a spy would wear, an American spy, or something a soldier would wear, an American soldier. He wore the coat all the time. To him it symbolized, and that is the correct word, his Ohio-ness. Oh, Ohio, Ohio, Ohio. That's all we ever heard about, that's all he ever talked about. Now, the state of Ohio occupies a very large area, and I did know that at the time, but in those first years when I knew Sandy Frazier, not Ian Frazier but Sandy Frazier, I came to really believe that Ohio was made up of a little bit of some unnameable area; Cleveland, which was bigger but not by too much than the unnameable area; and then, overwhelmingly, Hudson, the place where Sandy was born and spent his childhood and left when he went east to Harvard and which he returned to often when he was a young writer at *The New Yorker*.

I soon came to believe that anything claiming to be authentically American originated from Ohio and, in particular, Hudson, Ohio. The Rosenthals, parents of Sandy's girlfriend, Suzy. The Bartlows, parents of his best friend Ken. The Erskines, parents of his best friend Don. Particularly authentic were Mrs. Erskine's garden tips, which consisted mainly of getting Don and Sandy to weed her garden, and Mrs. Erskine listening to the opera broadcast on the radio every Saturday afternoon. His household cat, which he would terrify by crawling around the floor on his hands and knees while dressed in his mother's fur coat. His family's housekeeper, whom he insulted because he suspected she liked his brother best. (She did.) His parents were the most authentic parents in America, especially his mother, whom he adored and who adored him. But when he wrote a piece called "Dating Your Mom," a way of enshrining his adoration, while at the same time making fun of it, she was not pleased; he could tell, for she never mentioned it, she acted as if it had never happened. I loved his authentic family, made up of a brother, two sisters, and his mother and father. I loved them before I met them, particularly his mother. And my love for her turned out to be completely justified.

After she died and Sandy was going through her papers, he found a folder in which she kept everything I had published. Hard as he looked, he could find no such folder containing his own writing. To understand why this made us both laugh, it's important to know that he suffers from a serious case of sibling rivalry. From the earliest days of knowing Sandy, he has been my true, true brother, the only brother I have ever needed.

This authentic America that Sandy knew intimately because it emanated from Hudson, Ohio, because without Hudson, Ohio, authentic America could not exist, did not include the Southern states, the slave states. His father, David Frazier, once put some very close relatives (an aunt and uncle who were visiting from Alabama) out of his house because they used a derogatory word for African Americans in conversation in the living room. Once, George said there had been some good things about the institution of slavery as practiced in the American South before 1864 and this made Sandy so mad he walked all the way from midtown Manhattan up to the George Washington Bridge and hitchhiked to Hudson, Ohio.

The authentic America that Sandy knew (then) and knows (now) begins with Abraham Lincoln (excepting some small unpleasantness with the original Americans) and the right side of the Civil

War and the Emancipation and Lewis and Clark, whom he extracts from an earlier time and places in a more beautifully just America and also Crazy Horse and Sitting Bull and the vast, vast, vast openness of the West with its ancient history of unsettledness, settledness, and unsettledness again; and also fishing, fly-fishing to be exact; encounters with bears; an examination of life on a Rte., a major transportation artery, from which it is possible to return to Hudson, Ohio. The authentic America includes his immediate ancestors, Protestants all, seeking refuge in various American Christian sects as they tried to save themselves from their own certainties. How my dear friend and brother loves this act, a person, an individual, trying to save himself from their own convictions.

My friend Sandy's father was such a person. He was a chemist and worked for Standard Oil of Ohio, trying to make various forms of plastics from petroleum. He loved making plastics from petroleum. That was during the day. At night he read *The New Yorker* to his son, especially the writings of E. B. White. It was his father reading to him from *The New Yorker* that made Sandy want to leave Hudson, Ohio, and go to New York and become a writer. After he left Harvard, he applied for a job at *The New Yorker*. They offered him a job as a checker, that is, a person who would check the facts as they appeared in other writers' writing. Sandy refused it. *The New Yorker* then was a magical place: in whatever position you entered it, you were doomed to stay there. So if you entered *The New Yorker* as a checker, or as a writer, or as an editor, you were doomed to that role only. It was like life itself: no matter who you are in life, you are doomed to life itself. Not long after he rejected the position of checker, *The New Yorker* offered him a job as a Talk writer. It was right around then we met.

Sandy wore the green coat all the time. Other people wore clothes that were completely different. It was the disco era or sometime near it. No one we knew in New York did anything remotely serious, except for George's friend whose father had once been the mayor of New York, and there were some other people whom George knew who did serious things, or so George said, for he was always telling Sandy and me about the other serious people he knew. Many of the other people George knew we thought should be shot, though not shot dead, just shot in a Bugs Bunny sort of way, where they get up again. Sandy and I hated serious people. The exception was Mr. Shawn, the editor of *The New Yorker*. He was the only serious person we loved, and even better, he was the only serious person we took seriously. We took him so seriously that we often brushed him off. From time to time, Mr. Shawn would suggest ideas for Talk stories to Sandy and every time Sandy would say to him that his suggestions were terrible. Sandy would just say outright, over the telephone, in a note, or face-to-face with Mr. Shawn, that his idea was terrible. Mr. Shawn's ideas weren't terrible at all. How could they be? But we, Sandy and I, had decided, for reasons that we could not then articulate, never to agree to Mr. Shawn's suggestions. My own reasons for doing so are clear to me. Sandy's reasons for doing so reside for me with those obstructionist Protestants that he comes from and whom he has written about (see his book *Family*). How he liked defying then. He had convictions, I didn't know exactly what they were, but he felt compelled to save himself from them.

But that green cloth coat again, which made Sandy seem as if he were a spy or a lost agent of our government: it was an army surplus item. Sandy wore it and wore it, no matter what the season. One day, while he was wearing it, he came into my office at *The New Yorker* and said he had agreed to join the army or the navy or maybe it was the marines, I can't remember now, except that when he told me this, I said to him, Oh Sandy, you can't do that, you're too old. He said then, Yeah, you're right. It was quite complicated then to de-enlist but I didn't know that and he only told this to me not too long ago. There was a moment where we (George Trow and I, for the three of us were sometimes inseparable) thought he was a stranger from somewhere else. I came from Antigua, a small island in the West Indies, and George came from Connecticut, a small area of the original American enterprise, and dear Sandy from Hudson, Ohio, was a shock. It was because Sandy, while wearing the green cloth coat, which was authentically American (it too came from Hudson, Ohio), became sad that George suggested to him the possibility of the soothing entrée at the Payne Whitney psychiatric hospital, but at that time, because Sandy was authentically American, he was not so familiar with Payne Whitney and psychiatric hospitals.

The green cloth coat came to an end in this way: From time to time, as a joke and out of the blue, Sandy would say to George, "George, do you want a steak?" and George would say "Yes." This was a set piece. After a long set of back-and-forth humiliating one-upsmanship jokes between the two of them, Sandy would ask George if he wanted a steak and George would always answer that he did. One day, after George said yes, Sandy went down to the Jefferson Market, a fancy grocery store even then, and bought a very expensive steak, placed it unwrapped in the pocket of his green cloth coat, and presented it to George. That time, when he asked George, "Do you want a steak?" and George said yes, he took a piece of raw prime beef out of his green coat pocket and gave it to him. This all took place in George's office, an office he shared with Tony Hiss. I remember it because George, who was shocked by the actual appearance of the steak, did a good job of not showing how impressed he was by this whole brief gesture with its long preceding narrative; and I remember it because George gave me the steak and I took it to my little apartment which I rented on West Twenty-second Street, and cooked it according to a recipe in *Mastering the Art of French Cooking.* The steak made such a mess in the pocket of Sandy's green coat, he couldn't wear it anymore. I cannot remember what replaced it.

The authentic American hated English people. So did I. George wasn't an Anglophile, it was just that he liked aristocrats. The two of us now formed a camp: we couldn't understand how George liked Mrs. Vreeland, yet we loved George because he knew Mrs. Vreeland and a great many other people like her whom I personally wanted to place on a bonfire, but only if no one, no one on the face of the earth, could observe me. One day, when I was trying to read a biography of Lytton Strachey, written by another Englishman, Sandy was so outraged that instead of laughing at his antics I preferred to read this book, he tore it out of my hand and proceeded to read it himself. From this came a piece, a parody, a *New Yorker* casual titled "The Bloomsbury Group, Live at the Apollo." In this short, funny piece of writing, Sandy reduced two people who are a substantial part of modern consciousness, however you look at it (Virginia Woolf and Maynard Keynes), to desperate performers at the Apollo Theater, a venue for many black modern artists who were so beyond their time that there would never be a time for them. At that time in *The New Yorker*'s life, S. J. Perelman appeared in the magazine. Funny people wrote funny things and these funny things spilled over into the realm of literature. Yet when I saw that piece, knowing its origins as well as I did, I asked myself, How did he do that? And that thought has never stopped occurring to me; to this day, when I read something new that he has written, I think, How did he do that?

The collection begins with a couple of Talk pieces and ends with his memory of great Hudson, Ohio. But this end is really the beginning. It is from Hudson that he ventures forth into the wild lands of lower Manhattan, to live for a time or just to find a typewriter; to Brooklyn; to Queens; to invent a tool that will remove plastic bags from trees (his father did work in plastics), a tool so expensive that if he had not invented it he would not be able to own one. It is such a pleasure to read this collection of my dearest friend's work, and to see that it is meant to form an arc, an arc that has not yet begun its curve.

Captain's Farm

YEARS AGO Edward Lee Cave went to Connecticut to purchase some eighteenth-century furniture, the contents of an eighteenth-century farmhouse. When he got there, before going inside to look at his primary interest, he decided to buy the farmhouse itself and none of the furniture. The house came with a garden, an American country garden: herbaceous perennials, such as peonies and baptisia, and shrubs suitable for a New England climate—roses, lilacs, and laurels—and, of course, vegetables.

Cave until then had lived in New York City, but he grew up in the country, Virginia, in the Shenandoah Valley, and he was immediately reminded of this. "When I first saw the garden here," he says, "I thought of my youth. From the age of 12 I had my own garden, and I worked in it before school. My father had a victory garden, and my mother tended her flowers." From her, he says, he learned about the deep attention needed to make a garden seem as if there is nothing to it at all.

2006, June. "Captain's Farm." *Architectural Digest*. Vol. 63, iss. 6: 90–94.

All this rushed through him, he says, when he first saw Captain's Farm, for that is the name of his house and his garden, and he spent the first year looking out at the garden, just to get used to the way the land lay, the contours of it, the green empty space of the expansive lawns and the things that grew in the garden beds themselves.

It was lovely to begin with: There were wide swaths of lawn in which later he would plant thousands of daffodils. There were the roses, the peonies, and the old shrubs. These were all kept in the places he met them. But then after a year he began to expand. First he added patterned brick walks so that various parts of the garden became tied in with each other. Then he installed an extensive watering system; he says this was on advice from his banker.

He made new beds and filled them with the perennials he loves: geraniums, lilies, irises, poppies, veronica, dianthus, goat's beard, lady's-mantle, a garden that reaches a beautiful and high pitch of bloom and color around midsummer.

At the south side of the house, he made parterres of English box (and they are very sensitive to cold, so he builds them little jackets made of burlap to get them safely through a Connecticut winter), and he enclosed other beds with lavender. This part of the garden is formal and appropriately so, since it leads to some wonderful rooms inside.

On the other side of the house is a knoll, and this protects the house from some strong winter winds. He calls this area Spring Hill, for in spring it is abloom with primulas and early tulips.

The main project he undertook, he says, was enclosing his garden for privacy—that is, privacy from deer. There are plenty of those in Connecticut. Once he had put in a fence, he planted some good-size hemlocks, arborvitae, and birches, and he planted them in such abundance that they now seem to be the edge of a forest.

He carefully went through the apple trees on the property, culling some, and takes loving care of those that remain. Perhaps, for me anyway, the most beautiful aspect of the garden is the way he has various things climbing into them and spreading in their crowns: hydrangeas, roses, and clematis.

Just as I was leaving him and his garden, he said, almost mournfully, that he wished he had some things that would bloom in August. I immediately put on my gardening hat and went through a list of things I look forward to seeing blooming in my own garden come August. He listened to me patiently and then said, "Oh, but I am never here then." I laughed and left him, thinking to myself, Gardeners!

Foreword to Alexandre Dumas's *Georges*

GEORGES: Yes, it is a great joy to read this new translation of Alexandre Dumas's long-lost and forgotten novel, for it is fantastic, picturesque, almost believable, romantic, suspenseful, violent (as is to be expected when Africans, enslaved or not, are involved), sexy, naïve, and many more things besides.

And why do I think so? Here is an explanation: My mother, in an attempt to distract my young interest in her, taught me to read, and by the time I was three and a half years old, I could do so. This caused such a sensation among everyone, including and especially me. I then had very little to read: there was the tin of Ovaltine, the tin of butter from New Zealand, a book my mother owned which described the human body and the known tropical diseases that could destroy it, the King James version of the Bible. I read the writing on the tins over and over, each time as if they were new, each time as if I had never read them before; I read the book on the body and the tropical diseases that could kill it over and over be-

2007. Foreword to *Georges*, by Alexandre Dumas. New York: Modern Library. xi–xiii.

cause it was illustrated and the illustrations were described and the descriptions were fabulous, and better still, not understood by me; I read the King James version of the Bible because it was all of the above as it was also many things apart from all of the above. I soon came to think of reading as "sweet" and by that I was not referring to any relationship to the five senses (I knew then there were five of them), I was thinking of something that did include them but also something I had no real way of putting into words. At that time I could read but I was also learning to read; at that time the sensation that is reading became known to me.

Georges would have been so welcome to me then, for I would have approached it with complete freshness (reading was new, and the novel before me, *Georges*, was not imaginable; I was innocent of the intricate workings of the world in which I lived), taking it as it presented itself, a romance and all that comes with romance; a tale of adventure and all that comes with that; a narrative of the virtues and the virtuous explicated and exalted and then made shoddy and questionable and full of suspicion and then renounced and abandoned.

The world of *Georges* is an island, and that island is Eden before it was despoiled by European conquests and afterward the only thing left of it was, well, the vegetation, especially the vegetation. The landscape of Eden is the perfect landscape for this kind of situation: it offers the best sunsets against which murderous grudges take a short rest; the unprecedented hurricane will interrupt the outcome of the most successfully planned revolt; the trees are always overbearing in fruit and the enslaved escapee may be lost among their thick trunks but will never die of hunger; that thing called Time is not the same thing that is familiar through a wristwatch. Such is the physical world of *Georges*. Like Eden, too, this island is a source of contests of will, only not God and Lucifer, just England or France.

Georges himself (the hero, all of this novel comes from him, is about him) is not Adam (in any case Adam is not a hero of that story), he is not an original man, he is not the first of his kind, but he has the vanity to think himself so. As a child, he suffered an insult and this insult is new, unlike any insult visited on any child before; all life from then on is experienced and interpreted through this initial childhood event. Georges is not a slave but he is descended from slaves; Georges is not white but he could pass for white; Georges is not an entirely free man (he is partly descended from the enslaved) but his manners in every way are so correct that really free men (European) cede him a place in their presence and even their society.

In the world in which I was growing up, in St. John's, Antigua, the landscape of *Georges* was an everyday reality; the people inhabiting that landscape were familiar but not in real time; they were from yesterday, but as if yesterday were one hundred years ago before today.

This is, for me, the glory of *Georges*: I am reminded of an early pleasure and it so vividly portrays a long-ago recent past. The two are intertwined to such an extent that they are one: early, long ago, recent, past! It was been six hundred years now since Christopher Columbus left the coast of Spain and set off on a journey to find a new world, or was it to prove that the world was round, or was it to prove that people everywhere found a confounding and unrewarding curiosity in other people and places far removed from anything they knew. Within Dumas himself all of these things were true: he was a French man, and he was descended from Africans and Europeans, and he was a writer.

Writers need someone to read them, no matter what age they are writing in. More important, readers, budding or otherwise, need something to read. *Georges* was written over one hundred years before I was born and later learned to read. I am reading it now, and at my age it should be an old story, but an old story becomes a classic because it manages to bring up something new, something that it seems you have never heard of before.

Dances with Daffodils

I wandered lonely as a cloud
That floats on high o'er vales and hills,
When all at once I saw a crowd,
A host, of golden daffodils;
Beside the lake, beneath the trees,
Fluttering and dancing in the breeze . . .

Ten thousand saw I at a glance,
Tossing their heads in sprightly dance . . .
—William Wordsworth

WHEN I WAS A CHILD, a long time ago, I was forced to memorize this poem in its entirety, written by the British poet William Wordsworth. I had to memorize many things written by British people, since the place I was born and grew up in was owned by the British, but for a reason not known to me then, of all the things I had to memorize, I took an ill feeling to this piece of literature. And why should that have been so? Let me show you a picture of the little black-skinned girl, with hair strands curlier than wool, an imagination too vivid for the

2007, Apr. "Dances with Daffodils." *Architectural Digest*. Vol. 64, iss. 4: 78–82.

world into which I was born, my mind (whatever that meant and means) shining new and good, certainly good enough to know that there were things it was not allowed to know. The daffodil, for one: what was a daffodil, I wanted to know, since such a thing did not grow in the tropics.

In my child's mind's eye, the poem and its contents (though not its author) and the people through whom it came were repulsive. I had no rational or just way of arranging and separating the people who created the things to memorize from the people who made me memorize wonderful things, whether they were about daffodils, heaven and hell, or just the River Thames. And so for me, "I Wandered Lonely As a Cloud" became not an individual vision coolly astonishing the mind's eye but the tyrannical order of a people, the British people, in my child's life.

And yet, given all of that, what has the daffodil become to me, for memory is not set, no matter how we wish it to be so, and the past will intrude on the present new and fresh. I now live in a climate that has four seasons. When I was a child and memorizing the British literary canon, I lived in a climate of eternal summer, and the reality that, in England, four different climates existed filled me with sadness, succeeded by longing and, inevitably, curiosity.

Last fall I planted, without qualms, 2,000 daffodil bulbs, "Rijnveld's Early Sensation," in my lawn. This cultivar came on the market in the 1940s, and it is the only one I can find in any catalogue that brings to my mind that host that danced in the breeze. For 20 years now I have lived in Vermont, a state that falls in a climate suitable for this genus. For many of those 20 years I have gone back and forth with the daffodil: I love it, I do not love it. But I live in this place where there is true spring, a place where the four seasons repeat themselves one after the other in the usual order and the sight of the daffodil is a true joy. In any case, I view spring itself as such pleasure that I have come to believe that the earth and its workings are meant to result in this season, spring.

The 2,000 daffodils have joined 3,500. That is a little more than half of 10,000, but my aim is not Wordsworth's number, my aim is to cover my entire lawn and beyond that every nook and cranny that will receive some sun. I want to walk out into my yard, unable to move at will because my feet are snarled in the graceful long green stems supporting bent yellow flowering heads of daffodils. I will not have to come upon them suddenly; I have planted them myself, dug (with some help from a man named Paul) the 200 holes myself, placing 10 in each hole, making sure the holes are lined up just so for a visual show.

Somewhere I read that Wordsworth worried about misreadings of his poem. It can't be that he worried about the uses to which his countrymen would employ the product of his genius (they were busy trading slaves, not educating them). I believe it possible, though, that with his sensibility, so finely tuned to the unknown in the human realm, so finely tuned to our universal confusions and misunderstandings, he was, when worrying about misreadings, thinking of someone like me. There is no record as far as I can tell of Wordsworth and his sister, Dorothy, frantically planting daffodils anywhere hoping to be in touch again with that moment when they came upon them on their walk in the woods.

Her Infinite Variety

HERE IS A LIST, a long one, of flowers I have detested and then come to love so much, I could not live without them: marigolds, Asiatic lilies of every hue, even white ones; *Hibiscus syriacus* (rose of Sharon), *Salvia splendens*, cultivars of *Astilbe*, double-flowered hollyhocks, impatiens (excepting the Himalayan ones), celosias, cosmos, fuchsias, zinnias, spiraeas, weigelas, all *Berberis*, woody potentillas, hostas—excepting the British gardener Eric Smith's small blue-leaved hybrids—all daylilies except for the almost ancient "Mrs. Woodbridge," gaillardias, rudbeckias, *Alchemilla mollis*, daffodils, red and yellow triumph tulips, all of the penstemons, yellow flowers altogether and in general. And for a list of flowers I have loved without reservation and forever, see above and then some, for that list is longer than I am now able to remember.

I am constantly told that the garden is a place where the troubling thoughts of the world are suspended and then eventually erased, forgotten; that the garden is the sole place in the world where feelings of uncontested contentment can be realized; that the garden is the sole place in all of eternity to find perfection in every way imaginable. Very good, but why do I not find this to be true? I love the garden; I must, for I spend much of my time thinking of it, and this is for me a great pleasure: I often avoid life-sustaining, necessary efforts just so I can walk around in it and plot how to rob Peter to pay Paul, Peter being my children's well-being, Paul being the garden. And so there is the garden, a place I love very much—not as a refuge from all that is troubling and confounding about that general thing called life, but because all that is troubling about it, all that is confounding about it, is the source for me of multiple pleasures.

And what exactly am I thinking of? Here is what happened one afternoon in the middle of the ideal time to transplant things in the flower garden (that would be spring or autumn, but in this exact case, it was autumn): For years and years I had cultivated some peonies, "Mrs. Franklin D. Roosevelt," "Karl Rosenfield," "Festiva Maxima," and many others, all favorites, all much loved, of course, in a border that ran in front of the vegetable garden. It made that area look luxurious, with its extravagant blooms, huge goblets of petals, in hues that would be perfect for drawing room curtains or skirts worn solely when dancing. The vegetable garden had food growing in it, beautiful too, the pale blue or white star-shaped flowers on the potatoes, for instance, or the big, deep cut leaves and then fat flower buds of the artichokes.

For a long time, as I passed through one and entered the other (and then reversed course), I knew this arrangement of favorite flowers and favorite vegetables, aligned with each other in this particular way, to be completely perfect; two of my senses in a state of the sublime. And then one afternoon, in the middle of the transplanting season, I looked at the bed of peonies, their leaves blackened with age and lying low on the ground, and I thought how unjust it was that they only got to be seen on the way to the vegetable garden, and when they are in bloom, I suddenly remembered, I only go into the vegetable garden to plant things or to reap salad and cut herbs.

I promptly set about changing things. In the garden beds that offer me immediate enjoyment, the ones I could see just looking out any window of my house, there was a bed of hellebores of all kinds, and they all bloomed together, whatever kind they were, winter blooming, spring blooming, and they are shy in presentation, a roselike cluster of petals in delicate shades of green, white, pink, maroon, emerging cautiously out of the very earth; a bed of *Hibiscus moscheutos*, red and pink, in a glorious and successful struggle to bloom, as if blooming was all a plant should be, and in a hibiscus of any kind, blooms are all there is; a bed choked full of irises and aconitums I had collected in China, and amsonia and other little bits of things, scraps of my likes that I had separated from my dislikes; and then finally a bed that had a background of *Berberis* "Rose Glow" and in front of that a rose-pink persicaria that I had seen growing in a spectacular way in Daniel J. Hinkley's garden. This last entry is an example of the most lethal of the deadly sins, envy, for when I saw it in Dan's garden I didn't only admire it, I desired it and coveted it, wanting to have it instantly growing in its pink-lighted-candelabrum-glowing glory just outside in the garden bed I see as I sit down to eat something at the table.

The hellebores I have always loved and still love even now as I write this, and, as I write this, I cannot believe they will fall out of my highest favor. But as for the rest—the persicaria, hibiscus, aconitum, amsonia, sego lily, burnet, *Peucedanum*, inula, and so on and so on!—well, those all had to go! And so they did, not out of the garden completely, just to another area where I won't see them when I am looking out a window facing south in my house. I placed them where the peonies used to be. On my way to the vegetable garden, I will no longer see peonies, I will see all these other plants that at some time or other had a monopoly on my devotion, on my affection and my idea of all that is right in the world as I experience it in my creation of the vegetable kingdom. Yes, the gardener is a tyrant, and the baseness of this state to which she is confined cannot be disguised by any kind of ornamentation, verbal or vegetable. At this point, as far as I can see, tyranny in this guise is the only kind of tyranny to be accepted.

The Estrangement

THREE YEARS BEFORE my mother died, I decided not to speak to her again. And why? During a conversation over the telephone, she had once again let me know that my accomplishments—becoming a responsible and independent woman—did not amount to very much, that the life I lived was nothing more than a silly show, that she truly wished me dead. I didn't disagree. I didn't tell her that it would be just about the best thing in the world not to hear this from her.

And so, after that conversation, I never spoke to her, said a word to her of any kind, and then she died, and her death was a shock to me, not because I would miss her presence and long for it but because I could not believe that such a presence could ever be stilled.

For many years and many a time, her children, of which I was the only female, wondered what would happen to her, as we wondered what would happen to us; because she seemed to us not a mother at all but a God, not a Goddess but a God.

How to explain in this brief space what I mean? When we were

2009, Feb. "The Estrangement." *Harper's Magazine*: 24–26.

children and in need of a mother's love and care, there was no better mother to provide such an ideal entity. When we were adolescents, and embracing with adolescent certainty our various incarnations, she could see through the thinness of our efforts, she could see through the emptiness of our aspirations; when we fell apart, there she was, bringing us dinner in jail or in a hospital ward, cold compresses for our temples, or just standing above us as we lay flat on our backs in bed. That sort of mother is God.

I am the oldest, by nine, eleven, and thirteen years, of four children. My three brothers and I share only our mother; they have the same father, I have a different one. I knew their father very well, better than they did, but I did not know my own. (When I was seven months in her womb, my mother quarreled with the man with whom she had conceived me and then ran away with the money he had been saving up to establish a little business for himself. He never forgave her.) I didn't mind not knowing my real father because in the place I am from, Antigua, when people love you, your blood relationship to them is not necessarily the most important component. My mother's husband, the father of my brothers, loved me, and his love took on the shape of a father's love: he told me about himself when he was a boy and the things he loved to do and the ways in which his life changed for better and worse, giving me some idea about how he came to be himself, my father, the father of my brothers, the person married to my mother.

She was a very nice person, apparently; that is what everybody said about her at her funeral. There were descriptions of her good and selfless deeds, kindnesses, generosity, testaments of her love expressed in humor. We, her children, looked at one another in wonder then, for such a person as described was not at all known to us. The person we knew, our Mother, said horrible things to us more often than not.

The youngest of my three brothers died of AIDS when he was thirty-three years of age. In the years he spent actively dying, our mother tended to him with the greatest tenderness, a tenderness that was absent all the time before he was dying. Before he got sick, before he became afflicted with that disease, his mother, my mother too, quarreled with him and disparaged him. This was enabled by the fact that he did not know how to go off somewhere and make a home of any kind for himself. Yes, he had been unable to move out into the world, away from this woman, his mother, and become the sole possessor of his own destiny, with all the loss and gain that this implies.

The two remaining brothers and I buried her right next to him, and we were not sure we should have done that: for we didn't know then, and still don't know even now, if he wanted to spend eternity lying beside her, since we were sure we would rather be dead than spend eternity lying next to her.

Is this clear? It is to me right now as I write it: I would rather be dead than spend eternity with our mother! And do I really mean that when I say it? Yes, I really mean just that: after being my mother's daughter, I would rather be dead than spend eternity with her.

By the time my mother died, I was not only one of her four children, I had become the mother of two children: a girl and then a boy. This was bliss, my two children in love with me, and I with them. Nothing has gone wrong, as far as I can see, but tears have been shed over my not being completely enthusiastic about going to a final basketball game in a snowstorm, or my saying something I should have kept in my mind's mouth. A particularly unforgivable act in my children's eyes is a book's dedication I made to them; it read: "With blind, instinctive, and confused love to Annie and Harold, who from time to time are furiously certain that the only thing standing between them and a perfect union with their mother is the garden, and from time to time, they are correct."

I wrote this with a feeling of overbrimming love for them, my children. I was not thinking of my own mother directly, not thinking of her at all consciously at that exact time, but then again, I am always thinking of my mother; I believe every action of a certain kind that I make is completely influenced by her, completely infused with her realness, her existence in my life.

I am now middle-aged (fifty-nine years of age); I not only hope to live for a very long time after this, I will be angry in eternity if this turns out not to be the case. And so in eternity will my children want to be with me? And in eternity will I, their mother, want to be with them?

In regard to my children, eternity is right now, and I always want to be with them. In regard to my mother, my progenitor, eternity is beyond now, and is that not forever? I will not speak to her again in person, of that I am certain, but I am not sure that I will never speak to her again. For in eternity is she in me, and are even my children speaking to her? I do not know, I do not know.

Lack, Part Two

I LIVED IN AN EDEN made up of my mother's love for me until I was nine years of age and then was cast out of it by a transgression not of my own making (she became the mother of three other children, small boys, and had to take care of them). So true, so true, but that is the poetic part. Other people who can read between the lines often point out to me that at the same time I have been describing a romance, I was also giving an account of poverty. For instance, I have described my love of reading and will point out that I loved to read so much I would read in the dark, the dark being literal, no light, because the light in which I lived was provided mostly by the sun and when the sun set we lit lamps fueled by kerosene and my parents could not afford kerosene and so the lamp was kept lighted for no more than two hours after the sun fell below a horizon that coincided with another island I could see in the distance. Not only did I think this world good, I thought it fixed and me in it.

Here was that fixed world: The sun went down (and that was

2009. May 31. "Lack, Part Two." *Harper's Magazine*: 37–38.

just the way we talked of it) at about six o'clock and darkness fell over our world and so, therefore, our world in which we could move around freely ended. The sun came up twelve hours later, more or less, and the world began, again. That was one fixed point but here is another: water. We were surrounded by a sea and an ocean but potable water was scarce most of the time (drought) and could only be gotten through a common or public tap that was available to all the people who lived in my neighborhood (Ovals, it was called). No more than three people I knew had tap-water pipes that entered their private homes, and it was a deep longing of everybody I knew (unspoken) to have water, running freely, at your heart's desire and command. And so those were the fixed points of my young life and world: light and water; I had them in abundance (the sun always shining, the sea and the ocean a mere stone's throw away), but they were so useless, it amounted to a scarcity.

I was never in want of food then; in fact, I ate really good, fresh food. We ate fish for supper most nights (it was very cheap and plentiful) and fresh vegetables and delicious fruits that my mother bought daily from the market (we did not have a refrigerator). But I hated that kind of food. What I really wanted to eat was food that came inside a tin. I had once seen an advertisement in a magazine for Heinz Baked Beans, and the sight of those red beans in an orange-colored sauce, mounded up in a nice heap with an enormous piece of pork on top, was so appealing to me, for weeks I almost couldn't eat anything else. Finally, that poor woman (she would be my mother) grew so worried about me that she gathered up her pennies and bought me a small tin of the Heinz beans. Will I ever get over the deep disappointment I felt when the can of beans was opened before me and they looked nothing like the advertisement that made me love them and there was not even a sliver of pork on top of them or anywhere else? No!

I walked everywhere and cannot remember being in a motorcar before I was seven years of age. I took a full bath every morning and a sponge bath every night before I went to bed. I had whooping cough and almost died from it; I had typhoid fever and almost died from it; I had measles, chicken pox, but not the mumps (which I very much wanted because all my friends had it and the remedy for it was roasted sweet potatoes tied to your swollen jaw; I can say with certainty: roasted sweet potatoes are especially tasty after they have served that purpose). I had nice dresses, not too many, but they were always clean.

My childhood was a period of time that lasted until I was sixteen years of age and I left all that behind me and came to America, where I prospered in mind and material things. At this point in my life, I can imagine, really, really, that I have lost all my earthly possessions: my nice house in a little New England village, my well-made and expensive clothes, my car, and I am stricken with an easily cured disease but I can't afford to see a doctor. Such a calamity would plunge me deeper into my own mental depression, a state of existence I like, except when it is overwhelming.

This calamity calls for a simple life: eating true food that has been grown by someone I know or someone who doesn't live too far away from me; better would be growing it myself; wearing the same things over and over again, making the old clothes new, wearing the old clothes as if they were new; living in a sturdy dwelling that doesn't cost too much as it accommodates the elements; walking more and driving less; finding delight in the thing right next to me; minimizing conflict by accepting the person next to me, even if the person next to me is completely stupid. All of that I can do, for I have done it before. As I say, it sounds exactly like my childhood, except I couldn't actually afford my childhood then and I won't be able to afford it now.

I will give this era I am about to enter a name, one personal to me. I will call this time in my life: Lack, Part Two.

Tide

How to begin this? With common letters is very comforting, for I want to draw on memory and I make everything into memory, especially the present, for so it shall be soon, even when I am not capable of remembering, especially when I am not capable of remembering, and memory takes place in common letters; capitalization is never in memory, not even the proper arranging of words so that they are grammatically acceptable is in memory, words are not in memory, only a series of pictures are in memory and sometimes the pictures are still and sometimes they are not and when they move they are still and when they are still they are moving. Such is memory . . . . and so?

    1. I learned to read from a book but before I could do that, my mother read to me and all the words in the books from which she read to me did not exist before she read them to me, before that, they lay on the page, big and small, all lined up next to each other, never moving, stilled as if in death, without any responsibility for the joy or doom enfolded within them, impervious to the joy or

2011. *Tide*, with Silvia Bächli. New York: Peter Freeman, Inc.

wisdom hidden within them, so they were before my mother took them into her mouth and washed them and then clothed them and made them beautiful and then presented them to me and I regarded them carefully before taking them and making them central to my being, so it becomes clear that before that, I had nothing, I was nothing all before, all before.

2. before? Joel was not dead yet and his body was not tightly wrapped up in yards of white gauze and then placed in a coffin made of reinforced cardboard which was then covered over with synthetic velvet, colored mauve; and his dead body, which looked the same when he was actually dead as when he was alive for weeks before he died and then became dead, had not been consumed by flames from the fire in the oven that was the crematorium and all reduced to ashes and the ashes placed in an urn, though not all of the ashes all together, for the urn was not large enough to contain what remained of him after he had been reduced to ashes; and his friends, and his mother and father and sister too, were not yet crying and crying, crying so much that they had no tears left, no moisture anymore flowed down their cheeks, only they were crying and crying and the tears couldn't be seen, only just heard as they flowed down their cheeks; and before they said goodbye to him and then to each other and then to the moment, the moment being so big, the size of an immeasurable universe and unforgettable, and then disappearing into all the corners of the earth and never seeing each other again, as if they were dead like Joel, but Joel really was dead and they would never see him again, and they could see each other again though only by coincidence, by chance, and what a surprise that would be, will be, for it is to come and Joel died long before this coincidence, this by chance; before Joel was not yet dead and I had to borrow his razors which he used to shave the hair off his cheeks and chin and upper lip, to shave the hair off my eyebrows and the hair growing under my arms and between my legs and on my legs too, but not the hair on my head, I left that all alone, and it made him

annoyed at me, for I made his razor blades dull and he called me a disgusting name and then kissed me and dressed me up in a beautiful dress from one of the many beautiful dresses he collected and kept hidden away from me in a closet and I was forbidden to take a look at those dresses all by myself, when I was alone, and I had no interest in them, for I had my own dresses and it was when wearing his dresses that he studied me then and not before when I stood naked in front of him, putting on his dresses, removing my own.

3. before I accept that you don't know how to love me, that you don't know how to love anyone because no one had ever shown you how, before I accept that you don't know how to love me, that after you hadn't seen me for weeks, then you should have just held me close to you and so tightly as if your life depended on it, and my life depended on it for my lungs became empty and I gasped for air and before I had wondered if you loved me but then I was sure and now not too certain at the same time, before you walked in the door and said, Sweetheart are you in the sauce already, I was sitting at my desk looking through a series of catalogues that advertised plants that were native to and so grew wild in the Southwestern United States and they required good drainage, they cannot stand standing water, and they were beautiful in colors of tropical Africa or tropical anywhere and I was wondering if I should buy them and then I decided to buy them but I had no money and couldn't buy them and so they remained in my mind's eye and in the catalogue too, they remained there, just pictures of plants in flower and I turned the pages and then remembered the vegetables that were stewing on the stove for our dinner needed turning also and before all that, I had been looking at the red twig dogwood, so beautiful in the cold winter light, and this cannot be seen properly for later the Petasites with their thick stems and broad leaves, leaves the size of a child's umbrella, will overwhelm them and I will never know they are there..........

Before I knew Chilopsis and Fallugia and Shepherdia and Forestiera and really wanted to know them and know of them as if they were native to me, as if they were mahogany or as if they were mahogany again and again, an everlasting wood, wood from which an heirloom would be made—, I knew Heptacodium, Leucothoe, Styrax, Stewartia, Sophora, Schizophragma, and they were not native to me like Mahogany, like a special piece of furniture, they were not Native to me at all but they became familiar and I treasured them and did not know how to make furniture of them and never taught myself to make furniture from them;

4. before I had children, I believed no one should be born from me, that I must keep my womb empty—and I had been taught how to do that at the same time I was taught how to manage a house—, I didn't want to know anyone else—for children are the real and true other than yourself—, only myself, from which I could easily keep a great distance, for I could go to the ends of the whole world, all four corners or even if it were another configuration, and never let myself know and keep all the things I have seen and done separated from myself, my very own self, and I could view, even so regard, myself with indifference or sympathy, with love or without love, never hatred or anger or dissolution; before I had children, I must have wanted them, but before I had children I did not know that; before I had children, I was in bondage to freedom and would die for this state of bondage but did not have to do so, before I had children I could not even imagine them .... before I had children, I did not know that I had them anyway, and that they were a shadow of something that did not exist yet, and that shadow fell before me and after me and at my side too, though this shadow was not controlled by light coming from the daily progression of the sun in the sky above, and as a shadow, they were registering my ups and downs and keeping a score and would want to hold me accountable for all my laughter and my joys, for all my laughter and my joys would become a detriment to them and so they will remind me of before, before ....

5. before all that was so sweetly sad: the empty cup of coffee and all that remains is the foam and the sound of it dissolving; the empty

bed and all that remains are the dirty sheets; the empty room and all that remains is the dirt in the corners and the windowsills and spiders' webs on the ceiling full of all sorts of dried insects; before the front steps to the front door needed tending by the mason and the pathway leading away from those steps needed weeding; before the wood was not stacked up in the shed and lay there in a pile for so long that moss flourished all over it and someone might think it was worth rendering in charcoal on paper; before the Robins—the family, not the birds—appeared early and their appearance caused much worry, for what if the weather turned severely cold and they were not prepared for it and then the weather did turn severely cold and the Robins—the birds, not the family—seemed indifferent to it; before there was a long period in which no rain fell and then without warning, rain fell and fell and caused a deluge of water to appear on the face of the earth and change its contours completely and irrevocably, though not forever, for before will always modify and temper forever, before reigning tyrannically over forever and ever, eternally;

6. for it is before from which the present takes refuge, in the name of before an enormous enterprise is undertaken, what is to come will come after before; the present is to become before;

7. before? What came before? Before the void became chaos, before order was imposed on chaos, before order was made out of chaos, before chaos was judged imperfect and had to be dismantled again and again before it could be made perfect? Before Joel was dead and tears were made up only of sounds, just drops of sound after sound running down the cheeks, before all our lips were soiled from kissing love, before all our arms and feet tired from carrying each other from dance floor to dance floor and then to bed, before we buried each other at first with sorrow and then for duty and then with indifference; before we could say it is the end with a happy shrug and then say, it is the end, and pray that it not be so; before, what comes before? For before is the tyrant who reigns forever and ever over the eternal.

Introduction to Simone Schwarz-Bart's
The Bridge of Beyond

A work of art is good if it has arisen out of necessity. That is the only way one can judge it.
—Rainer Maria Rilke

SIMONE SCHWARZ-BART'S *The Bridge of Beyond* (originally titled *Pluie et vent sur Télumée miracle*) is a seminal work of literature that cannot be contained within the usual confines of "the novel" or "a work of fiction." It arises, as Rilke says a true work of art must, out of necessity, telling the story of a little-known island and the long-lasting effects of slavery through the eyes of a woman. It is profoundly original. It is exceptionally good. That a book so radical in style, in form, and in content is not widely known in this country, and its influence not deeply felt, is one of those unfortunate mysteries of Time and Place. Literature like this does not offer the comfort of an already digested plot. It seeks out the

2013. Introduction to *The Bridge of Beyond*, by Simone Schwarz-Bart, trans. Barbara Bray. New York: NYRB Classics.

truth of history, which turns out to be most powerfully and effectively conveyed through fiction.

Here is the book's wonderfully evocative and memorable opening paragraph, as conveyed from the original French by the extraordinary translator Barbara Bray:

"A man's country may be cramped or vast according to the size of his heart. I've never found my country too small, though that isn't to say my heart is great. And if I could choose, it's here in Guadeloupe that I'd be born again, suffer and die. Yet not long back my ancestors were slaves on this volcanic, hurricane-swept, mosquito-ridden, nasty-minded island. But I didn't come into the world to weigh the world's woe. I prefer to dream, on and on, standing in my garden, just like any other old woman of my age, till death comes and takes me as I dream, me and all my joy."

The narrator is a woman and the characters in Schwarz-Bart's story with heart and courage are mostly women. The people of Guadeloupe are lost just as many people who were forcibly brought from Africa and deposited throughout the West Indies are lost. This chain of islands that make up the Lesser Antilles was formed by multiple ancient volcanic eruptions; and on a few of them the volcanoes are not entirely dormant—there the violence of man and the violence of nature take turns causing sorrow. In *The Bridge of Beyond* the reader learns of the sorrows of lost-ness as they are passed down through the generations. We see them disperse and mingle, sometimes in the same paragraph, the same sentence, the same breath. These sorrows are the sorrows of mothers and daughters, who then become mothers themselves—mothers and daughters who continue to pass down traditions and rituals that are part of everyday existence. Each daughter will be a mother, each mother has been a daughter: a bond that is never broken and persists in the presence of love or its opposite.

Schwarz-Bart tells the story of five generations of Lougandor women. In their names are echoes and commemorations of a multicultural past: Minerva who is the mother of Toussine, also called Queen Without a Name; Toussine is the mother of a pair of twins, Eloisine and Merance, who perish in a blaze they cause while not being able to share the lamplight as they learn their alphabet, and is also the mother of great Victory; Victory is the mother of Regina, who is the mother of Tulemee. Their names make the past present and so do their actions: when Queen Without a Name dies, people make the sign of the cross and sprinkle holy water in the four corners of the room in which her body lies; a group gathers and the individuals pass a rock between them from one hand to the other while chanting:

> Accursed one, accursed one
> Even if your mother is accursed too
> Say a prayer for her.

Catastrophe follows the women closely almost as if they had invented it but they are never vanquished. As the late scholar of Caribbean literature Bridget Jones once noted, they continue to rebuild their village communities in spite of the threats presented by social discrimination and by the plantation system. Love is like a ghost haunting their past, present, and future—and sometimes it's solid and good and they experience a moment of lightness:

> As we stood in the door and watched the people going, one of them gave a little shout and pointed to a patch of pink sky that had just appeared over the highest peak of the mountain, above the volcano. The rosy light soon spread over half the sky, and seeing it, the one who had shouted murmured as if in a dream: "And now may ugly souls be absent."

The islanders meet the unchanging duplicity of the world around them, be it from faraway France or across the road, with humor and wisdom and resignation, but never defeat.

Simone Schwarz-Bart was born in 1938 in Charante-Maritime on the southwest coast of France. When she was three months old her mother, a schoolteacher, took her to live in Guadeloupe; her father was in the French army and absent for the first six years of her life. It was on his second voyage to a world new to him that Christopher Columbus found the island of Guadeloupe—he was looking for drinking water. He found some, for Guadeloupe has lots of it, and he also came across the pineapple for the first time. The people who lived on the island at the time (the Caribs) were not as pleasant and innocent as those he had met on his first voyage (the Arawaks). On that Sunday of November 4, 1493, he named the island, like the other islands he found, after the Virgin Mary, Santa María de Guadelupe de Extramadura. Later Guadeloupe was claimed by Spain, then for some years traded hands between France, England, and Sweden. From early on, African slaves tended to the sugar production. Guadeloupe was ceded to France in the Treaty of Paris in 1814 and though it is a vast ocean away France still claims the island as its own.

In *The Bridge of Beyond*, Schwarz-Bart's lyrical, incantatory words create a lush, nuanced world that exists between dream and memory. This is a book that might be difficult to read for someone who is at the beach to sun and sip and stop thinking. (By the way, the characters in this story are very familiar with the beach, and yet remarkably no one ever goes there.) The characters head into the mountains, they cross many rivers for which Guadeloupe is famous, they walk through forests of flowering trees, the names of which they do not know. It is as if they are on a journey farther inward to hold on to the last threads of their spoiled civilization.

The cultural traditions and historical events from which this work of art springs cannot be contained in a strict linear narrative. In fact, such a device might even lend a veneer of inevitability to them. For a narrative that began with a search for fresh water on an island one Sunday morning has no end—it circles back on itself, it begins again, it staggers sideways, it never lurches forward to a conclusion in which the world where it began is suddenly transformed into an ideal, new world. Schwarz-Bart's prose awakens the senses and enlarges the imagination; it makes me anxious for my own sanity and yet at the same time certain of it; her sentences, rooted in Creole experience and filled with surprising insights and proverbs, resonate in my head and heart.

Some writers make a fetish of that edifice called "the Novel." They write to reinforce this edifice down to the last full stop. But the novel, like the essay, or the poem, isn't subject to formulae or laws. A book like *The Bridge of Beyond* establishes its own order, its own sense of being, tugging one way into the painfully personal and then taking another turn into the joys and sufferings of the community.

Here I've tried to express my deep admiration and love for this courageous book, a book that is Fiction, Nonfiction, and History, categories that are of little use if they interfere with the greater truth of a work of art. As if from out of the blue, from the Great Beyond, from the margins, a woman from Guadeloupe has given us an unforgettable hymn to the resilience and power of women.

The Kind of Gardener I Am Not

ONE TIME, when our four children were ages eleven, six, six, and three, my friend Sandy Frazier and I took them for a trip to Glacier National Park. We came in through the main entrance, meaning to go up to the Continental Divide by way of the "Going-to-the-Sun" Road. First we took a walk through a path to see some trees, but I was only interested in the *Tiarella* at their feet, since I had never seen that shade plant growing in its natural habitat before. Then we drove off on the road to the sun, going uphill, passing miles and miles (or so it seemed) of burnt trees and scorched landscape, the remains of a notorious fire; sometimes there was nothing to protect us from falling off either side of the road and the road itself was very narrow and winding, each twist revealing some natural spectacle liable to distract and perhaps lead to your doom; a road meant for a pilgrimage. Sandy then remembered a time not too long before this trip we were on with our children when he and George Trow had taken this very

2018, Jul. 27. "The Kind of Gardener I Am Not." *Book Post.* https://books.substack.com/p/diary-jamaica-kincaid-the-kind-of-gardener-i-am-not.

road and somewhere midway up, at what Sandy believed to be the most dangerous part, George began to recite the words to a song by Noel Coward, "I Went to a Marvelous Party."

> I went to a marvelous party
> With Nounou and Nada and Nell
> It was in the fresh air
> And we went as we were
> And we stayed as we were
> Which was Hell.

He wasn't able to recall the song in its entirety but he came up with enough that the children asked him to stop. He then decided he should explain to them the meaning of the Continental Divide and so went into the whole business of pouring a glass of water onto the ground and how half would end up in the Gulf of Mexico and the other half would end up near Alaska. That was met with a seemingly polite silence but when we got to the top of the Going-to-the-Sun Road and got out of the car, my daughter Annie, the eleven-year-old, looked around her, saw the sign that announced our geologic position, looked at the two adults, and said, in that forever annoying high-pitched voice of just-before-adolescence: "What's a Continental Divide?"

After wandering around a bit in the park, hearing about roads closed because of the sightings of grizzly bears and baby elks out for a swim whose mothers were dragged out of the lake by grizzly bears, and seeing meadows of flowers I was not familiar with, we headed off to our rooms in one of the park's lodges, ate dinner, and slept soundly. The next morning I walked up to an alpine meadow where I was assured there were no grizzly bears. That was very nice. Everything was small-growing and intense in color: the *Castilleja* in particular were wonderful, especially since they were so new to me; *Pulsatilla vulgaris*, yellow *Aquilegia flavescens*, and so on. Awed and frightened by all this newness, I made my way back to breakfast and the rest of my traveling companions. I could see and smell breakfast as I approached our dwelling place, the kitchen was very busy. Just outside it, in the middle of loose rocks and gravel, I saw a clematis, the *C. columbiana*. I knew it immediately from pictures in the various books of flowers endemic to the area I had carried with me from my home in Vermont. To see a picture of anything that you imagine or know for certain that you will never see in real life and time (an angel, for instance, or a moon in one of the planets in our solar system that rotates on its side) creates in me (and perhaps, you) a realization of the incompleteness of my whole existence, the fragility of everything I know (the little island in the Caribbean I grew up on, for instance), the grandness of a living member of the vegetable kingdom blooming without wanting to be cared about by me or anyone who came before me. The columbine grew here with abundance and generosity, as if it knew that growing so near the kitchen might bring at least one admirer: four narrow petals of a light blue, like the January sky in New England on a sunny day, not the everyday sky of the Caribbean that I want all things blue to be. It is because of *C. columbiana* that I remember that kitchen.

Leaving the park just before noon, I did not see *Lilium philadelphicum* growing in a ravine, though I did two years later when Sandy and I took our children to the Canadian side of Glacier.

All the same we exited the St. Mary area of the park and made our way to Browning, Montana, the place the Blackfeet Indians were consigned to for living by European migrants who had murdered many of them and stolen their land. At the museum we bought bracelets and hair ornaments and also admired the many examples of Blackfeet art and craft. Approaching the reservation from one side or the other, that is coming and going, small crosses festooned with plastic flowers appear in frightening numbers. Sandy drove carefully even though he knew that careful driving has never prevented the death of anyone.

We went on to Cut Bank, a town on the plains in Montana, some miles off. Along the way, from time to time, Sandy would stop the car to point out to us some relic of the journey of Lewis and Clark or some devilish installation of weapons related to the Cold War. At first, the children got out dutifully and seemed to listen to his little lectures. At around the fourth stop, after hearing a few sentences of what he had to say, they started to chant in unison: "Back-in-the-car! Back-in-the-car! Back-in-the-car!"

Humiliated and defeated, we entered Cut Bank. There was still quite a bit of daylight so Sandy, who had been to Cut Bank before, drove us around the small town and then we got out and walked a bit. It was in Cut Bank that I saw the garden and the kind of gardener that I am not. In the front yard of each little house—the houses were small, bungalow-like, a style of architecture very much suited to vast expanses of landscape—were little gardens blooming with flowers. The flowers, almost without exception, were petunias (red, purple, white), impatiens, portulaca, and short, red salvia. There was one garden that seemed more cared for than the others and that had a plaque placed prominently in a garden bed that read: GARDEN OF THE WEEK.

And that is exactly the kind of gardener I am not and exactly the kind of garden I will never have. A garden made for a week is unknown to me. For years I have been making a garden and unmaking it too. It isn't out of dissatisfaction that I do and undo, it is out of curiosity. That curiosity has not led to stasis. It has led to a conversation. And so it is, I have been having a conversation in the garden. And so it will be until I die.

The Walk to Robert Frost's House

To Robert Woolmington of North Bennington, Vermont

Robert Frost lived in many places and didn't live in them for very long, but the house he lived in for the longest time was a house in Shaftsbury, Vermont, a lovely old-fashioned modest house made from stone and wood, all of which must have come from the immediate vicinity. You can take a drive up Route 7A in southern Vermont and you will come to it, on the line that divides the city of Bennington from the town of Shaftsbury, if you stay within the speed limit. If not you will find yourself, well, not there.

Every summer, sometime between the last week in June and no later than the Fourth of July, I like to go for a walk through the woods to his old house, which has now been declared to be the official Robert Frost Stone House Museum. In it are all the sort of things you would expect in a shrine to a great poet: pictures on the walls, pictures of the especially great and much revered poem he

---

2019, Jan. 19. "The Walk to Robert Frost's House." *Book Post.* https://books.substack.com/p/diary-jamaica-kincaid-the-walk-to.

wrote while living there, "Stopping by Woods on a Snowy Evening"—and annotated at that—and other such things.

Visitors are restricted to the downstairs, excluding the room in which Carol Frost, a son of the poet, killed himself with a gun. Frost's two most prominent biographers, Lawrance Thompson and Jay Parini, disagree about the events that led up to this tragedy, Thompson being frank about Frost's personality, for he knew him well; Frost had designated him his official biographer. The Parini version is meant to be a corrective: the great poet was a horrible husband and father. Robert Frost's father tried to join the wrong side of the Civil War, and when he was deterred from that, he moved to San Francisco, and when his child was born he named him after the traitor: Robert E. Lee. And so, Robert Lee Frost.

But what I wonder, as I set off from my house to walk the trail to his house/museum, if his father had named him Nat Turner Frost or Frederick Douglass Frost, would his epic, glorious poem "New Hampshire" begin this way?

> I met a lady from the South who said
> (You won't believe she said it, but she said it):
> "None of my family ever worked, or had
> A thing to sell." I don't suppose the work
> Much matters. You may work for all of me.
> I've seen the time I've had to work myself.
> The having anything to sell is what
> Is the disgrace in man or state or nation.

I once saw Jay Parini and when I told him that I liked his biography a lot, for it was so instructive and far more easy to read than the Thompson, but I thought the Thompson was more accurate about Frost, he said that Thompson had a tin ear for Frost's poetry. But Thompson's account of Frost's life isn't only about the poetry, he seems to take it as a given, something we all know from the beginning: Frost was a great, very great, poet, but he was not a nice man. Not being a nice man but a great poet is perfectly fine, as long as such a person is not your husband.

The walk to Robert Frost's house begins on the man-made sandy beach of the man-made lake called Lake Paran. Walking around the upper circumference of the lake I encounter many beautiful flowers—some clover, some silene, some centaurea, some achillea—but these hold no real interest for me and when I see them in my own human-made garden I go into a huge fret and rip them out without a thought, for in a garden, they are weeds, which only means I have not yet the intelligence to understand their place in my cultivated landscape, my garden.

The path then forks: the high meadow, which calls for a steep walk up, or the lower meadow, which follows the shoreline of the man-made lake. In the high meadow I have seen a family of bluebirds (there were eight of them, so they seemed like a family to me), and I have seen the outline of the Taconic range rising far away in New York. Onward then, and the upper and lower meadow converge at a newly made wooden bridge that has two benches for resting, so necessary, for no matter how many times I have done this walk, I am always grateful for the bridge with its benches. Sitting there, I can see trout happily moving about in the stream, innocent of the thought that I might need them for dinner or just the pleasure of saying I caught them. Also on the opposite side of the river, still going toward the Frost house, are tall bundles of Joe Pye Weed (*Eutrochium purpureum*), taller than any I have ever seen in a cultivated garden, and then beyond that a moist woodland of beeches shading colonies of ginger (*Asarum canadense*), maiden hair ferns (*Adiantum*), *Actea* (baneberry), and skunk cabbage (*Symplocarpus foetidus*). Right around here suddenly is an outcropping of rock, a cliff all jagged and layered in brown and white stone that I was once told was in the middle of something geologists call uplift.

A short climb up and then on the right is the wetland meadow, then turning right from that is another glorious bit of foresting but dry, and then after half a mile or so, a descent into a lower wet meadow, and there I have seen swaths of marsh marigold (*Caltha palustris*) blooming so seductively that in my mind I have found a place for them in my own garden, though when I have tried to put this vision in front of me, a mere two and a half miles away, the result was a gradual diminishing of the plants and then one year they just did not turn up at all. And this has been true of so many plants I love: I see them in their natural habitat and I immediately imagine them in my own garden and put them there, and then they disappear. And this is why there is such a thing as a plant-order nursery, for many things that thrive happily in the wild will have to be slightly manipulated to thrive in the contrivance of a garden.

This path along the profusion of marsh marigolds is narrow and apparently Frost wandered along during his epic attempts to be a farmer. This farming business is thought to be a failure in his life, but it seems to me that it is one of the most important pieces of his greatness as a poet. A great writer always, mostly, needs to do something that has nothing to do with writing, or so it seems, but that thing they are involved with is the very place in which they write; while farming, a poet is writing. Writers go to parties, great writers do something else.

After that walk among the marsh marigolds, a quarter of a mile or so are some younger woods and old apple trees, and apparently this is the source of "Stopping by Woods on a Snowy Evening." The funny thing is that no matter what time of day I pass through this particular path of the walk, it always seems like evening: the path here is tranquil in a way the other parts of the walk are not; here is where I want both to linger and to run at the same time and also wish the woods would tell me whatever memory they have of him.

I went into the house/museum once and then never again. My walk to the Frost house ends in an orchard of apple trees he is said to have planted. The apples are inedible, as they should be, for they were planted for some other reason than the pleasure to be found in eating them.

Going backward, going back along the path that has become familiar in your mind's eye, especially if it has been a recent encounter, always seems unfamiliar and so even more frightening, for it should be familiar, but the way back is a new way too and will have its own pleasures and anxieties; the pleasure and the terror of going back on any path is always a surprise. Here is a pleasure and a terror: in the second year of my five-mile pilgrimage to the Frost house, while returning home I found growing, in a dry part of the meadow that slopes down toward the stream that feeds Lake Paran, a patch of *Lilium philadelphicum*; in a large patch of flowers long past bloom were these little heads of open-faced orange (not recurved like *L. superbum* or *L. canadense*) popping up here and there. And how did I recognize them? A long time ago my friend Sandy and I took our children to the Canadian part of Glacier Park. It was a disagreeable trip, the children hated all the hiking, and at the border crossing back into the United States the guards suspected us of smuggling children. Sandy was quite agitated, the children were silent, and I was trying to identify the many new flowers I saw in bloom. Suddenly I saw a swatch of reddish orange flowers that I had never seen before and I wanted to examine them but the driver wouldn't stop. Not too far from that first sighting, I saw another batch of these same flowers, and I insisted that we stop not only to look at them but also for me to pick some for decorating the dashboard. We stopped, I picked the flowers, and we resumed our journey to Sandy's family's home in Missoula, Montana. I then got out my little flower guidebook for plants native to Glacier Park, and I soon found it. I read happily of its beauty and rareness, feeling very proud of myself to have noticed it, but then I came to the last sentence and it was more or less this: unfortunately this beautiful plant is in danger of extinction because it has so many thoughtless admirers. Sandy, who at that time was annoyed with my obsession, laughed at me and to this day when I approach something with a dangerous amount of enthusiasm he only has to say, "Thoughtless admirer," and I grow silent.

Nothing on the walk to and from the Frost house stirs in me such a feeling of what is known as the sublime as seeing the *Lilium philadelphicum*. The thing is I only see them on my return and each year I am surprised that they remain. Sometimes there are more of them than the year before, and sometimes there are fewer. When I see fewer of them, I wonder about the other thoughtless admirers and pray there are not many of them.

A Letter to Robinson Crusoe

The true symbol of the British conquest is Robinson Crusoe, who, cast away on a desert island, in his pocket a knife and a pipe, becomes an architect, a carpenter, a knife grinder, an astronomer, a baker, a shipwright, a potter, a saddler, a farmer, a tailor, an umbrella-maker, and a clergyman. He is the true prototype of the British colonist, as Friday (the trusty savage who arrives on an unlucky day) is the symbol of the subject races. The whole Anglo-Saxon spirit is in Crusoe: the manly independence; the unconscious cruelty; the persistence; the slow yet efficient intelligence; the sexual apathy; the practical, well-balanced religiousness; the calculating taciturnity.
—James Joyce

DEAR MR. CRUSOE,

Please stay home. There's no need for this ruse of going on a trading journey, in which more often than not the goods you are trading are people like me, Friday. There's no need at all to leave your nice bed and your nice wife and your nice chil-

---

2019, Jul. 22. "A Letter to Robinson Crusoe," in introduction to *Robinson Crusoe*, by Daniel Defoe. New York: Restless Books.

dren (everything with you is always nice, except you yourself are not) and hop on a ship that is going to be wrecked in a storm at night (storms like the dark) and everyone (not the cat, not the dog) gets lost at sea except lucky and not-nice-at-all you, and you are near an island that you see in the first light of day and then your life, your real life, begins. That life in Europe was nice, just nice; this life you first see at the crack of dawn is the beginning of your new birth, your new beginning, the way in which you will come to know yourself—not the conniving, delusional thief that you really are, but who you believe you really are, a virtuous man who can survive all alone in the world of a little godforsaken island. All well and good, but why did you not just live out your life in this place, why did you feel the need to introduce me, Friday, into this phony account of your virtues and your survival instincts? Keep telling yourself geography is history and that it makes history, not that geography is the nightmare that history recounts.

Perhaps it is a mistake to ask someone like me, a Friday if there ever was one, a Friday in all but name, to consider this much loved and admired classic, this book that seems to offer each generation encountering it, sometimes when a child and sometimes as an adult who becomes a child when reading it, the thrill of the adventure of a man being lost at sea, then finding safety on an island that seems to be occupied by nobody, and then making a world that is very nourishing to him physically and spiritually.

I was a ravenous reader as a child. I read the King James version of the Bible so many times that I even came to have opinions early on about certain parts of it (I thought of the Apostle Paul as a tyrant and the New Testament as too much about individuals and not enough about the people); I read everything I could find in the children's section of the Antigua Public Library, situated on a whole floor just above the Government Treasury. If there was something diabolical or cynical in that arrangement, I never found it, but if it does turn out to be so, I will not be at all surprised.

Among the many things that would haunt me were these three books: *Treasure Island* by Robert Louis Stevenson, *The Water-Babies* by Charles Kingsley, and *Robinson Crusoe* by Daniel Defoe. Yes, yes, my early education consisted largely of ignoring that native Europeans were an immoral, repulsive people who were ignorant of most of the other people inhabiting this wonderful earth. Also, they were very good writers, that was true enough.

What made a native of Europe, less than two hundred years after Christopher Columbus wandered into the mid–Atlantic Ocean (where he found a paradise and proceeded to undo it), imagine himself alone on an island far away from his home? Had his world, the world of Europe, become so burdensome to him, and the presence of all those new people and the things to be done to them in their "New World" become so overwhelmingly burdensome, that "all alone" became a heaven and a haven, a metaphor for becoming a new person, a perfect person? What makes such a person imagine himself (for it would be a him) the only survivor of a catastrophe at sea, and finding himself alone on an unknown island (unknown to him) construct a self that is confident, complete, and reasonable (within such boundaries), assured of his place in the order of things, in command of the order of things? For there are no real moments of doubt in this narrative that all will be well, or that he will emerge from this catastrophe enhanced in all the ways his enhancement requires.

Alone is always accompanied by loneliness, at least if you are an English person of a certain time. There doesn't seem to be a single one of them who does not need a companion. Somebody has to polish his shoes or make her tea or at least listen to tales of things the listener will never know. An English person of a certain time must have a Friday. Christopher Columbus ambled into the Caribbean archipelago on a Thursday in October 1492. He met people who seemed to look remarkably like Friday. Columbus immediately began to make a detailed list of their physical characteristics and their ways (they were so amiable, even their dogs didn't bark) and immediately judged them beneath him: Columbus gave a man a sword; the man, having never seen a sword before, held it by the blade.

So just how did Daniel Defoe conceive of a parable for the 1492 adventure? What if Christopher Columbus and his gang of hardened criminals and cold-hearted adventurers had arrived in the Antilles and found themselves stranded with no way of going back whence they came? Would Columbus then have been a refugee dependent on the kindness of these strangers? Crusoe, though, is that rare kind of refugee: the refugee who is not suffering from hardship of the usual kind attached to a refugee: economic hardship, political persecution; he is having an existential crisis, a crisis seemingly known only to the privileged person from Europe, having come along with their Enlightenment. You know who doesn't have such a crisis? A person living quite comfortably in a climate that is called paradisaical and who has no need for much clothing, with, not far away in the background, a jungle, not a forest.

Ennui, a domesticated, localized version of an existential crisis, is not for the Fridays of this world. We are vulnerable to the insane needs and greed of our own Other, that native of Europe; we have our flaws, but at this point we Fridays, when we are spoken of, are not regarded as part of the vast array of human experience, we are regarded as wanting, as illegitimate forms of the human family, as forms of Being meant to tend sugarcane and reap cotton, mastering the role of performing in perpetuity the Other, the Other that is always lacking in the full form and dignity that is the human condition.

The vivid, vibrant, subtle, important role that the tale of Robinson Crusoe, with his triumph of individual resilience and ingenuity wrapped up in his European, which is to say white, identity, has played in the long, uninterrupted literature of European conquest of the rest of the world must not be dismissed or ignored or silenced. Quite the opposite: it is evidence of the ignorance, the absence of moral knowledge and feeling, the realization once again that the people who lay claim to the "Enlightenment" needed enlightenment and that the rest of us were perfectly okay and that because of them we are in search of something that some of us already knew: when confronted with a sword, accept it by the blade, for the handle only leads to more blades, and the more blades and better blades that await in the long run—and life is the long run—are of no use at all.

So Dear Mr. Crusoe,

Please don't come. Stay home and work things out; your soul, a property you value very much, will be better off for it.

Sincerely,
Jamaica Kincaid

I See the World

IT BEGINS IN THIS WAY:
It's as if we are dead and somehow have been given the unheard-of opportunity to see the life we lived, the way we lived it: there we are with friends we had just run into by accident and the surprise on our faces (happy surprise, sour surprise) as we clasp each other (close or not so much) and say things we might mean totally or say things we only mean somewhat, but we never say bad things, we only say bad things when the person we are clasping is completely out of our sight; and everything is out of immediate sight and yet there is everything in immediate sight; the streets so crowded with people from all over the world and why don't they return from wherever it is they come from and everybody comes from nowhere for nowhere is the name of every place, all places are nowhere, nowhere is where we all come from; the dresses hanging in a store window that are meant for people half my age are so appealing and the waist of this dress is smaller than my upper arm

2020, Apr. 28. "I See the World." *The Paris Review* (*The Daily*). https://www.theparisreview.org/blog/2020/04/28/i-see-the-world/.

and I walk on; the homeopathic combination of vitamin C and bioflavonoids and zinc are on a shelf in the Brattleboro Co-op and I let them remain there, but in the Brattleboro Co-op are cuts of meat that used to be parts of animals and these animals were treated very well and given the best food to eat and that is why they are on the meat shelf of the Brattleboro Co-op; the blue sky, the blue sky and the white clouds are made less so even, modified really, when I place them next to the blue of the sky and the white of the clouds I know exist in the place where I was born and grew up, St. John's, Antigua, nowhere, nowhere; the long lines in/at the airport and the people manning the various portals of entry and then exit to allow me to attend my oldest brother's funeral, though he was nine years younger than I was at the time he was born but how much younger is he now that he is dead, he is dead and I am alive in the time of the dead, the time of the dead being the time in which to be alive is a form of being dead, we are dead right now for we cannot be all our ways that are ways of being alive that is familiar; I can hear Martha and the Vandellas singing backup to Marvin Gaye as he sings, close my eyes at night, though to close my eyes at night does not bring sleep or dreams of being loved, only how it came to be that I thought being dead would come about by nuclear bombs, not from something my eyes cannot even see; that very shaded part along the banks of a small stream, which feeds into a larger stream, which feeds, all ending in the Atlantic Ocean, that very shaded area is beginning to be filled up with ramps; there were funerals, there were weddings, there were bar mitzvahs, there were meetings I never attended and was penalized, there were evaluations and I thought hard and did my best to be fair; there were sentences that could not be completed for long periods of time; bells, all kinds of bells, in churches, at dinners, in gardens, when someone was hung at Her Majesty's Prison at eight o'clock on a Wednesday morning; girls with small bosoms, ladies with large bosoms, men who couldn't stand up straight, the phone ringing, somebody telling me that my mother had died; the fear of using public toilets because people I didn't know had used them before; one thing I would have loved: sailing across the southern Atlantic Ocean from Argentina to Cape Town, South Africa, and making a little detour to the Drake Passage; the wonder of this world, the wonder of this world and there are no words for it, every word spoils it; the prison for women on the corner of 8th Street and Sixth Avenue and in it were women who had violated all sorts of rules: sexual, which were political, and political: Grace Paley and Angela Davis, a writer of one kind and a writer of another but thinkers observing the same thing and not being heard and not being heard is in the land of the dead where I am now; Jean and Dinah, Rosita and Clementina; walking so closely to someone just to hear what they are saying and then telling someone else what was overheard, so I could make fun of it; the joy of ridiculing someone I don't know and will never meet again; there was that time when I told my best friend that if I got married and had children that he should commit me to an institution for the insane because this meant that I would never be a great writer and I did get married and had children and never became a great writer, that thing, the great writer, now looks so ridiculous, like a clown or something unworthy of human attention, not garbage, not that at all, just something to be but, but, I was young and didn't understand anything at all, though I knew everything all and danced in the streets while wearing pajamas that had been issued to me by a cancer hospital, where it was found I did not have cancer at all but after I left the hospital I continued to wear the pajamas for they had been so comfortable; and having children, how difficult to see that they were not me and that their comfortable childhood was not mine and my girl daughter, oh how she suffered from my confusion and that world is separated from me, lost forever because of that thing that came from nowhere, like the rest of us it comes from nowhere, China, the United States of America, Antigua, all of that is nowhere, we are all of us from nowhere, and nowhere is where we end up, it is our destiny; alive but dead, dead but alive; a great divide has fallen on our life, on my life certainly and on the way I see the world: in life itself there are lots of dead in it, the kingdoms of mammals, vegetable, mineral, and all the others, are all in the living sometimes but in the dead all times.

Inside the American Snow Dome

DEAR READER,
Do you know what a snow dome is? I believe you do not so I will tell you. It is this: a snow dome is an object, dome-like in shape, resting on a flat piece of material that is fitted to it and sealed perfectly to its base. The entire structure is made of a material that is easily shattered. Inside, the dome is filled about three-quarters of the way up with water. Scenes of one kind or another are created and fixed to the bottom of the dome. Flakes of something white made to resemble snow are settled at the bottom of the dome, and when the dome is shaken, as it often is by a playful hand passing by, the flakes rush up in a flurry around the scene that has been fixed to the bottom of the dome. All the figures and objects are lost in a blur of the pretend snow, they are consumed by it, and for a moment, it seems as if this will be the new forever: they will never be seen clearly again. Then the false snow slowly settles back

2020, Nov. 11. "Inside the American Snow Dome." *The Paris Review* (*The Daily*). https://www.theparisreview.org/blog/2020/11/11/inside-the-american-snow-dome/.

to the bottom of the dome and everything returns to the way it was. The scene remains just as it was before, fixed, fixed, and fixed! The snow dome is usually found at the destinations of grim family vacations: Disneyland, the Bronx Zoo, the Empire State Building, the Statue of Liberty, the area of airports near the gates of departure, places you very well might never visit again because you never wish to visit these places again. Such is the existence of the snow dome.

For the past four years, starting sometime in early November 2016, I have been living in a snow dome that resembles the United States of America. I have been a figure in this snow dome. The color of the water in it was sometimes orange, sometimes a rage red, and the color of the snow was never white. It has been a shameful experience. I have been trapped here. The United States of America is to me the most wonderful country in the world, and it really is, but only if while you live there you attach yourself to the best people in it, and the best people in it are Black people, African American people. If, when you go to the United States, you attach yourself to the group of people who call themselves "White" you will consign yourself to misery and minor and major transgressions against your fellow human beings and also greediness and everyday murder. And more. Here's how you live in America: your children must go to the best schools and the best schools are always for white children and you'll completely forget the best schools have never helped anybody be a good person (see George W. Bush, just for a passing reference). With the exception of most likely John Adams (second president of the United States for one term) and most certainly Barack Hussein Obama, all the presidents of the United States of America were racists and their racism was especially and particularly directed at Black people of African descent. The great Abraham Lincoln, a president I am so deeply attached to I grow roses named in his honor in my garden, was a racist but he abhorred slavery and that's good enough for me, being that I am most blessedly descended from the enslaved (I say blessedly but I really mean accidentally because blessings are so random, they are in fact accidents). The United States of America, before it even became such a thing as the United States of America, was a roiling unsettling snow dome of transgression, and from the beginning that transgression was caused by people immigrating from Europe.

Perhaps this land has been inside a snow dome since August 3, 1492, but right now, let me look at the one I am in that appeared in early November 2016. All at once the open skies under which I lived in the state of Vermont closed up, which was very odd, for in September of 2001, which was a time of darkness, the open sky in the state of Vermont under which I lived couldn't have been more open, more blue, more inviting and welcoming. But now, or then, however I want to regard it, the sky above me in 2016, that November, grew dark: words do change the color of things. Shortly after November of 2016, the people who were not allowed to come into the United States of America could trace their exclusion to the America of the slave states, which, after they were defeated, found a way to rise again. That particular snow globe is the one most of us are in. To make groups of people feel they are less than who they are, to make groups of people feel they are more than who they might be, to make groups of people teeter between more or less is an American idea, an American aspiration. But nothing is permanent, even in a snow globe, for sometimes a stray arm will knock it off its shelf (the shelf is the permanent home of the snow globe). There was the ban on people from "Islamic" countries. But what countries were those? In the Elizabethan era, after the defeat of Spain, Catholics more or less became racialized; when I was growing up as a little girl on a British-ruled island in the Caribbean, I was told that Catholics—that is, people from Italy and Spain and places like that—were not really white people and that idea was so strong in me that when I came to the United States, and met so many people who said they were white (Italians, Spaniards, just about anyone

Catholic), I lost any fear I might have had of white people. This was a great comfort for me personally: I met plenty of racism but usually the people directing it toward me, I knew them to have had their own difficult encounters with the permanent impermanence of the snow globe. And so the people from countries where Islam was the dominant belief were like Catholics and also they were like Black people in America: segregation is an American ideology. Only African Americans/Black Americans instinctively understand this and that is why we are the true Americans. It is also why many immigrants to America try to get as far away as they can from identifying themselves with African Americans (the Irish, the fair-skinned immigrant from India, the fair-skinned immigrant from China, Korea, Japan): because the African American is American for the long haul, there is no America without the African American/Black people. Everyone loves what Black Americans are and do, they just don't want to be them. The American obsession with freedom is simply because we have lived so intimately with people we made "not free." We know very well the situation of the "not free." The African American is the definition of the "not free." America is a peculiar place: it has fifty states, half of them named after the Native people who inhabited the land called America; it goes from Alabama to Wyoming. The American national motto could easily be "Kill the people, keep their names."

On a morning over this past weekend, in early November 2020, someone passed by the table where the snow dome I have been living in for four years lay and just deliberately knocked it to the floor. It shattered into many pieces, the water disappeared, soaked into the wooden floor. The phony snow did not melt, of course, but all the figurines were broken. I picked up the pieces of the good ones, myself included (yes, it's my snow dome and I get to decide). I would mend them back and try my best to make them whole again. I then took a hammer, one I use in the garden to hammer stakes into the earth, and I ground and ground the rest of them into dust.

I was never really making a garden so much as having a conversation

BUT I WAS NEVER REALLY making a garden the way that most people, who are intent on making a garden and who will have ideas at the outset about what it should mean in some way that they might not even be conscious of; I was never really making a garden in that way so much as I was having a conversation, a conversation with all the components, all the attributes, all the dangers, all the failures and pitfalls, all the moral and immoral dilemmas, all of the history of the garden and the way it has formed, starting with the Edenic prelapsarian ideal/idyll and its postlapsarian catastrophe. There isn't a garden that I have ever encountered, whether it be one created by a king in France or a woman raising children in Cut Bank, a small town on the Great

---

2020, May 8. "I was never really making a garden so much as having a conversation (Part One)." *Book Post.* https://books.substack.com/p/diary-jamaica-kincaid-i-was-never. 2020, May 9. "I was never really making a garden so much as having a conversation (Part Two)." *Book Post.* https://books.substack.com/p/diary-jamaica-kincaid-i-was-never-e11.

Plains of northern Montana, who in her spare time made a garden of flowers, annuals that were foreign in origin to her region of the United States—nasturtiums, petunias, zinnias, portulaca, marigolds—that I haven't, however unknowingly, involved in this ongoing conversation I have in my head: before the Fall, after the Fall.

I grew up on a small island with the Atlantic Ocean on its north side and the Caribbean Sea bordering its south. I saw an ocean and a sea every day of my small child's life but I hardly saw fresh water for the island had been denuded of trees by colonial settlers from England in the seventeenth century. The garden, that place in which things were grown in an enclosed area and were meant to excite at least two of the senses, the eye and the nose, existed for me only in a book. In a book, people walked in them, sometimes in silence and alone, sometimes in silence but with a companion, sometimes to make mischief, sometimes to just show off how rich they were. Gardens were separate from the place where food was grown. Where food was grown was associated with labor. Gardens were the place where flowers were grown, the place where the plants existed for the sole purpose of pleasure and thoughtfulness and reflection. Later when I myself began to happily drown myself in the world of the garden I saw how that division between sustenance (food) and knowledge is reflected in the creation story. In Eden, the first garden in Christianity's mythology, the Tree of Life (agriculture) comes before the Tree of Knowledge (horticulture); and that place called the garden comes with an explicit suggestion of there being plenty to eat and so thinking can begin. In the world of the garden someone who looks like me is associated with agriculture. I am descended mostly from enslaved Africans, the people whose forced labor made the world of the garden as we have come to know it possible, the people whose very presence itself makes the modern world possible.

I came to see all this and so many other ways of looking at the world in the garden. Why are the people who now inhabit that little island I am from so averse to field labor? They will not be employed in cotton fields nor will they cut sugarcane for money. Such work was the work of slaves, our ancestors. The first gift God gave to Adam was the pleasure of naming things and in that way he gave Adam a sense of power, for to name things or people is a way of possessing them. This revelation (for to me standing in the garden with a plant in my hand, wondering why it was called by this or that name, and then suddenly going back to the creation story, was a revelation) led to Carolus Linnaeus, the great Swedish doctor and botanist and the inventor of the binomial system for naming living things. So much of the unwelcome European intrusion in the lives of people living more or less quietly by themselves in the other places in the world is entangled in his little life. It is like this: Linnaeus was on his way to London for one reason or another when he stopped off in Holland to see his friend, an Anglo-Dutch businessman named George Clifford who was associated with the Dutch East India Company. Clifford had a greenhouse filled with plants native to East India, tender plants, and to him they had no names. Linnaeus spent two years examining them and giving them names based on his ideas regarding classification. And that act/game of classifying, which they extended to people, led to race and racism, a way of looking at people and judging them to be worthy or not-worthy. That spell of Linnaeus staying with George Clifford led to his great work *Hortus Cliffortianus*, a book I spent hundreds of dollars acquiring because I wanted to read it. I then had to purchase a Latin dictionary and a botanical Latin dictionary, for it is written in Latin.

Linnaeus is not the least of the troubling people I have met in the garden. The modern garden is full of the history of the last five hundred years, at least since 1492. What were the Dutch people like before they met potatoes and the tulip? Are there any flowers native to Holland, for though their main export is plants, in particular bulbs, none of these are native to Holland. The Dutch iris comes from somewhere in Spain. The tulip comes from Turkey, Afghanistan, Iran, and those areas. And yet Dutch national identity seems to be very wrapped up in the tulip. It's a common way Europeans have of looking at the world: love the plants, hate the people.

This is what I mean when I say that I have not been making a garden so much as having a conversation with the idea of the garden. In the year that the Golan Heights were still considered part of Syria, I was in Israel and went up there to see some flowers in bloom. I came across a beautiful iris that looked so much like a variety of *Iris germanica*, but it was really *Iris hermona*; the *hermona* must have been because it was in the vicinity of Mount Hermon, a mountain on the border of Syria and Lebanon. It was so beautiful, abundant in form and color. The day after I left Israel, the Golan Heights, according to the American president, were no longer a part of Syria. The Mount Hermon iris, I imagine, is indifferent to this. But will I be?

If I had not made a garden, I would not have read *The Travels of William Bartram*, an eighteenth-century American plant gatherer (or plant hunter, if I didn't like him so much) who wrote an account of his travels to the southern part of the United States. This book is said to have been an influence on William Wordsworth and his friends. Bartram's father John had been a botanist to King George III of Great Britain and he found a plant that he named after the American diplomat Benjamin Franklin, *Franklinia alatamaha*, a plant that was never again seen in its natural habitat, all Franklinia grown today being descended from that collection. I fall into a huge dream if I think about that too much.

I would not have understood the third president of the United States, Thomas Jefferson, or understood the journals of Lewis and Clark, whose mission was really to make a claim to the contiguous northern part of that region of North America that was under Thomas Jefferson's instructions; a great influence on Jefferson's instructions to Lewis and Clark was the first journey that Captain Cook had made circumnavigating the world, and that journey of Captain Cook led to sending breadfruit to the West Indies, where it was to be cultivated as a cheap source of food for the enslaved. I would not have known that Indians didn't drink tea until the British sent it to them from China (*Camellia sinensis*). I would not have understood the first paragraph, chapter 3, in *Narrative of the Life of Frederick Douglass*:

> Colonel Lloyd kept a large and finely cultivated garden, which afforded almost constant employment for four men, besides the chief gardener, (Mr. M'Durmond.) This garden was probably the greatest attraction of the place. During the summer months, people came from far and near—from Baltimore, Easton, and Annapolis—to see it. It abounded in fruits of almost every description, from the hardy apple of the north to the delicate orange of the south. This garden was not the least source of trouble on the plantation. Its excellent fruit was quite a temptation to the hungry swarms of boys, as well as the older slaves, belonging to the colonel, few of whom had the virtue or the vice to resist it. Scarcely a day passed, during the summer, but that some slave had to take the lash for stealing fruit. The colonel had to resort to all kinds of stratagems to keep his slaves out of the garden. The last and most successful one was that of tarring his fence all around; after which, if a slave was caught with any tar upon his

person, it was deemed sufficient proof that he had either been into the garden, or had tried to get in. In either case, he was severely whipped by the chief gardener. This plan worked well; the slaves became as fearful of tar as of the lash. They seemed to realize the impossibility of touching tar without being defiled.

I would not have known, I would not have known, oh the list goes on and on, and it would end with: I would not have known myself but who can know themselves?

The Disturbances of the Garden

MY OBSESSION WITH THE GARDEN and the events that take place in it began before I was familiar with that entity called consciousness. My mother taught me to read when I was very young, and she did this without telling me that there was something called the alphabet. I became familiar with words as if they were all wholly themselves, each one a world by itself, intact and self-contained, and able to be joined to other words if they wished to or if someone like me wanted them to. The book she taught me to read from was a biography of Louis Pasteur, the person she told me was responsible for her boiling the milk I drank daily, making sure that it would not infect me with something called tuberculosis. I never got tuberculosis, but I did get typhoid fever, whooping cough, measles, and persistent cases of hookworm and long worms. I was a "sickly child." Much of the love I remember receiving from my mother came during the times I was sick. I have such a lovely memory of her hovering over me with cups of

2020, Sept. 7. "The Disturbances of the Garden." *The New Yorker*.

barley water (that was for the measles) and giving me cups of tea made from herbs (bush) that she had gone out and gathered and steeped slowly (that was for the whooping cough). For the typhoid fever, she took me to the hospital, the children's ward, but she visited me twice a day and brought me fresh juice that she had squeezed or grated from fruits or vegetables, because she was certain that the hospital would not provide me with proper nourishment. And so there I was, a sickly child who could read but had no sense of consciousness, had no idea of how to understand and so make sense of the world into which she was born, a world that was always full of a yellow sun, green trees, a blue sea, and black people.

My mother was a gardener, and in her garden it was as if *Vertumnus* and *Pomona* had become one: she would find something growing in the wilds of her native island (Dominica) or the island on which she lived and gave birth to me (Antigua), and if it pleased her, or if it was in fruit and the taste of the fruit delighted her, she took a cutting of it (really she just broke off a shoot with her bare hands) or the seed (separating it from its pulpy substance and collecting it in her beautiful pink mouth) and brought it into her own garden and tended to it in a careless, everyday way, as if it were in the wild forest, or in the garden of a regal palace. The woods: the garden. For her, the wild and the cultivated were equal and yet separate, together and apart. This wasn't as clear to me then as I am stating it here. I had only just learned to read and the world outside a book I did not yet know how to reconcile.

The only book available to me, a book I was allowed to read all by myself without anyone paying attention to me, was the King James version of the Bible. There's no need for me to go into the troubles with the King James version of the Bible here, but when I encountered the first book, the Book of Genesis, I immediately understood it to be a book for children. A person, I came to understand much later, exists in the kingdom of children no matter how old the person is; even Methuselah, I came to see, was a child. But never mind that, it was the creation story that was so compelling to me, especially the constant refrain "And God saw that it was good." The God in the Book of Genesis made things, and at the end of each day he saw that they were good. But, I wondered, for something to be good would there not have to be something that was not good, or not as good? That was a problem, though I didn't bother myself with it at the time, mainly because I didn't know how to, and also because the story had an inexorableness to it: rolling on from one thing to another without a pause until, by the end of six days, there were a man and a woman made in God's image, there were fish in the sea and animals creeping on land and birds flying in the air and plants growing, and God found it all good, because here we are.

It was in the week after this creation, on the eighth day, that the trouble began: loneliness set in. And so God made a garden, dividing it into four quarters by running water through it (the classic quadrilinear style that is still a standard in garden design) and placing borders, the borders being the eternal good and evil: the Tree of Life and the Tree of Knowledge. One tree was to be partaken of, the other forbidden. I have since come to see that in the garden itself, throughout human association with it, the Edenic plan works in the same way: the Tree of Life is agriculture and the Tree of Knowledge is horticulture. We cultivate food, and when there is a surplus of it, producing wealth, we cultivate the spaces of contemplation, a garden of plants not necessary for physical survival. The awareness of that fact is what gives the garden its special, powerful place in our lives and our imaginations. The Tree of Knowledge holds unknown, and therefore dangerous, possibilities; the Tree of Life is eternally necessary, and the Tree of Knowledge is deeply and divinely dependent on it. This is not a new thought for me. I could see it in my mother's relationship to the things she grew, the kind of godlike domination she would display over them.

She, I remember, didn't make such fine distinctions, she only moved the plants around when they pleased her and destroyed them when they fell out of favor.

It is no surprise to me that my affection for the garden, including its most disturbing attributes, its most violent implications and associations, is intertwined with my mother. As a child, I did not know myself or the world I inhabited without her. She is the person who gave me and taught me the Word.

But where is the garden and where am I in it? This memory of growing things, anything, outside not inside, remained in my memory—or whatever we call that haunting, invisible wisp that is steadily part of our being—and wherever I lived in my young years, in New York City in particular, I planted: marigolds, portulaca, herbs for cooking, petunias, and other things that were familiar to me, all reminding me of my mother, the place I came from. Those first plants were in pots and lived on the roof of a diner that served only breakfast and lunch, in a dilapidated building at 284 Hudson Street, whose ownership was uncertain, which is the fate of us all. Ownership of ourselves and of the ground on which we walk, ownership of the other beings with whom we share this and see that it is good, and ownership of the vegetable kingdom are all uncertain, too. Nevertheless, in the garden, we perform the act of possessing. To name is to possess; possessing is the original violation bequeathed to Adam and his equal companion in creation, Eve, by their creator. It is their transgression in disregarding his command that leads him not only to cast them into the wilderness, the unknown, but also to cast out the other possession that he designed with great clarity and determination and purpose: the garden! For me, the story of the garden in Genesis is a way of understanding my garden obsession.

The appearance of the garden in our everyday life is so accepted that we embrace its presence as therapeutic. Some people say that weeding is a form of comfort and of settling into misery or happiness. The garden makes managing an excess of feelings—good feelings, bad feelings—rewarding in some way that I can never quite understand. The garden is a heap of disturbance, and it may be that my particular history, the history I share with millions of people, begins with our ancestors' violent removal from an Eden. The regions of Africa from which they came would have been Eden-like, and the horror that met them in that "New World" could certainly be seen as the Fall. Your home, the place you are from, is always Eden, the place where even imperfections were perfect, and everything that happened after that beginning interrupted your Paradise.

On August 3, 1492—the day that Christopher Columbus set sail from Spain, later having a fatal encounter with the indigenous people he met in the "West Indies"—the world of the garden changed. That endeavor, to me, anyway, is the way the world we now live in began; it not only affected the domestic life of Europeans (where did the people in a Rembrandt painting get all that stuff they are piling on?) but suddenly they were well-off enough to be interested in more than sustenance, or the Tree of Life (agriculture); they could now be interested in cultivating the fruits of the Tree of Knowledge (horticulture).

Suddenly, the conquerors could do more than feed themselves; they could also see and desire things that were of no use apart from the pleasure that they produced. When Cortés saw Montezuma's garden, a garden that incorporated a lake on which the capital of Mexico now sits, he didn't mention the profusion of exotic flowers that we now grow with ease in our own gardens (dahlias, zinnias, marigolds).

The garden figures prominently in the era of conquest, starting with Captain Cook's voyage to regions that we now know as Australia, New Zealand, New Guinea, and Tahiti, its aim, ostensibly, to observe the rare event of the transit of Venus. On this trip, in 1768, the first of Cook's three voyages around the world, he brought with him the botanist Joseph Banks and also Daniel Charles Solander, a student of Carolus Linnaeus. The two took careful notes on everything they saw. Banks decided that the breadfruit of the Pacific isles would make a good food for slaves on British-owned islands in the West Indies; the slaveholders were concerned with the amount of time it took the enslaved people to grow food to sustain themselves, and breadfruit grew with little cultivation. And so the Pacific Islands came to the West Indies. Banks also introduced the cultivation of tea (*Camellia sinensis*) to India.

Then there is Lewis and Clark's expedition from the Mississippi River to the Pacific Northwest. On that adventure, which was authorized by President Thomas Jefferson and was inspired by Cook's scientific and commercial interests, the explorers listed numerous plant species that were unknown to John Bartram, botanist to King George III, who ruled the United States when it was still a colony. Bartram's son, William, a fellow botanist, later wrote a book about his own explorations, which is said to have influenced Wordsworth, Coleridge, and other English Romantic poets.

There now, look at that: I am meaning to show how I came to seek the garden in corners of the world far away from where I make one, and I have got lost in thickets of words. It was after I started to put seeds in the ground and noticed that sometimes nothing happened that I reached for a book. The first ones I read were about how to make a perennial border or how to get the best out of annuals—the kind of books for people who want to increase the value of their home—but these books were so boring. I found an old magazine meant to help white ladies manage their domestic lives in the 1950s much more interesting (that kind of magazine, along with a copy of *Mrs. Beeton's Book of Household Management*, is worthy of a day spent in bed while the sun is shining its brightest outside). But where did plants, annual and perennial, pristinely set out in something called a border, and arranged sometimes according to color and sometimes according to height, come from? Those books had no answer for me. So one book led to another, and before long I had acquired (and read) so many books that it put a strain on my family's budget. Resentment, a not unfamiliar feeling relating to the garden, set in.

I began to refer to plants by their Latin names, and this so irritated my editor at this magazine (Veronica Geng) that she made me promise that I would never learn the Latin name of another plant. I loved her very much, and so I promised that I would never do such a thing, but I did continue to learn the Latin names of plants and never told her. Betrayal, another feature of any garden.

How did plants get their names? I looked to Linnaeus, who, it turned out, liked to name plants after people whose character they resembled. Mischievous, yes, but not too different from the doctrine of signatures, which attempted to cure diseases by using plants that resembled the diseased part of the body. I was thinking about this one day, stooped over and admiring a colony of *Jeffersonia diphylla*, whose common name is twinleaf. *Jeffersonia diphylla* is a short woodland herbaceous ephemeral whose leaf is perforated at the base so that it often looks like a luna moth, but the two leaflets are not identical at the margins, and each leaf is not evenly divided: the margins undulate, and one leaflet is a little bigger than the other. But isn't Thomas Jefferson, the gardener, the liberty lover and slaveowner, often described as divided, and isn't it appropriate that a plant such as the twinleaf is named for him? The name was bestowed by one of his contemporaries, Benjamin Smith Barton, who perhaps guessed at his true character. It was through this plant that I became interested in Thomas Jefferson. I have read much of what he wrote and have firm opinions about him, including that his book *Notes on the State of Virginia* is a creation story.

It was only a matter of time before I stumbled on the plant hunters, although this inevitability was not clear to me at all. Look at me: my historical reality, my ancestral memory, which is so deeply embedded that I think the whole world understands me before I even open my mouth. A big mistake, but a mistake not big enough for me to have learned anything from it. The plant hunters are the descendants of people and ideas that used to hunt people like me.

The first one I met, in a book, of course, was Frank Smythe. No one had ever made me think that finding a new primrose—or a new flower of any kind—was as special as finding a new island in the Caribbean Sea when I thought I was going to China to meet the Great Khan. A new primrose is more special than meeting any conqueror. But Smythe gave me more than that. I noticed, when reading his accounts, that he was always going off on little side journeys to climb some snow-covered protuberance not so far away, and then days later returning with a story of failure or success at reaching or not reaching the peak, and that by the way he had found some beauty of the vegetable kingdom on the banks of a hidden stream which would be new to every benighted soul in England. But his other gift to me was the pleasure to be had in going to see a plant that I might love or not, growing somewhere far away. It was in his writing that I found the distance between the garden I was looking at and the garden in the wilderness, the garden cast out of its Eden which created a longing in me, the notion of "to go and to see." Go see!

I end where I began: reading—learning to read and reading books, the words a form of food, a form of life, and then knowledge. But also my mother. I don't know exactly how old I was when she taught me to read, but I can say for certain that by the time I was three and a half I could read properly. This reading of mine so interfered with her own time to read that she enrolled me in school; but you could be enrolled in school only if you were five years old, and so she told me to remember to say, if asked, that I was five. My first performance as a writer of fiction? No, not that at all. Perhaps this: the first time I was asked who I was. And who am I? In an ideal world, a world in which the Tree of Life and the Tree of Knowledge stand before me, before all of us, we ask, Who am I? Among the many of us not given a chance to answer is the woman in the library in St. John's, Antigua, two large rooms above the Treasury Department, a building that was steps away from the customs office and the wharf where things coming and going lay. On that wharf worked a stevedore who loaded onto ships bags of raw sugar en route to England, to be refined into white sugar, which was so expensive that we, in my family, had it only on Sundays, as a special treat. I did not know of the stevedore, the lover of this woman who would not allow her children to have much white sugar because, somewhere in the world of Dr. Pasteur and his cohort, they had come to all sorts of conclusions about diseases and their relationships to food (beriberi was a disease my mother succeeded in saving me from suffering). Her name was Annie Victoria Richardson Drew, and she was born in a village in Dominica, British West Indies.

Acknowledgments

For Ann Warner Arlen who was like a mother to me and showered me with the love and support I should have had from my own mother, even though I was only a servant in her household; for Karen Durbin, M. Mark, Ellen Willis, and Richard Goldstein, and I am remembering that time when I lived at 284 Hudson Street in New York and on Sunday afternoons I cooked and we all danced, especially I am remembering the Rolling Stones album *Some Girls*, which was very nice for them because they didn't really like disco but I loved disco and the Rolling Stones too; and Ellen, always so brilliant with her many contradictions, then wrote an article titled "Can a Feminist Love The Rolling Stones?" and she found the answer to be maybe, maybe not, but that essay led George W. S. Trow to write a casual titled "At Lunch With the Rock Critic Establishment"; and for Ellen Willis again (I cannot mention Ellen enough for she had such a brilliant mind and also was so beautiful with her pale-pink-tinctured skin and her late-sunset-colored Pre-Raphaelite hair), we shared an office at *The New Yorker* and I was often alone in it for she almost never came in; for Michael O'Donoghue whom I met in the elevator, he on his way to his office at *National Lampoon* where he was the editor and I on my way to the offices of *New Ingenue*, a magazine for teenage girls, both magazines owned by the same person, but I was still innocent of the chaos (not the cruelty) of capitalism, my response was an enthusiastic "yes" to his invitation to dinner at his home where he lived with the writer Anne Beatts and it was there I met George Trow, who over dinner had a very loud almost violent argument with Henry Beard, another writer. Tim Mayer was there also but I saw all of them together over and over again after that and they were still rowing with each other about old grudges that would turn into new ones, the old ones had begun when they were students at Harvard and members of something called *The Harvard Lampoon* where women were not allowed to become members; and for Michael Arlen, who walked me around the block that was and still is Madison Avenue and 90th Street and up to 91st Street and then turned and walked over to Park Avenue and then turned and walked down to 90th Street back to the apartment where I was the maid to his four daughters and all that time convincing me that I should go to college even if all I did there was sit under a tree and read Shakespeare and so I did go off to Franconia College in New Hampshire and to support myself cleaned a house that was not far from a farm that the poet Robert Frost had lived in but I did not know who Robert Frost was at the time and in any case I left Franconia College after one year and moved back to New York City where I declared myself a writer and no one disagreed with me; and for Kennedy Fraser who wrote about fashion with such seriousness as if the end of the world could be avoided by her observations and insights; for Vince Aletti and the many midnight reveries we had at The Loft, though before we went off to that venue we would meet up at his apartment and have dinner with someone named Manni who was married to someone who lived in the Bronx and a photographer named Peter Hujar, a seemingly shy person whose shyness I believed I respected; and for Sherman and Albert who were extraordinary in a way I did not fully understand but knew somehow they could teach me something, for instance Sherman always wore a ladies' housecoat after he came from work, though at work he wore the clothes that men wore but when he came home to his apartment which was under the bridge that connected the isolated little protuberance of rock and soil that is now called Queens, an important part of New York City, he wore this garment and also collected large jars in the shape of fat women in which sweet biscuits were meant to be stored though his own jars remained empty; Albert was French; for Mark Singer, and he and Sandy (Ian Frazier) shared an office that was separated from Kennedy Fraser's office by eighteen stories of empty space, and one day when Mark was not yet in their shared space, Sandy saw Kennedy writing away at her desk and decided to remove all his clothes, to tunes accompanied by me in what I imagined to be striptease music and it went on for quite a while until Sandy got down to his underwear at which point Kennedy dramatically drew her blinds down and Sandy did not remove any more of his clothes and I stopped singing and then he and I laughed until our jaws ached; and when I told Kennedy I had a crush on Allen Shawn, she said, "Oh no, he is too short," but I hadn't noticed that and so I married him; and Hilton Als, whom I met when he was seventeen and I was twenty-seven, though he was really sixteen; and, oh I almost forgot, for Helen Wilson, who found an old chair on the street outside her loft where she lived in Tribeca and she painted it white and gave it to me for my birthday, and for Tim Woodman who made me a brooch from tin in the shape of an elephant and though it was very nice, I never wore it because I didn't want people to think I was a Republican and Tim's cousin Francesca made us dress up in our wedding garments days after we were married so she could make a photograph in which she wasn't in the picture but she failed for thin wisps of her gold-colored, threadlike hair can be seen in the photograph; and for Veronica Geng, who made me swear I would never learn the Latin names of plants and I did swear to that and then learned the Latin names of plants and never told her that I did, not even when I knew she was dying; and for Pat Strachan who wrote to tell me that if I ever wanted to collect the little almost sentences that I had written in a book, she would like to publish them and so she offered me the least money, less than other people who said they were interested in publishing the little book I had written and offered me more money and I accepted her offer because even then I knew that writing was not a career, that a writer's first consideration could not be about the weight of your money bag, that if you wanted to make money as a writer, you should become a thief in a small way or a big way, legal or illegal; and for Jeff Posternak; and Candace King Weir; and Jill Fox; and Annie Woodhall; and Fred Seidel; and Mac Griswold, who made me understand things about the Italian garden I would not have known no matter how many books I could have read; and for Jonathan Galassi and Andrew Wylie or should it be for Andrew Wylie and Jonathan Galassi, I can't decide; and for William Shawn, what can I say (Boz Scaggs), for words from me cannot ever be enough; and then that time when my status as an immigrant had become illegal and as it became clear to George and Sandy what that meant, George said to Sandy, "You know one of us is going to have to marry Jamaica," and Sandy said, "I know"; and especially to Allen Evan Shawn, who at that time, whenever I showed him anything I had written would say, "That's great!"

Thank you!